DIVE
ARUBA, BONAIRE AND CURAÇAO

JACK JACKSON

Series Consultant: Nick Hanna

Interlink Books

An imprint of Interlink Publishing Group, Inc.
Northampton, Massachusetts

Diving legend Jack Jackson is the author of 12 books and hundreds of magazine articles. His other titles have included *The Dive Sites of the Philippines*, *The Dive Sites of Malaysia and Singapore* and the award-winning *Top Dive Sites of the World*, for which he acted as principal consultant. He is a fellow of the Royal Photographic Society in underwater photography.

This edition first published in 2008 by

INTERLINK BOOKS
An imprint of Interlink Publishing Group, Inc.
46 Crosby Street, Northampton, Massachusetts 01060
www.interlinkbooks.com

10 9 8 7 6 5 4 3 2 1

ISBN 978-1-56656-707-7

Project development: Charlotte Parry-Crooke
Series editor: Pete Duncan
Copy editor: Richard Hammond
Design concept: Philip Mann, ACE Ltd
Design: Chris Aldridge, Alan Marshall
Cartography: William Smuts
Index and proofread: Jennifer Mussett

Reproduction by Hirt and Carter, South Africa
Printed and bound in Singapore by Kyodo Printing Co (Pte) Ltd

Photographic Acknowledgements
All photographs taken by Jack Jackson except for the following: Les Kemp 28, 41, 43, 98, 109 (bottom); Steve Powell 4, 34, 37, 47, 57, 64, 65, 77, 79, 80 (top), 89, 91, 96, 97, 101, 106, 109 (top), 130 (top and bottom), 135, 136; Lawson Wood 8, 26, 29, 68, 116, 121, 149.

Title page: *Azure vase sponges are notably common around the ABC islands.*
Contents page: *Sea fans are always set perpendicular to the current.*

The author and publisher have made every effort to ensure that the information in this book was correct when the book went to press; they accept no responsibility for any loss, injury or inconvenience sustained by any person using this book.

To request our complete 40-page full-color catalog,
please call us toll free at 1-800-238-LINK, visit our website at www.interlinkbooks.com, or write to Interlink Publishing, 46 Crosby Street, Northampton, MA 01060
e-mail: sales@interlinkbooks.com

AUTHOR'S ACKNOWLEDGEMENTS
Compiling a book of this nature requires the help and goodwill of tourist boards, local experts, dive operators and divemasters who contribute their time and knowledge. I would like to give special thanks and appreciation to the following people who helped me with my diving and research in the ABC islands.

Aruba Rafael V. Estrada and René Nieuwkerk of the Aruba Tourism Authority in Holland. Castro E. Perez, Ecotourism Project Manager of the Aruba Tourism Authority in Aruba, who also acted as my dive buddy when local operators' regulations prevented me from diving solo. Alex Nieuwmeijer of the Divi Aruba and Tamarijn Aruba Beach Resorts. Howard Maduro, Angela Tromp and the divemasters of Red Sail Sports. Martin G. Molina and the divemasters of Pelican Tours and Watersports, and Emmit and Su Zanne Kimble, Richard L. Dunstan and the divemasters of Unique Sports of Aruba.

Bonaire Patricia P. Henderson of the Bonaire Tourist Office in Holland. Elsmarie Beukenboom, Director of Tourism of the Tourism Corporation Bonaire, and Nick Davies, Jack Chalk, Silvia Haansen and the divemasters of Captain Don's Habitat Bonaire – Nick Davies was especially helpful. Captain Don Stewart and Dee Scarr for giving me some of their valuable time.

Curaçao Sophia Bradly, Deïdre Keegan and Nina Viner of the Curaçao Tourism Development Bureau in London. Erwin Eustacia of Curaçao Tourism Development in Holland, Chernov Rozier of Curaçao Tourism Development in Curaçao. Albert E. J. Romijn, Mike T. Stafford and Chris Richards of Habitat Curaçao. Anne-Marie Vermeer, Harry Francissen and Anton Miltenburg of Easy Divers; Richard Smit, Hans van den Eeden and Manuela Berends of All West Diving; Jürgen Krause, Harald Weinrich and Marion Mendler of Eden Roc Dive Center, and Eva van Dalen of Curaçao Seascape.

PUBLISHER'S ACKNOWLEDGEMENTS
The publishers gratefully acknowledge the generous assistance during the compilation of this book of the following: Nick Hanna for his involvement in developing the series and consulting throughout and Dr Elizabeth M. Wood for acting as Marine Biological Consultant and contributing to The Marine Environment.

PHOTOGRAPHY
The author's photographs were taken using Nikonos III, Nikonos V, Nikon F-801S and Nikon F90X cameras.
    The Nikonos cameras were used with 15mm and 28mm Underwater Nikkor lenses, sometimes with a Nikon Close-up lens and a home-made framer attached to the 28mm – the framer having only two sides to avoid the shadow of the framer showing in the picture.
    The two Nikon F90X cameras were housed in either of two waterproof aluminium housings made by Subal of Austria and used with 14mm, 24mm, 55mm Micro-Nikkor macro and 105mm Micro-Nikkor macro lenses.
    All the author's underwater photographs were taken with the addition of electronic flash, to replace the colour filtered out by the water. The electronic flash units (strobes) were either a Nikon SB-24 Speedlight in a Subal housing, a Sea & Sea YS-300TTL or a Sea & Sea YS-350TTL/PRO.
    Underwater the housed cameras were always operated in manual mode with shutter speeds of either 1/125th or 1/250th of a second. This avoids the double images that can occur when balancing the flash exposure with the ambient daylight. Through-the-lens (TTL) flash synchronization was sometimes used.
    The Nikon F-801S camera was used for land shots, with a Nikon SB-24 Speedlight attached when required.
    The film stock used was Fujichrome Velvia, Fujichrome Astia and Fujichrome Provia.

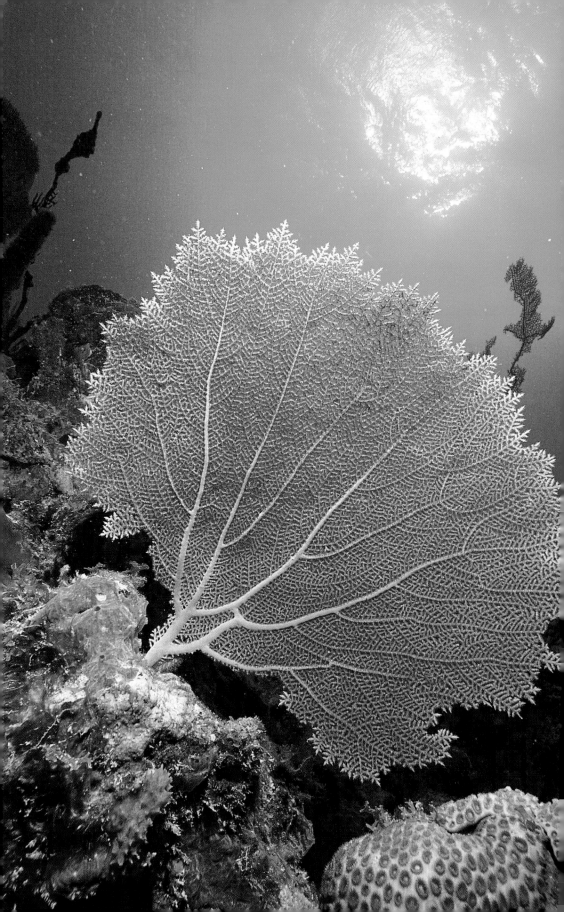

CONTENTS

FEATURES

How to Use this Book

THE REGIONS

The dive sites of the islands covered in this book are divided into eight areas: Aruba, North Bonaire, Central Bonaire, South Bonaire, Klein Bonaire, West Curaçao, Central Curaçao, and East Curaçao/Klein Curaçao. Regional introductions describe the key characteristics and features of each island and provide background information on climate, the environment, points of interest, and advantages and disadvantages of diving in the locality.

THE MAPS

A map is included at the beginning of each sub-section to identify the location of the dive sites described and to provide other useful information for divers and snorkellers. Although certain reefs are indicated, the maps do not set out to provide detailed nautical information, such as exact reef contours. In general the maps show: the locations of the dive sites, indicated by white numbers in red boxes corresponding to those at the start of each dive site description; the locations of key access points to the sites, such as ports and beach resorts; and wrecks. (Note: the border round the maps is not a scale bar.) Each site description gives details of how to access the dive site.

MAP LEGEND

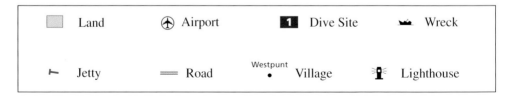

| Land | ⊕ Airport | ▮ Dive Site | ⚓ Wreck |
| ⊢ Jetty | ▭ Road | Westpunt • Village | 🗼 Lighthouse |

THE DIVE SITE DESCRIPTIONS

Within the geographical sections are the descriptions of each region's premier dive sites. Each site description starts with a number enabling the site to be located on the corresponding map, a star-rating and a selection of key symbols, as shown opposite. (Note that the anchor used for live-aboards is merely symbolic: no boat should ever drop anchor over a reef.)

Crucial practical details on location, access, conditions, typical visibility and average and maximum depths precede the description of the site, its marine life, and special points of interest. In these entries, 'average visibility' assumes good conditions.

THE STAR-RATING SYSTEM

Each site has been awarded a star-rating, with a maximum of five red stars for diving and five blue stars for snorkelling. (Note that the author has graded the dive sites in this book on a world scale. When assessing a star-rating, readers should add one star to those given if they wish to compare the star-rating on a Caribbean scale.)

Diving			*Snorkelling*		
★★★★★	**first class**		★★★★★	**first class**	
★★★★	**highly recommended**		★★★★	**highly recommended**	
★★★	**good**		★★★	**good**	
★★	**average**		★★	**average**	
★	**poor**		★	**poor**	

THE SYMBOLS

The symbols placed at the start of each site description provide a quick reference to crucial information pertinent to individual sites.

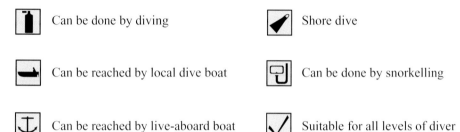

Can be done by diving

Shore dive

Can be reached by local dive boat

Can be done by snorkelling

Can be reached by live-aboard boat

Suitable for all levels of diver

THE REGIONAL DIRECTORIES

A regional directory, which will help you plan and make the most of your trip, is included at the end of each regional section. Here you will find practical information on how to get to an area, where to stay and eat, and available dive facilities. Local non-diving highlights are also described, with suggestions for excursions.

OTHER FEATURES

At the start of the book you will find practical details and tips about travelling to and in the area, as well as a general introduction to the islands. Also provided is a wealth of information about the general principles and conditions of diving in the area. Throughout the book there are features and small fact panels on topics of interest to divers and snorkellers. At the end of the book are sections on the marine environment (including coverage of marine life, conservation and codes of practice in the ABC islands) and underwater photography and video. Also to be found here is information on health, safety and first aid, and a guide to marine creatures to look out for when diving in Aruba, Bonaire and Curaçao.

INTRODUCTION TO ARUBA, BONAIRE AND CURAÇAO

Aruba, Bonaire and Curaçao – popularly known as the ABC islands – lie deep in the south of the Caribbean, some 25–80km (15–50 miles) off the coast of Venezuela and well below the hurricane belt. For several centuries colonies of the Netherlands, the three islands became an integral part of the Kingdom of the Netherlands in 1954. Today Bonaire and Curaçao officially comprise part of the Netherlands Antilles – which includes a second group of islands 880km (550 miles) to the northeast, namely Saba, Sint Eustatius, and the south part of Sint Maarten. Aruba seceded in 1986 from the Netherlands Antilles to became self-governing, though it remains within the Kingdom of the Netherlands.

The people of the ABC islands enjoy a higher standard of living than many others in the Caribbean; most goods have to be imported and prices are not always cheap. However, the Dutch influence lends a special atmosphere to these fascinating islands. The buildings, for example – rather than being painted light pastel shades as on other Caribbean islands – sport rich, striking colours: the result of a decree in 1817 by the Governor, Vice-Admiral Kikkert, who found that whitewashed walls hurt his eyes in the strong sun. Lying close to South America, there is also a tangible Latin influence, particularly evident in the local music.

Aruba, Bonaire and Curaçao are so near the mainland that on a clear day the mountains of Venezuela are visible. The islands are not, however, geologically connected to the continent, but were formed by ashes and lava pushed up from the sea floor. The climate is semi-arid and the countryside, or *cunucu* as it is known in the local dialect, Papiamento, is covered in thorny scrub. It is nearly always sunny, with temperatures averaging 28°C (82°F), though the trade winds help moderate the heat. These winds are very strong in the early months of the year and provide ideal conditions for windsurfing. The winds pass over without forming rain clouds, as all three islands are low-lying. Freshwater run-off is therefore minimal and the waters around the leeward coasts remain clear and calm all year round. The consistency of these conditions helps make the ABC islands a diving paradise.

Opposite: *Ironshore, or eroded limestone, is typical of Bonaire's coastline.*
Above: *The islands' flora, such as this prickly pear cactus in flower, reflects the largely dry conditions.*

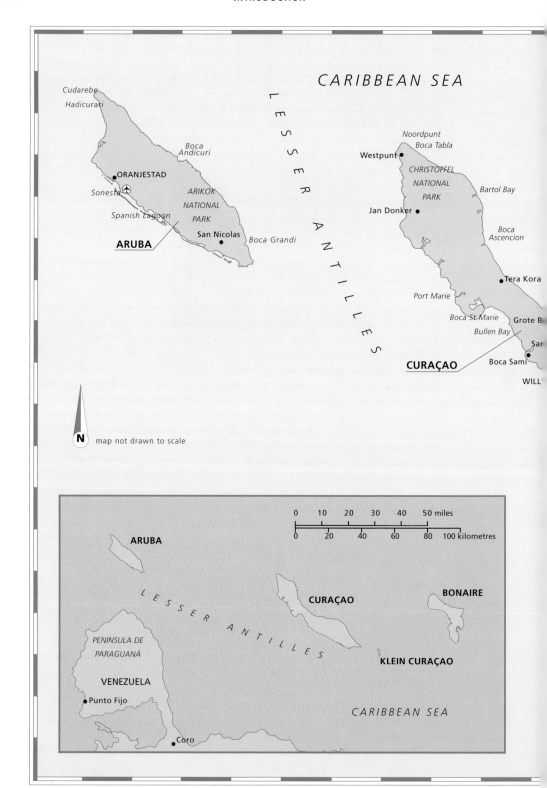

ARUBA, BONAIRE AND CURAÇAO

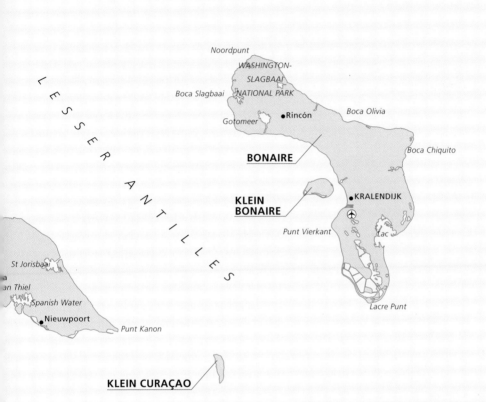

L E S S E R   A N T I L L E S

Noordpunt

WASHINGTON-
SLAGBAAI
Boca Slagbaai NATIONAL PARK

Gotomeer ●Rincón

Boca Olivia

Boca Chiquito

BONAIRE

KLEIN
BONAIRE

●KRALENDIJK

Punt Vierkant *Lac*

St Jorisbaai
an Thiel
Spanish Water
●Nieuwpoort
Punt Kanon

Lacre Punt

KLEIN CURAÇAO

CARIBBEAN SEA

UNITED
STATES OF
AMERICA

BAHAMAS

CUBA

DOMINICAN
REPUBLIC

US & UK
VIRGIN
ISLANDS

CAYMAN
ISLANDS

HAITI

PUERTO
RICO

GUADELOUPE

MARTINIQUE

JAMAICA

CARIBBEAN SEA

HONDURAS

GRENADA

BARBADOS

NICARAGUA

CURAÇAO

ARUBA   BONAIRE

TRINIDAD

COSTA RICA

COLOMBIA   VENEZUELA

PANAMA

TOPOGRAPHY

Curaçao is the largest and most populated of the Netherlands Antilles, and is situated between Aruba and Bonaire, some 55km (35 miles) off the northern coast of Venezuela. Aruba is the westernmost of the ABC islands, lying less than 35km (20 miles) north of the Paraguaná peninsula of Venezuela and 68km (42 miles) west of Curaçao. Bonaire, the second largest of the ABC islands, lies 48km (30 miles) east of Curaçao, 80km (50 miles) north of Venezuela and 129km (86 miles) east of Aruba.

Curaçao is approximately 61km (38 miles) long, 5–14km (3–9 miles) wide at its widest point and has a total surface area of 44,400 hectares (110,000 acres). Its highest point is at Mount Christoffel, at 375m (1230ft). Nearby Klein Curaçao is a tiny, desolate volcanic island 1^1/$_2$ hours by boat off the southeast coast of the main island. Bonaire, shaped like a boomerang, is 39km (24 miles) long by 5–11km (3–7 miles) wide, and covers an area of 29,000ha (71,680 acres). Its highest point, Brandaris Hill, is 240m (784ft) high. West of the main island, one kilometre (half a mile) offshore, is Klein Bonaire (Little Bonaire), a tiny circular island of 600ha (1480 acres). The smallest of the ABC islands, Aruba, is 35km (20 miles) long, 10km (6 miles) wide, and has a total surface area of 19,300ha (48,000 acres). Its highest hill is Yamanota.

Aruba, Bonaire and Curaçao all have a semi-arid climate, with the constant salt-laden trade winds producing a landscape of cacti, dramatic boulders and *watapana* (divi-divi) trees. Aruba used to suffer from severe water shortages. These, however, were overcome when refineries were constructed to process oil from Venezuela – with the refineries came the resources necessary to provide a secure supply of desalinated water, as well as a significant source of economic security for the island's residents. As a result, Aruba's population increased significantly, though so did its dependence on the outside world.

Bonaire's landscape features an ironshore, or eroded limestone coastline. This limestone often has sharp edges and can be difficult to walk across without hard-soled wet suit booties. Thousands of years ago the continental shelf, now located close to Montserrat, moved along this region and volcanic activity forced rock to the surface, creating the islands of the Lesser and Greater Antilles. Some of these volcanic eruptions produced molten lava, leading to the volcanic formations visible on Bonaire. Needless to say, there is no threat of volcanic activity on Bonaire today.

The most exciting feature of Bonaire, however, is its fringing reef. Many millennia ago sea levels were higher than today and the ocean covered the island, so coral grew on top of it. As the waters later dropped, the coral that became exposed to air died and formed surface limestone deposits. Nevertheless, the coral that was still underwater around Bonaire continued to grow, resulting in Bonaire's fringing reef. Off the calmer leeward side of the island, the reef begins right at the water's edge; with a tidal range of only around 60cm (2ft), live corals can be found immediately below the low tide line. Klein Bonaire, the small island off the sheltered west side of Bonaire, has the same geological history but with a land surface only just higher than high tide. It has not been developed, so its fringing reef is pristine.

LEEWARD/WINDWARD

There is confusion regarding the terms 'Leeward' and 'Windward' when applied to the Netherlands Antilles. The locals refer to the ABC islands as the Leeward Islands and the three remaining Netherlands Antilles to the north as the Windward Islands – Aruba, Bonaire and Curaçao all lying roughly downwind of Saba, Sint Eustatius (Statia) and Sint Maarten in the trade winds. However, this is in contrast to another meaning that developed elsewhere in the Caribbean and gained political currency during the British Empire – where the terms denoted an island's position in relation to European ships' usual point of arrival in the Caribbean, around Dominica or Martinique. This second meaning is still used extensively in describing the Lesser Antilles and confusingly places Saba, Sint Eustatius (Statia) and Sint Maarten as 'Leeward Islands', lying as they do slightly downwind of Dominica and Martinique.

Many beaches line the coastline of the ABC islands. Curaçao has no less than 38 distinct beaches. Some, like Westpunt Beach, are sheltered by towering cliffs and have become famous for high diving; others range from wide expanses of sand with modern facilities to small, secluded coves. On Aruba, beautiful white, palm-fringed beaches stretch along the leeward south and west shores, sloping gently toward the calm turquoise of the Caribbean. In contrast on the northeast coast, the waves collide with the cliffs, where they have carved out eight arched coral bridges, secluded coves and limestone grottoes. Bonaire is less known for its beaches – the best beaches can be found on the windward side, especially near Lac Bay.

SALIÑAS

Saliñas (salt pans) are a prominent feature of Washington-Slagbaai National Park in Bonaire. These areas of saltwater and mud are a reminder of the island's geological history. The sea was once 6m (19ft) higher than today, and much of present-day Bonaire would have been underwater. When the water level dropped, saltwater was left behind in valleys that silted up. Salt used to be extracted and exported from these salt pans, but nowadays the *saliñas* are good places to watch birds feeding, especially flamingos. The area of the *saliñas* varies according to rainfall, but even in the dry season the ground encircling them is treacherously soft and often wet; drivers should stick to the main roads.

HISTORY

Various Indian tribes lived on the islands before Christopher Columbus reached the New World. For the preceding 300 years it had been the Caiquetios, a group of Arawak Indians who lived there under the control of a *cacique* (chieftan) on the mainland. They mainly existed by subsistence farming and fishing, trading some of their catch for other goods. When Alonso de Ojeda (one of Columbus' lieutenants) and Amerigo Vespucci (the Florentine whose name was later given to the whole American continent) explored the South American coast in 1498/9, Vespucci referred to Curaçao as 'The Land of the Giants' because the Indians were comparatively tall.

Initially the islands were considered *islas inútiles* (useless) by the European newcomers. With poor soil for cultivation and no gold to be found, the islands were left to the Indieros,

Below: *Divi-divi trees are bent by the constant winds into striking shapes and forms.*

INDIAN PAINTINGS

The Caiquetios, a tribe of Arawak Indians from the nearby mainland, inhabited the ABCs long before the Spaniards arrived. They lived in areas that had enough freshwater to maintain their communities, but also left rock frescoes on the walls and ceilings of caves that were positioned well away from their settlements.

Some of the rock drawings seem to have a religious significance, while others are of annual events such as turtle nesting. Many have not yet been deciphered, though it is possible to make out features such as human hands and snakes.

slave traders who dealt in South American Indians. Most of the local Indians were shipped off to work in the gold mines or cattle and horse farms of Hispaniola, while those who were left were expected to resist any other Europeans who invaded. However, in 1527 the Spaniards settled in Curaçao to breed cattle. The English pirate Jack Hawkins found Curaçao to be 'one great cattle ranch' when he landed on the island in 1565.

During the early 17th century the Dutch began using Curaçao as a base to harass the Spanish, and in 1634 the Dutch West India Company took over; in 1636 they built garrisons on Aruba and Bonaire to protect Curaçao's approaches. The Spaniards attacked Bonaire in 1642 but found that the Dutch had fled, so they burned the settlements. However, the Spaniards soon left and the Dutch were able to return.

In 1638 Peter Stuyvesant became the governor of Curaçao – and later Director General of all the Dutch possessions in the New World. Administering the Dutch possessions from Nieuw Amsterdam, which was to become New York, Stuyvesant ushered in a new prosperity based on the Dutch Fleets. The main trade underlying Curaçao's success was in slaves to work the Caribbean sugar plantations. In time, South American Indians were replaced with West Africans, and buyers came to Curaçao from all over the Caribbean. In the 18th century 40 per cent of all the slaves brought to the New World came via Curaçao.

Aruba and Bonaire were used as farmland to supply Curaçao, their poor soil being worked to grow maize. Aruba also became known for breeding horses, with Paardenbaai

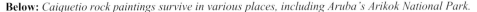

Below: *Caiquetio rock paintings survive in various places, including Aruba's Arikok National Park.*

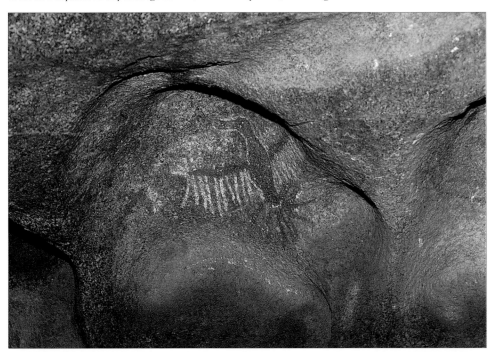

Above: *The tiny Alto Vista chapel on Aruba was constructed on the site of a chapel built in 1750.*

(Horses' Bay) forming the original harbour off Willemstad. Bonaire was home to some cattle ranching but its most important export was salt, an essential commodity before the days of refrigeration for trading ventures to far-off Europe.

Curaçao's fortunes varied with the politics of Europe. The British invaded twice during the Napoleonic Wars, but by 1816 the Dutch were back in control. Being near to South America meant that the islands were often used as a political sanctuary – particularly the closest island, Aruba, where Simón Bolívar took refuge in 1812.

During the 19th century trade declined and various schemes were tried to keep the islands going financially. Cochineal insects were bred to make a dye for inks, cosmetics and food colourings; aloe plants were grown for use in cosmetics and medicine; and sisal was grown for making rope. The salt workings continued in Bonaire, and gold was found in Aruba in 1825; but Bonaire remained so poor that in 1863 the government offered it for sale. By the end of the 19th century the islanders were forced to find work abroad, either in the then Dutch colony of Surinam or helping to dig the Panama Canal.

The Panama Canal, locally referred to as 'The Ditch', reinforced Curaçao's status as a port, but it was the discovery of oil in nearby Venezuela in the 1920s that gave Aruba and Curaçao prosperity in the 20th century. With a stable political climate and steep shores that allowed the approach of larger oil tankers than could approach the nearby South American coast, the two islands were ideal for oil refineries. Shell and EXXON set up refineries and workers flooded into the islands, increasing their populations by a multiple of five. However, the dependence on oil refining was short-lived. In the 1950s and 1960s automation cut the workforce drastically, and during the 1980s OPEC raised oil prices, reducing consumption and causing a glut. The ageing refineries, able to refine only one type of crude oil, floundered. The oil companies sold up and the islands turned to tourism to survive. Today, oil is again being refined

THE WEST INDIA COMPANY

The Dutch West India Company was a trading company set up by the Netherlands in 1621 to share world trade with the Dutch East India Company. In return for subsidies to the government, the company was granted the Dutch trading monopoly for Africa and the Americas, with the right to colonize. The company started colonies in the New Netherlands (later New York), Curaçao, Surinam and for a limited period, in parts of Brazil. The Netherlands armed forces were used to enforce the company's position and to plunder Portuguese and Spanish settlements.

The Dutch West India Company was not as successful as the Dutch East India Company. By 1674 it was in financial difficulty and was dissolved. A new company lasted until 1795, then collapsed during the French invasion of the Netherlands. Another West India Company was formed in 1828 but it too was unsuccessful.

but the islands have moved into tourism in a big way as a dependable income for the future.

THE PEOPLE

The people of the ABC islands are of mixed descent. Those on Aruba and Bonaire descend from about 40 different ethnic backgrounds and 80 nationalities, while the people of Curaçao claim descent from over 50 different ethnic backgrounds. Influences from around the world have combined successfully to form a fully integrated society on all the islands. Broadly speaking, the population today derives from a mixture of European settlers (Dutch, English, French, Portuguese and Spanish), Southeast Asians, South Americans and imported Africans. None of the original South American Indians survive, but there is more of their heritage on Aruba than on the other islands. On Bonaire, the harsh living conditions during slavery produced resilience in the character of the people and a richness in Bonairean culture. Less cosmopolitan than the Curaçaoans and less Americanized than the Arubans, Bonaireans are said to be the most Antillean of the ABC islands' people.

Although the official language is Dutch, the native language across the ABC islands is the Creole dialect, Papiamento (Papiamentu). Most speak English and Spanish as well. On Curaçao the population exceeds 170,000, on Aruba the figure is 91,000 and on Bonaire roughly 15,000.

CLIMATE

The weather is guaranteed to be sunny almost all the time in the ABC islands. The trade winds, mostly blowing from the east, keep the humidity low and moderate the average temperature to 28°C (82°F); the difference between daytime and night-time temperatures and between summer and winter temperatures is 2°C ($3^1/_2$°F). The hottest months are August–October and the coolest December–February, but the temperature rarely goes over 32°C (90°F) or below 26°C (80°F). The average water temperature is 27°C (80°F).

What little rain does fall, occurs in short showers mainly from October to December. Curaçao averages 550mm (22 inches) of rain a year, while Aruba has less than 430mm (17 inches). The average yearly rainfall on Bonaire, 65 per cent of which occurs between October and the end of January, is 560mm (22 inches). On Bonaire, the wind speed averages 12 knots, 15 per cent less than on Curaçao and 40 per cent less than on Aruba, with the wind at its strongest in February, March and June. Lighter winds and occasional reverses in wind direction occur during October and November. For most of the year, however, the trade winds make for a windsurfing Mecca, as well as helping to evaporate salt, which is still produced on Bonaire, and to sustain the salt beds of Pekelmeer, home to populations of flamingos.

In November 1999 Hurricane Lenny moved from west to east across the central Caribbean. Although well to the north of the ABC islands it generated wave surges that caused unusually rough seas on the islands' normally sheltered south- and west-facing coasts. Apart from boat damage, on Aruba there was some loss of sand on beaches and some jetty damage. On Bonaire there was damage to jetties and some low-lying buildings fronting the

Above: *A windsurfer attempts an aerial gybe on the flat water off Sorobon Beach, Bonaire.*
Below: *Aruba is lined with stretches of sandy beach, such as here at Sonesta Suites Hotel.*

Above: *Traditional cacti fences are still used to protect crops from meandering goats.*
Opposite: *The islands' plentiful birdlife includes the brown pelican, found along the seashore.*

sea, while some of the dive sites on the west side of Klein Bonaire lost their moorings. On all three islands, where dive sites had coral heads on sand in less than 6m (20ft) of water, there are now broken corals stacked in piles, creating ideal shelter for eels, juvenile fish and lobsters. Dive Masters have noticed a considerable increase in the fish life of these areas.

FLORA

The ABC islands' flora largely reflect the dry conditions and the constant trade winds that blow across this region. Divi-divi trees are bent by the wind in the direction of the southwest, forming living sculptures everywhere. On Aruba, columnar (organ pipe) cacti grow to 12m (40ft), living for 4–5 years without water, their flowers blossoming when it rains. When there is unusally excessive rain, the cacti soak up so much water that they become heavy and often break – the broken branches can be replanted and will root again, so they are used as fences. The once plentiful kwihi tree, which almost disappeared in a building boom but is now a protected species, is a source of hardwood. Aged naturally for years, the wood is used to produce unique tables and decorative pieces.

On Bonaire, the most obvious plants are cacti. The two main species are the yatu (*Lemaireocereus griseus*) and the kadushi (*Ceres repandus*), easily distinguishable by their thorns, those of the yatu forming neat rows of rosettes, while those of the kadushi are denser and stick out in all directions. The fast growing mesquite tree or indju (*Prosopis juliflora*) used to be burnt to produce charcoal. The tree would be cut down to about 30cm (12 inches) above the ground, and within five years would grow back to its previous size. With selective coppicing and the aid of this rapid growth, Bonaire avoided deforestation. The divi-divi tree (*Caesalpinia coriaria*) has pods containing tannin, which was exported to Holland for use in tanning hides for leather until the 1950s – as in Aruba, the constant winds have forced the trees to bend sideways as they grow. Aloe plants (*Aloe barbadensis*) were cultivated for use in the pharmaceutical industry, while the dyewood, or Brazil wood tree (*Haematoxylon brasiletto*), with its twisted shape and deeply grooved trunk, was used to produce a red fabric dye, and its commercial value lasted well into the 19th century. It was grown on all the ABC islands, but because the tree was rarely replanted it is now close to extinction on Aruba, although it remains abundant on Bonaire and Curaçao. The matapiskà tree (*Jacquinia barbasco*) was used by the original Indians for fishing: it produces chemicals that paralyse fish, but are harmless to man. The Indians would put the branches, leaves or berries into the water and then collect the fish floating on the surface.

ARUBAN ISLAND RATTLESNAKE
The Aruban Island rattlesnake has been declared a national wildlife symbol. It has been shown on postage stamps and is portrayed on the 25Afl. banknote.   To ensure the survival of the Aruban Island rattlesnake, there are captive breeding programmes carried out at zoos in Aruba and in America. Scientists have implanted radio transmitters in 20 of the reptiles to help find out more about their microhabitat. In Aruba, the most likely place to encounter rattlesnakes is south of Yamanota. In the unlikely event that you get bitten, the hospital holds the necessary anti-serum.

Despite the dry conditions, there is a variety of other plants on the islands. On Aruba, with the advent of the second largest water desalination plant in the world, pure water produces a flourishing display of tropical flowers. Bougainvillea (brought to the West Indies in the 1700s from Brazil), hibiscus and oleander from tropical Asia grow alongside ixora, frangipani and poinsettia, which in Aruba grow 5m (16ft) high. There are also coconut, date and royal palm trees, while lemon trees brought by the Spanish grow alongside mangoes from tropical Asia and papayas.

On Curaçao the vegetation differs according to the geological substrate: on lava, vegetation is largely deciduous, while on calcium carbonate formations it is largely evergreen. Columnar (organ pipe) cacti are found on both. Centuries of uncontrolled grazing by livestock has had a large effect on the species composition, and thorny acacia trees, prickly pear cacti and the introduced aloe and rubber vine are common. The agave has a 9m (30ft) stem that flowers after rain.

BIRDLIFE

Birdlife is abundant on the ABC islands. On Aruba 170 resident water and land birds (of which 50 breed there) are augmented by those migrating between North and South America; others are blown off course and settle at the Bubali Bird Sanctuary or along Spanish Lagoon at Frenchman's Pass. From November to January the total rises to about 300 species. The small yellow-breasted bananaquit has taken advantage of tourism and is now also called the sugar bird or sugar thief for its habit of stealing anything sweet from outside tables. The southern mockingbird, known in Aruba as the *chuchubi*, sings all day long in gardens with fruit. Giant green parakeets may be heard calling, troupials flash brilliant orange against the sky and brown pelicans are

ALOE

Aloe is a plant of the *Liliaceos* genus, which has more than 150 species, mostly native to South Africa. Usually they have short stems, fleshy, spiny leaves crowded into rosettes at the end of the stem and red or yellow flowers in dense clusters. Species vary in height from several centimetres to more than 9m (30ft). The leaves can retain water in warm and dry climates and their bitter tasting sap has a strong laxative effect.

When the green skin of the leaf is removed, a mucilaginous substance emerges containing fibres and the constituents that retain water. These ingredients have been known for at least 2000 years as good for healing wounds, sunburnt skin and stomach ailments.

During the 19th century the aloe vera plant was brought from Africa for cultivation in the Caribbean, Mexico and Venezuela. In the 20th century it was also grown in Texas, USA but frost killed most of the plants in 1984, 1985 and 1989. At the start of the 20th century aloe was widely used as a laxative. In the 1920s Aruba raised 70 per cent of the world's production, most of it going to England. Nowadays it is used as a moisturising ingredient in cosmetics, particularly hand creams and sunburn creams as well as being added to health drinks.

common along the south shore. At the Bubali Plassen, opposite the Olde Molen (windmill), is a viewing platform where you can see cormorants, herons and fish eagles. Snowy egrets and scarlet ibis settle down on Bubali Lake, the only freshwater wetland in the southern Caribbean, while Aruba is also a breeding ground for many sea birds and is the only area in the Western Hemisphere where black noddies breed. Some 45 per cent of the world's Cayenne terns nest in San Nicolas Bay in front of the refinery.

Bonaire is probably the most popular of the islands for birdwatchers. Over 170 species of birds can be observed, many of them at Goto Lake, Pekelmeer, Cai and Dos Pos. Bonaire is one of only a few places in the world where flamingo colonies breed, and the flamingo is the island's national symbol. They can be found at the Pekelmeer Sanctuary to the south, where the birds flock around the salt ponds, and at Lake Gotomeer in the Washington-Slagbaai National Park. The most common sea bird spotted offshore is the magnificent frigate bird. Its wingspan is the largest in relation to bodyweight of any bird; it is also known as the 'man of war' for its habit of tormenting other birds until they give up their catch. Other sea birds include the olivaceous cormorant, the brown pelican and the brown booby. Bonaire also has five different species of heron. The largest is the great blue heron. Other common wading birds include the snowy egret, the reddish egret and the great white egret. Known for their loud cries, laughing gulls are seen on Bonaire in late March or early April. Least terns and common terns invade the island in the spring and summer, while royal terns reside all year round. Peeps, a local term for all small shore birds, include the semi-palmated plover, the snowy plover and the semi-palmated sandpiper. On land, two birds are indigenous to Bonaire – the Caribbean parakeet and the yellow-shouldered parrot. Raptors include ospreys, crested caracaras and white-tailed hawks, while there are two species of hummingbird: the ruby-topaz hummingbird and the common emerald hummingbird. Belted kingfishers, southern mockingbirds and bananaquits are also common.

On Curaçao 168 species of birds have been recorded, 51 of which breed on the island, 90 are migrants and 19 are seabirds. As well as the ubiquitous bananaquit there are doves, hawks, hummingbirds, troupials and yellow orioles; flamingos have their own sanctuary in Banda Abao. The parakeet and the barn owl are subspecies restricted to Curaçao and 14 other birds are endemic to the Leeward Netherlands Antilles and nearby Venezuelan islands as subspecies. The barn owl, the caracara, the white-tailed hawk, the scaly-naped pigeon and several species of tern are endangered.

OTHER FAUNA

A surprising amount of other animal life is also present on the ABC islands. On Aruba the boulders and crevices between the various rock formations create a microclimate that supports unique examples of indigenous flora and fauna. As a result, Arikok National Park is the habitat for several animal species that are found only in Aruba, including two snake species, the cascabel (Aruban Island rattlesnake), which does not use its rattle, and the harmless santanero (Aruban cat-eyed snake); the kododo blauw (Aruban whiptail lizard); and two bird species, the shoco (Aruban burrowing owl) and the prikichi (Aruban parakeet). As well as many species of lizards there are large iguanas, which are hunted for soup.

On Bonaire there are iguanas and lizards of all shapes and sizes. The large blue lizards are endemic to Bonaire, while the anolis, a tree lizard with a yellow dewlap (a loose fold of skin hanging below the throat), is related to the Windward Islands *anolis* species – rather than to the neighbouring Venezuelan species. The most common mammal is the goat, which may be found roaming the island eating everything except the cacti. All goats on Bonaire are actually owned by someone, and provide a staple food. There are also donkeys left over from hauling salt at the old salt workings.

Eleven native mammals are found on Curaçao: the Curaçao white-tailed deer, the mouse, the cotton-tail, and eight species of bat. The deer, the cotton-tail and four of the bats are endemic to the Leeward Dutch Antilles as a subspecies, while the baiomys mouse is endemic. The deer and all of the bats are endangered species – Curaçao is the only Caribbean island where the white-tailed deer has been present since pre-Columbian times, yet few of these goat-sized animals are left, despite protection from hunting since 1936. Nine species of native reptiles are found on Curaçao, two snakes and seven lizards; four of the lizards are endemic to the Leeward Netherlands Antilles. Early Arawak Indians brought iguanas to Curaçao from mainland South America as food. These herbivorous creatures can live up to 30 years, grow up to 120cm (47in) long, and change their skin colour to match their background. Females can lay 30 eggs in a year, and the bright green hatchlings live in trees for the first year and a half.

Below: *Various reptiles, such as these iguanas, can be found in Curaçao's Christoffel National Park.*

TRAVELLING TO AND IN THE ABC ISLANDS

From Europe the major airline carrier is KLM, with services via Amsterdam from major and many regional airports. Other services include TAP Air Portugal via Lisbon and British Airways via Miami or Caracas with connections on Curaçao's national carrier, ALM.

From North America there are direct flights from various cities including Atlanta and New York, while other flights connect via Miami with American Airlines, United Airlines, Air Aruba, ALM, Air Jamaica or Guyana Airways. From Latin America there are regular services from Columbia, Guyana, Surinam, Venezuela and other Central American countries on carriers such as Aerorepublica, Avensa, Avianca, Aserca, SAM, Servivensa and VASP. Numerous connections are available from other Caribbean islands, including Saba and St Eustatius.

Aruba and Bonaire are also major ports of call on the itinerary of over 200 cruises from America and Europe. For more detailed information on travelling to the islands, see the directory at the end of each regional chapter.

ENTRY REQUIREMENTS

All visitors must have an onward or return ticket together with identity documents and sufficient funds for their stay on the island. Citizens of most countries do not need a visa for entering the islands. Those who do need a visa include citizens of Afghanistan, China, Cuba, Dominican Republic, Iraq, Iran, Cambodia, Korea, Libya, Mauritania, Mongolia, Burma, Syria, Vietnam, Peru, Haiti, Albania, Croatia, Serbia and Bosnia – except in cases where such travellers are in transit and staying for less than 24 hours.

All visitors are issued with an immigration card, which must be returned to immigration on departure. Length of stay is usually granted for two weeks and up to 90 days may be granted by airport immigration officials upon request at arrival. A visa is required for stays of more than 90 days.

A valid passport is required except by nationals of Belgium, Germany, Luxembourg, The Netherlands, San Marino, Brazil, Mexico, Trinidad & Tobago, and Venezuela, for

Opposite: *A boat approaches Santa Martha Bay on Curaçao's leeward coast.*
Above: *Car number plates on Bonaire draw attention to the importance of diving locally.*

> ### DIVERS' BAGGAGE
>
> Airlines vary in their provision for divers' baggage. Travellers from Europe wishing to take full diving equipment with them should note that KLM in London stick rigidly to the 20kg (44lb) baggage limit (unlike other airlines), even when a higher allowance is specifically requested in advance.
>
> If time is not a problem, American Airlines fly via Miami or New York at a cheaper price and with enough baggage allowance to cover divers' equipment (including any camera equipment). The onward connections from Curaçao to Bonaire with ALM do sometimes charge for the extra baggage but it is a flat fee of US$10 not per kilogram.

whom a national identity card is sufficient. US and Canadian citizens only require proof of identity (although a passport is recommended) in one of various forms: a valid passport; an official birth certificate and a photo identity card (for persons born in the USA or Canada), or a certificate of naturalization and a photo identity card (for citizens born outside the USA or Canada). Non-US or Canadian citizens who are legal residents of either country must submit one of the following: a re-entry permit, a valid non-quota immigration visa, or an Alien Registration green card.

CUSTOMS

In addition to articles for personal use, persons 18 years old or over are allowed to bring in two litres of alcohol, 200 cigarettes, 50 cigars and 250 grams of tobacco. Ensure that prescription drugs are clearly marked.

HEALTH

A certificate of vaccination against yellow fever is needed by vistors coming from endemic zones. Vaccinations are not required for any other diseases, although typhoid and polio vaccinations are recommended.

Generally, however, tropical diseases are practically absent from the ABC islands (malaria is unknown), and biting insects are far less of a problem than they are on most other Caribbean islands. Remember that the sun burns, so come prepared with high-factor sun-block, especially if you are fair-skinned. The water on the islands is desalinated and purified, and is safe for drinking; imported water is also available.

Note that, unlike in Holland, marijuana and other such recreational drugs are illegal.

ACCOMMODATION

A wide range of accommodation is available to suit most tastes. Suggestions for where to stay in Aruba, Bonaire and Curaçao are given in the directory at the end of each regional chapter. There are also some condominiums available throughout the ABC islands. If you want to rent a condominium (or 'condo'), it is the same as renting an apartment or villa, sharing the use of facilities such as a swimming pool and any bars or restaurants.

The 'high season' runs from late December through to March. This has more to do with North Americans escaping winter in the northern hemisphere than the weather in the ABC islands. Rainfall is not much of a problem, and the ABC islands lie completely outside the hurricane belt, so there isn't actually any one time of year to avoid. The 'low season' extends from mid-April through to September. At this time of year there are generally less people and the prices are lower (sometimes dropping by as much as 50 per cent).

> ### TIME
>
> The ABC islands are on Atlantic Standard Time, one hour ahead of Eastern Standard Time and the same as Eastern Daylight Saving Time. To Europeans it is GMT minus 4hr, BST minus 5hr.

Regardless of season, hotels add 10–15 per cent as a surcharge for service and 11 per cent for room tax. It is customary to tip porters an average of 50 cents US$ per bag; other gratuities are left to the discretion of guests.

Above: *Oceans Bar and Restaurant is one of numerous quality dining establishments on Bonaire.*

Transport

Driving is on the right-hand side of the road. Cars, four-wheel drive vehicles, motorcycles (dirt-bikes), scooters and bicycles may be hired for getting around and a limousine service is available. Car hire companies, both international and local, are located at the airport, in the capital and in the main hotels. Note that only a few fuel stations are open late at night or on Sundays, on a rotating basis. International, US, Canadian, and European driving licenses are all valid for use on the islands. Generally, local drivers are extremely courteous, but be careful of the goats, donkeys and pedestrians that roam the islands' roads.

Renting motorized aquatic or land transport should be approached with caution. Some companies offer self-insured policies, so when accidents occur exorbitant charges may be levied against the hirer's credit card for repairs or replacement of the transport. Also, car theft, especially of rental vehicles left unattended (a 'V' on the numberplate gives away that it is a hired vehicle), is on the increase.

Taxis have TX on their license plate, but are not metered and should have a fixed price schedule for most destinations on the islands. Make sure you fix the price of the journey with the driver before you set off. Fares are for a maximum of four passengers and 20–25

Above: *A dive boat from Captain Don's Habitat on Bonaire approaches the shoreline.*
Below: *Many hotels have good facilities, such as the pool at the Tamarijn Beach Resort on Aruba.*

per cent is added for each additional passenger and during late hours – generally after 23:00, though on Curaçao fares are surcharged by 25 per cent between 20:00 and midnight and 50 per cent between midnight and 06:00. Also, US$1 is added on Sundays and official holidays and another one dollar if the boot cannot close normally due to the amount of luggage within. Tipping is usually 10 per cent of the fare.

Taxis can usually be found at any hotel, or ordered through the central despatch office when in Bonaire (tel 869 0752) or Curaçao (tel 8100). Taxi drivers can also provide a half-day tour of the island. On Curaçao shared taxis operate within Willemstad.

SUNDRIES
Before your visit make sure you purchase and take with you antihistamines, anti-misting agents, decongestants, pain killers, mosquito repellent, suntan lotion, Swim-Ear type ear drying aids, any necessary prescription medicines, spare prescription spectacles if worn, and anything else that may be important to your welfare. These items may not always be available locally and will cost more as they will have been imported.

There are a number of bus services on the islands. On Aruba, buses run on a regular daytime schedule between San Nicholas, Oranjestad and the resorts along Eagle and Palm Beaches. On Bonaire minibuses run from central Kralendijk to Rincon but none go south past the airport. On Curaçao large blue or yellow buses run every half an hour on the most used routes. There are two bus terminals in Willemstad; the main one, serving the harbour area and the east of the island, is found outside of the Post Office on the Waaigat Inlet in Punda. The second terminal, which serves the hotel area, the airport and the west of the island, is by the underpass in Otrobanda. Private minibuses follow routes at the driver's whim – look for the word BUS on the license plate. Many of the main hotels provide their own minibus services to Willemstad.

MONEY

The official currency of Aruba is the Aruban Florin, whereas the official currency of Bonaire and Curaçao is the Netherlands Antilles Florin (guilder). The Netherlands Antilles Florin is not accepted in Aruba, and the Aruban Florin is not accepted on Bonaire or Curaçao, although both currencies can of course be changed in banks. The Venezuelan Bolívar and the US dollar are accepted on all three islands.

Both ABC island currencies are pegged to the US dollar. The Aruban Florin is divided into 100 cents, with coins of 5, 10, 25 cents and 1 Florin, and banknotes of 5, 10, 25, 50 and 100 Florin denomination. The Netherlands Antilles Florin (abbreviated as NAG, NAFl, NFl, or just Fl) is also divided into cents, with coins of 1, 5, 10, 25, 50 cents and 1 guilder. Paper money is available in 5, 10, 25, 50 and 100 guilder notes. Higher value paper money does exist, but is not particularly common. Note that Bonaire follows a particular tradition in the way that numbers are displayed: thousands are separated from hundreds with a decimal point, and guilders are separated from cents with a comma; so, for example, thirty six thousand, one hundred and twenty one guilders and thirty cents would be written as NAFl 36.121,30.

Most larger hotels provide foreign exchange facilities, but with the economy so dependent on the US dollar there is little need to carry local currency. Travellers' cheques and US dollars are accepted virtually everywhere, even in buses and taxis. However, you may have difficulty changing large denominations such as US$100 or US$50 bills in shops and restaurants, and are likely to require identification and proof of purchase to change travellers' cheques. Buses will not take bills larger than US$5. Note that on Bonaire and Curaçao the import and export of local currency is limited to NAFl 200, and that the importation of Dutch or Surinam silver coins is forbidden throughout the ABC islands.

BONAIRE AND CURAÇAO ELECTRICITY

Bonaire and Curaçao have mains electricity supplies that operate on 120/127 volts with an alternating current of 50Hz. On these islands equipment designed for European 220 volts, 50Hz will require a transformer unless the appliance is of the multi-voltage type. Visitors with American equipment should note that this is not 110 volts, 60Hz as in the USA. American appliances with electrical motors will run slower than normal because of the 50Hz and run hot because of the higher voltage. Strobe (flash gun) chargers or other battery chargers designed for 60Hz may take up to four times as long to recharge. Power surges and brownouts are not uncommon. If you plug anything electronically delicate into a standard wall outlet, it is sensible to have a surge protector in between. Most hotels, diving operators and dive shops have transformers or controlled power outlets for charging purposes. There are only two cycle formats around the world, 50Hz or 60Hz, and chargers labelled 50/60Hz are usable anywhere without problems.

All major credit cards are accepted at most commercial establishments, even in supermarkets. Usually when buying with a credit card, your card will be charged in the currency of the issuing country. Occasionally, shopkeepers may charge the card in the local currency: if they do, make sure that the use of the local currency is clearly marked on the charge slip, and a special charge slip which allows the shop to select a currency next to the total is used. Travellers carrying Automatic Teller Machine (ATM) cards bearing the MasterCard, CIRRUS, NYCE or other ATM network logos can withdraw cash in Aruban Florins (on Aruba) and Netherlands Antillean Florins (on Bonaire and Curaçao). The home bank account will be debited in the currency where the cards were issued, though service charges will be deducted.

BANKS

On Aruba banks are open on weekdays from 08:00 to 12:00 and 13:30 to 16:00, although some branches stay open until 18:00 on Friday. Money transfer services are available via Western Union Money Transfer Service; for information call De Palm Tours on (297) 824400. On Bonaire and Curaçao banks are open on weekdays from 08:00 or 08:30 to 15:30 or 16:00. The airport bank in Curaçao is open from 08:00 until 20:00 Monday to Saturday and 09:00 until 16:00 on Sunday. All other banks on the ABC islands are closed at the weekend.

Above: *Pottery is laid out for sale in Willemstad, the administrative centre of the Netherlands Antilles.*
Opposite: *The imposing Queen Juliana Bridge rises high above the entrance to Willemstad's harbour.*

ELECTRICITY

On Aruba electricity supplies operate on 110 volts with an alternating current of 60Hz, whereas on Bonaire and Curaçao the electricity supplies operate on 120/127 volts with an alternating current of 50Hz. European 220-volt appliances and many South American electrical appliances require a voltage adapter (unless they are of the multi-voltage type) and a surge protector should be used for delicate equipment. While the majority of US appliances will run safely without transformers or adapters, electric razors and hair-dryers should not be left on for too long as they may overheat. Dive shops have regulated outlets for safe charging.

COMMUNICATIONS

The ABC islands all have modern international communications for telephone calls, including direct dial, person to person and collect calls, as well as telex and telegrams, email and marine telephone calls.

The international dialling code for Aruba is 297, followed by the local six digit number. When telephoning from within

NUMBERS IN PAPIAMENTO	
0	Zero, Nul or Nada
1	Unu
2	Dos
3	Tres
4	Kwater
5	Sinku
6	Seis
7	Shete
8	Ocho
9	Nuebe
10	Dies

the island you need to dial only the local six-digit number. Local numbers used to be five digits but were changed in 1997 to include the prefix 8. The international dialling code for Bonaire and Curaçao is 599, followed by 7 for Bonaire and 9 for Curaçao, then the local number (on Bonaire the local number is only four digits). As in Aruba, local telephone numbers can be reached by dialling just the local number.

Calls from hotels or resorts are expensive so it is advisable to use the other telephone services available. On Aruba it is cheaper to use Servicio di Telecomunicacion di Aruba (SETAR), to be found next to the Aruba post office at the Irausquinplein, at the SETAR Teleshop at Palm Beach across from the Hyatt Regency Aruba Beach Resort & Casino, and at the SETAR Teleshop, Schelpstraat, around the corner from Le Petite Café in Oranjestad. On Bonaire you can call from the Telbo building in Kralendijk, and on Curaçao it is cheaper to use the offices of the telecommunications company (Setel).

Internet access is available on Aruba through the Cyber Cafe, located at the Royal Plaza Mall in Oranjestad. On Bonaire there is an internet kiosk available at the Harbourside Mall in Kralendijk. The cost for using the kiosk is NAFl 1 for 3 minutes, and you need to feed coins into a machine to pay for access; plastic cards or paper money are not accepted.

Personal cellular phones will not work on the ABC islands (unless the personal phones are on satellite), since local cellular service providers have no reciprocal agreements with other carriers.

LANGUAGE

Dutch is the official language of the ABC islands but most locals also speak English and Spanish as well as Papiamento.

Papiamento (also spelt Papiamentu) is a kind of Creole language indigenous to the Netherlands Antilles. The word is a derivation of the old Spanish verb *papear*, which meant 'to converse', though nowadays the word is thought of as meaning 'babble'. There are numerous theories on the origins of Papiamento but it is most likely that it began as a Portuguese-based Creole derived during the slave trade from early contact between the Portuguese and West Africans in the 15th century. Since the Portuguese colonized a wide area of the West African coast, the slaves came from far apart and did not speak a common language. A pidgin language developed from African and Portuguese vocabulary, which became the mother tongue of a generation that settled on the ABC islands. The resulting Creole often served as a secret language shared by the slaves while not understood by slave owners who only spoke Portuguese.

PAPIAMENTO PHRASES			
Good morning	Bon dia	At the port	Na waf
Good afternoon	Bon tardi	The road	Caminda
Good night	Bon nochi	Police	Polis
Welcome	Bon Bini	I am hungry	Mi tin hamber
Please	Por fabor	Food	Cuminda
Thank you	Danki	Fish	Pisca
How are you?	Con ta bai	Chicken	Galinja
Goodbye	Ajo	Lobster	Kreeft
Me	Ami	Crab	Kangrew
You	Abo	Conch	Calco
I, I am	Mi	Salad	Salada
Miss	Yufrow	Bread	Pan
Mrs	Señora	Cheese	Keshi
Mr	Mener	Milk	Lechi
How much does	Kwanto esaki	Sugar	Suku
this cost	ta costa	Salt	Salo
Bank	Banco	Pepper	Pika
Money	Plaka	Soft drink	Soda
Water	Awa	Beer	Cerbes
Beach, ocean	Lama	Wine	Binja (also Purple)

Opposite: *Aruba's cruise ship terminal is visible from the footbridge of the Sonesta Suites Hotel.*

Papiamento also includes Dutch, English, Portuguese, Spanish, West African and Indian words. It is only spoken on Aruba, the Netherlands Antilles and Surinam (formerly the Netherlands Guiana). In Curaçao Papiamento has a strong Dutch influence, while in Aruba it has more Spanish influence. An official spelling for Papiamento words has been established and dictionaries are available on the islands. However, on Aruba different spellings are used for some words, so that while people of all three islands can communicate well via the spoken language, differences in the written language can cause problems.

Unlike other Caribbean islands where the Creole dialects are often treated with disdain, Papiamento is spoken across the social spectrum and is even the language used in debates by the Aruban parliament. The many differences in accents and vocabulary that have developed over the years has meant that Papiamento is becoming a symbol of cultural identity throughout the islands.

Modern Papiamento has a structural similarity to Crioulo, the Portuguese Creole that is still spoken on the West African coast in parts of the Cape Verde Islands, Gambia, Guinea Bissau and Senegal. Other Portuguese-based Creoles connected with early Portuguese colonization include Cafundo (Brazil), Korlai (Bombay, India), Macanese (Macao, China), Kristang (Melaka, Malaysia), Ternateno (Maluku, Indonesia) and Indo-Portuguese (Sri Lanka). However, only Cafundo shares West African origins.

HOLIDAYS AND CARNIVAL

Carnival time in the ABC islands is the week before Lent, when there are parades, elaborate costumes and constant partying, culminating on the Sunday before Ash Wednesday. The birthplace of Aruba's exuberant carnival is San Nicolas, while more parades are now held

Below: *Aruba is best known for its carnival, though there are plenty of other performances here as well.*

in Oranjestad. Easter is also a time of celebration when there is a Harvest Festival (Simadan).

Other holidays when banks, offices and shops are closed are Christmas Day, Boxing Day, New Year's Day, Ash Wednesday, Good Friday, Easter Monday, the Dutch Queen's Birthday on 30th April (Rincon Day), International Labour Day on May 1st and Ascension Day.

Aruba also celebrates Betico Croes day on January 25th, an official holiday in memory of the political leader who attained 'Status Aparte' from Holland, as well as Flag Day on March 18th, a national holiday. Bonaire national holiday for Flag Day is on September 6th, while on Curaçao Flag Day is on July 2nd; both Bonaire and Curaçao celebrate Antillean Day on October 21st.

January 1st is celebrated on Bonaire with midnight fireworks and groups of musicians called 'Dande' wandering from house to house singing good luck greetings. Bonaire also hosts a number of traditional festivals, including the Mascarada (Masquerade), celebrated from New Years Day to the 'Twelfth Night' (January 6), the Feasts of San Juan and San Pedro, celebrated in June, and Bari, which occurs from the end of October until the end of December.

> ### CASINOS
>
> Gaming is legal in the ABC islands. Gambling activities range from one-arm bandit machines to very up-market casinos. Most are open from midday till just before dawn, although Aruba's Crystal Casino runs 24 hours a day.
>
> As well as all the common betting games, the casinos offer Caribbean Stud Poker, which was invented in Aruba in 1988. As in Blackjack, each player competes only with the dealer, and there is a progressive jackpot that can reach hundreds of thousands of US$.

> ### RELIGION
>
> Most of the population is Roman Catholic but there are followers of many other creeds, including Protestants, Jews, Hindus, Muslims and Confucians.

All the islands hold various windsurfing and fishing competitions. During June, Bonaire hosts an annual international sailing regatta, combined with windsurfing and fishing competitions. Usually in October, Curaçao hosts a music festival when well-known artists are invited from other countries to contribute to a lively celebration of jazz and Latin music.

SHOPPING

Stores are generally open from 08:30 till noon, and then from 14:00 till 18:00 Monday to Saturday. Some shops are open on Sundays and holidays, though others only open on Sundays and holidays if cruise ships are in port. There is more variety on Aruba than in the so-called duty-free shops of Bonaire and Curaçao, but what is available is still mainly designer fashions, jewellery and electronic or camera equipment.

Curaçao prides itself on having the lowest prices for luxury items in the Caribbean. It is not technically a free port but taxes are very low and there are no duties on electronic products. There are also plenty of fashion items, jewellery, tourist curios and the famous Curaçao Liqueur, made from the dried peel of bitter oranges and a mixture of spices. Most of the duty-free shopping malls are located in a five square-block area in the Otrobanda and Punda districts of Willemstad; the two districts are separated by Saint Anna Baai (Bay) and connected by the Queen Emma Pontoon Bridge.

WHAT TO WEAR

Dress is casual, informal summer wear. Shorts and T-shirts are the norm for day wear while most visitors dress up in the evening for casinos, nightclubs and the more elegant restaurants. The air-conditioning in some places can be quite cold so a sweater is advisable. Bathing suits or skimpy outfits (for both sexes) should be confined to the beach and poolside only; it is illegal to wear these when shopping or sightseeing.

DIVING AND SNORKELLING IN THE ABC ISLANDS

Compared with the vast oceans the Caribbean Sea, a mere arm of the Atlantic, is minute – roughly 2415km (1500 miles) east to west and between 640 and 1540km (400 and 900 miles) north to south. Still, it contains more than a thousand different islands. Served by the Equatorial Current and the Gulf Stream it offers warm waters and a mild tropical climate, and is firmly established as the world's most frequented holiday diving destination.

The Caribbean was formed quite late in geological time. Some 200 million years ago, the earth's surface consisted of a supercontinent, Pangaea, surrounded by a great primordial ocean, Panthalassa, that covered the rest of the globe. Another 400 million years earlier there had been a proto-Atlantic Ocean, but tectonic plate movements had closed it. Pangaea, which consisted of Laurasia (Europe, North America and Asia) and Gondwanaland (the southern continents), slowly broke up to form the continents that we recognize today. Then three million years ago South America welded itself to North America, closing the Isthmus of Panama and delimiting the Atlantic Ocean. Cut off from the Pacific, the currents and species interaction in the Caribbean and North Atlantic were substantially reduced. Consequently the Caribbean has only a tenth of the marine species found in the much larger (and older) Indo-Pacific. Absent from the Caribbean are the ever-popular clownfish, lionfish and brightly coloured soft corals, but these are partly made up for by a profusion of other fish, gorgonians, rich coral reefs and colour from a myriad of sponges.

What the Caribbean lacks in species it compensates for in being diver-friendly. The islands and connecting ridges of the eastern Caribbean prevent the interchange of deep water from the Atlantic, so tides are smaller and the visibility good, sometimes approaching the near mythical 60m (200 ft). Apart from Cozumel's high-voltage drift diving, most Caribbean destinations including the ABC islands are relatively free of strong currents, and therefore well suited to novices and casual divers. Resorts throughout the Caribbean tend to be well organized and are often at the forefront of eco-tourism. In general, they have good facilities, introductory courses, a good selection of diving and camera equipment for hire

Opposite: *A dive boat floats above a typical ABC islands reef scene with various sponges.*
Above: *A mixed shoal of grunts and snappers shelter in the safety of a wreck.*

and a great variety of non-diving and after-dive activities, ideal for accompanying non-divers. You don't even have to get wet, as some have tourist submarines to take you down. Several destinations where diving is important to the economy have marine reserves, with fixed mooring buoys to minimize anchor damage.

For photographers, the Caribbean offers tame animals, maximum water clarity and minimum back scatter. And if the profusion of marine life is not enough, there are plenty of wrecks. During the Spanish colonial period the world's richest maritime trade was often prey to pirates, naval engagements and storms. Various 'treasure ships' have been located, while more modern wrecks are also regularly dived. Some islands have initiated artificial reef programs by sinking cleaned-up ships and aeroplanes.

DAN

The Divers Alert Network (DAN), based in North America, provides a 24-hour emergency hotline on diving related problems or injuries and recompression chamber assistance.

DAN is a publicly supported, non-profit membership organization for sport divers and research into diving medicine. Dubbed 'The Divers Safety Net', membership benefits include DAN's Diving Accident Manual.

Divers Alert Network, PO Box 3823, Duke University Medical Center, Durham, NC 27710, tel (919) 684 2948; websites, DAN America: www.diversalertnetwork.org; DAN Europe: www.daneurope.org

DIVING IN ARUBA, BONAIRE AND CURAÇAO

The waters around the ABC islands are influenced by the Southern Equatorial Current, which comes up from Antarctica. This current is full of nutrients that help enrich the coral reefs around the islands. The Equatorial Current later turns north when it reaches Panama and becomes the Gulf Stream.

Thanks to their colourful marine life and the consistency of diving conditions, the ABC islands are one of the Caribbean's top diving destinations. With majestic reefs, shoals of colourful fish, large pelagics, abundant invertebrates, wrecks, caverns and breathtaking visibility, the ABC islands guarantee an excellent diving holiday whether you are a snorkeller, novice diver, or seasoned veteran. An arid environment, minimal rainfall and a location outside the hurricane belt ensure that the underwater visibility is excellent. Among the friendly creatures you are likely to encounter are tarpon *(Megalops atlanticus)*, black grouper *(Mycteroperca bonaci)*, tiger grouper *(Mycteroperca tigris)*, great barracuda *(Sphyraena barracuda)*, and green moray eels *(Gymnothorax funebris)*. French angelfish *(Pomacanthus paru)* and queen angelfish *(Holacanthus ciliaris)* are common, while frogfish *(Antennarius multiocellatus)*, seahorses and numerous other small creatures are found.

DAN EMERGENCY LINES

DAN America
Peter B. Bennett Center, 6 West Colony Place, Durham, NC 27705, USA; tel 1 919 6842948, 800 446 2671; fax 1 919 4906630
USA and Canada and regional responsibility for Central and South America, the Caribbean, Polynesia, Micronesia and Melanesia (except Fiji).

DAN Europe Central Office
PO Box DAN 64026 Roseto (Te), Italy; tel 39 085 8930333; fax 39 085 8930050
Geographical Europe, European territories and protectorates, with regional responsibility for the Mediterranean Sea and Shore, the Red Sea, the Arabian Gulf, Ethiopia, Kenya and the Maldives.

Dawn and dusk are the times when predators are most active and several creatures of the night begin to appear at dusk. The ambient light in the water is highest between 10:00 and 14:00, so photographers using wide angle lenses may choose to dive hard between 09:30 and 15:00 and miss out on the afternoon's siesta.

THE STAR GRADING SYSTEM FOR DIVE QUALITY

While the quality of diving in the ABC islands is high, no dive site in the Caribbean can fully compare with the best of the Indian Ocean, South Pacific or Red Sea for species diversity. However, dives in the Caribbean can make up for this with their ease of diving, the quality of the reef, fish habituation to divers' presence and any unique small or rarely noticed creatures that can be easily found. Themed dives such as Dee Scarr's 'Touch the Sea' in Bonaire, Stingray City in the Cayman Islands, shark and dolphin dives in the Bahamas and specially sunk wrecks are other alternatives.

The author has graded the dive sites in this book on a world scale. When assessing a star-rating, readers should add one star to those given if they wish to compare the star-rating on a Caribbean scale.

LEARNING TO DIVE

While many people wish to upgrade their existing diving skills, others come to the ABC islands to first learn to dive. The most popular way to learn whether diving is for you is to enrol in a Discover Scuba programme. This 2–4 hour basic instruction course is a combination of lectures and swimming pool techniques designed to give you a taste of diving, fire your enthusiasm and teach basic water safety and conservation. If you decide to take up diving you can then take a resort course or an Open Water certification course. This gives you tuition by fully qualified dive instructors and teaches you to dive safely. A popular variant on this is the referral course, whereby much of the classroom work and pool training is done at home before travelling out to the ABC islands to complete the open water dives.

Below: *A queen angelfish explores the surroundings of Salt Pier (Bonaire, Site 46).*

CERTIFYING DIVING ORGANIZATIONS

There are several diver training organizations, with varying degrees of international coverage.

PADI	Professional Association of Diving Instructors
BSAC	British Sub-Aqua Club
NAUI	National Association of Underwater Instructors
SAA	Sub Aqua Association
SSI	Scuba Schools International

Under the PADI system, divers qualified in the Open Water course are then able to go on to an Advanced Open Water course. Thereafter, a wide variety of speciality courses become available to divers, including wreck diving, cave and cavern diving, underwater photography and dive instruction. Similar speciality courses are available through other training agencies. The BSAC has two types of instruction, one similar to that of PADI and another where more detailed training is included in the basic course to enable divers to dive safely in cold water and challenging conditions. Several agencies affiliated to the World Federation (CMAS) also include diving in challenging conditions among their basic training.

Once you are fully qualified, your certification or 'C card' serves as your diving passport and is recognized worldwide. It is valid for life, but, if you are unable to dive from one year to the next, it is recommended that you enrol on a refresher course. As with most sports, your confidence and awareness will increase the more you partake of the sport. Also always ensure that any equipment you own is serviced at least yearly and especially after a lengthy break.

When choosing a dive operation on the ABC islands, make sure that it is affiliated to one of the major schools of instruction, such as PADI, SSI, NAUI, or BSAC International. These are the world's leading diver training organizations and all train to the highest standards. Most diver training in the ABC islands is to American training

Below *Divers from Captain Don's Habitat are asked to sign in as soon as they board the dive boat.*
Opposite: *Divers load gear on to the dive boat at the jetty of Easy Divers on Curaçao.*

agency standards such as NAUI, PADI or SSI. However, there are some European-run operators training divers to the CMAS system, while the BSAC system is widely recognized; most operators have staff who can teach in English, Dutch, German, Spanish, French or Papiamento.

You must gain certification before you are allowed to rent equipment and head off to dive independently with a buddy. Most diving operators and live-aboard boats require proof that you have been properly trained by a recognized training agency – a diver's certification card ('C card'), logbook of recent dives and the date of your last dive. A check-out dive may be required if you cannot produce these documents and operators may insist that you dive with an instructor.

DISABLED DIVERS

A few diving operations in Aruba, such as Red Sail Sports, are specifically geared to cater for disabled divers. Certain boats are specially adapted for wheelchairs, and such dive centres are able to certify people of all disabilities, including paraplegics, quadriplegics and those with impaired hearing or sight, provided that the individual is medically able to dive. Any prospective student must consult a doctor prior to taking a certification course. As a general rule, any dive operator

STATEMENT OF ALTERNATIVE TRAINING (SALT) TABLE

The British Sub-Aqua Club accepts the following qualifications by other diver training agencies to be roughly similar:

Entry Level: (these qualifications do not usually include rescue training)
BSAC Club Diver/Ocean Diver
NAUI Scuba Diver & Advanced Diver
PADI Open Water Diver & Advanced Open Water Diver
SAA Open Water Diver
SSI Open Water & Advanced Open Water Diver

Second Level: (these qualifications must include rescue training)
BSAC Sports Diver
NAUI Scuba Rescue Diver
PADI Rescue Diver
SAA Club Diver
SSI Advanced Open Water Diver with Stress & Rescue Speciality

Third Level:
BSAC Dive Leader
NAUI Master Scuba Diver
PADI Divemaster
SAA Dive Leader
SSI Master Diver

with its own jetty will be accessible for disabled divers, whereas smaller operators whose access to their dive boat is by beach cannot offer the service.

Facilities for divers with disabilities are not yet available on Bonaire and Curaçao.

Snorkel Tips, Techniques and Equipment

Entering the water for the first time wearing a mask, snorkel and fins can be quite daunting, but with the correct techniques you will quickly discover that snorkelling requires little physical effort. Only the ability to swim is essential.

Instruction is offered at nearly all top hotels and dive resorts and may take place in a dive centre's swimming pool.

With instruction you will quickly be able to enjoy the many excellent snorkelling sites around the ABC islands. It is wise to check with the local dive shop whether the area you are planning to snorkel in is safe enough for you and your family. If in any doubt, do not enter the water – seek advice first.

Snorkellers should take care to stay in deep enough water when snorkellng over shallow reefs, as it is easy to cause damage to the fragile corals or inflict personal injury. Never snorkel or tread water in a vertical position as flapping fins can easily break coral or disturb sediment which may in turn smother coral polyps. For the same reasons, never adjust snorkelling equipment near coral – always swim away into a 'safe' area.

Equipment can normally be rented from a dive centre, though snorkelling is not an expensive sport and it is simple to purchase your own. Snorkelling equipment consists of a mask with an adjustable retaining strap and tempered glass, snorkel, fins and, if the snorkeller intends to descend below the surface, a weight belt. The snorkel should have a bore of approximately 25mm (1in), but should not be too long, as you must be able to clear the water out of it with a single breath. Some snorkels have a self-draining valve, which will allow some of the water to drain out. Some feature top vent systems to limit surface chop entering, though these can restrict breathing. The angle of the mouthpiece can make a big difference to comfort, so it helps if this is adjustable.

Fins come in two different styles. The open-heel foot pocket type, incorporating an adjustable ankle strap, is often worn over diving bootees. The smaller, softer kind features a moulded shoe fitting that fits snugly around the foot. Buoyancy vests may also be worn as an additional safety measure, but for general shallow water snorkelling these are rarely used.

In addition to the basic equipment of mask, snorkel and fins, it is sensible to wear either a Lycra skin suit or a thin full wet suit. This will not only shield you from the sun's rays but also afford protection against any stinging microscopic plankton which may be found in the water. If you have no other protection, at least wear a T-shirt to keep off the sun.

Diving Equipment

Supplementing the basic snorkelling equipment, diving equipment consists of a scuba cylinder and air; a regulator or demand valve through which you breathe; a contents gauge (pressure gauge) to indicate how much air you have left in your scuba cylinder; an easy-to-read depth gauge to indicate your current depth and maximum depth reached; a

Opposite: *A useful guided snorkelling programme is available on Bonaire.*

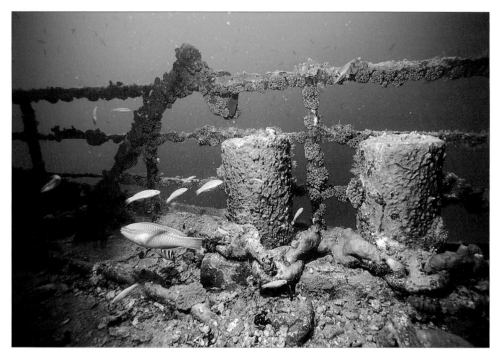

Above: *A parrotfish swims across the beautiful Jane Sea Wreck (Aruba, Site 12).*

watch with an adjustable bezel or timer device to let you know the duration of your dive; a weight belt and weights, which help counteract the body's natural buoyancy; and a buoyancy compensator or adjustable buoyancy life jacket of some description that allows you to adjust buoyancy at depth in order to remain at that depth or keep off the corals.

Because of the warm water temperatures all year round in the ABC islands, most divers do not require a full wet suit; a shorty wet suit is usually sufficient. However, thin divers and underwater photographers, who move around less, may want to wear a light full wet suit. Those who do not require a wet suit at all will find a Lycra skin useful as protection against fire coral and stinging plankton when underwater. A small knife may be worn, in case you need to use it to cut yourself free from impediments such as fishing line loose in the water. A computer is recommended for more experienced divers who are on an unlimited dive package, to assist them with repetitive dive profiles.

When storing diving equipment at the end of a dive vacation, make sure that it is rinsed thoroughly and that all salt concretions have been removed. Have your regulator serviced and pack equipment carefully: remove any batteries from electronic equipment and torches; clean knife blades; hang dive suits on thick or padded coat hangers and store everything away from heat or direct sunlight.

SILICONE MASKS

Most divers' masks are now made of silicone since divers prefer that the material pressing against their face is soft, lasts longer and can be made opaque, coloured or black. Many wearers feel less restricted in opaque masks and photographer's models certainly look more eye-catching in a clear or brightly coloured mask. However, photographers themselves often find that clear masks reflect onto the eyepiece of their camera or camera housing, particularly when the sun is behind them; for this reason many photographers opt for a black mask.

PERSONAL VISION

Poor personal vision underwater can not only decrease your appreciation of the marine world but also compromise your safety. Eyesight problems are exacerbated in the lower light conditions prevalent underwater. Bear in mind that if you cannot read a diving gauge or dive computer display properly you will be putting yourself and your diving companions in danger.

If you do have a problem with your sight, consider investing in optical lenses ground directly into or bonded to the mask faceplate. This method ensures that the alignment of the lenses is set very accurately. Lenses that are not centred accurately can cause eyestrain, perceptual changes or double vision. This is at its worst with stronger pre-scriptions and in conditions of low light, low visibility or with nitrogen narcosis.

Using corrective lenses in a mask, however, does mean that you also require spectacles handy when you are not wearing the mask. If you find this an overwhelming hassle, consider wearing contact lenses. There used to be some fears over the use of contact lenses for diving but these have now been dispelled. When properly fitted, rigid gas-permeable contact lenses are rarely lost underwater, and although on ascent from a deep dive there is sometimes a build-up of microscopic bubbles between the lens and the eye, these bubbles out-gas slowly through the lens and generally clear within 15–30 minutes. Soft lenses fit the eye differently and there are differing opinions as to whether they can be lost easily. If your mask floods or is lost it is best to only partially open your eyes to prevent loss of the lenses.

> **ANTI-MISTING AGENTS**
>
> A good and very cheap anti-misting agent for diving masks is washing up liquid detergent. Rub a very small amount of it onto the inside of the mask and rinse it out with seawater immediately before diving or snorkelling. As with commercial mask-clearing agents, make sure you rinse your mask very thoroughly since any residues can sting your eyes. Veteran divers also swear by human saliva – it is free and always available!

Below: *Water temperatures are generally warm all year round in the ABC islands.*

Modern diving computers have made diving far easier by virtue of one not having to spend time working out decompression tables or other systems. They are particularly useful when checking for a suitable dive profile for your next dive, when diving more than twice a day or for underwater photographers, enabling them to concentrate on their photography while the computer does the necessary calculations.

A great advantage of some modern diving computers is the ability to interface them with a personal computer. With this system you can upload your previous dive profiles, which is very useful for maintaining your logbook and indispensable for doctors if you get a decompression sickness problem. You can also alter some of the diving computer's functions.

However, diving computers are not infallible. They were originally calculated on a mathematical model based on research done by the navy on fit young men. Some diving computers may make allowances for cold water and higher-than-normal work rates, but they do not allow for people who are over-weight, over fifty or female, so be conservative. It is worth remembering that a warmer diver has a faster rate of blood circulation and therefore more exchange of nitrogen between the blood and the tissues, thereby increasing the chance of getting a bend – it makes sense not to rush about and overheat.

A few diving computers are designed to stop supplying information if you go into decompression; such computers are best avoided as they become unusable when you most need them – when you have made a mistake! Some diving computers switch off soon after surfacing to save on the battery. These are also best avoided, as a diving computer should really remain switched on until it has calculated that all of the nitrogen in your tissues has been out-gassed. This of course is heavy on batteries, as such computers may be switched on for more than a week at a time.

BATTERIES

Carrying spare batteries is essential, especially if you are travelling to dive areas where backup is minimal or non-existent. Battery failure can be a major problem, not just with diving computers but with any equipment that relies on them. I have often been let down with little warning. Also, diving computers can occasionally switch themselves on in humid climates, and in hot countries batteries discharge more quickly. To safeguard against battery failure it is sensible to carry two diving computers or take decompression tables, a watch and a depth gauge as backup.

Most diving computers have to be returned to a qualified technician for battery replacement. The connections are usually soldered on and there can be a problem with over-tightening of the battery compartment, which allows water to leak into the unit. There have been a couple of models that were designed for owners to replace their batteries, but they were dogged by leakage due to split battery compartments – or by the parent company going out of business. The Nitrox version of Cochran's Commander is one exception, and is easy to use in the field for replacing batteries. Even if the battery compartment does flood, it is safely sealed away from the diving computer's electronics and only requires flushing out with fresh water, drying out and fitting with new batteries to get the unit working again.

PRACTICAL HINTS

Use a computer with displays that are large enough for you to read when underwater. This is especially important for divers with poor eyesight. Also make sure the displays of numbers and icons are easy for you to understand. In the event of experiencing mild nitrogen narcosis, or if you become stressed, you do not want to have to try to understand ambiguous figures.

A computer that switches itself on in one metre of water will eliminate any chance of forgetting to switch it on. It is also useful if your computer gives out an audible warning at any time you violate the rules of diving. However, do not wave your arms about during a dive as the unit will assume that you are ascending too fast and react with audible warnings.

For underwater photographers, with their hands full of photographic equipment, it is more convenient to read from a wrist-mounted unit than from computers that are fitted into consoles. A back light feature is useful for dim-light, night or cave diving.

There is no need to pay high prices for a protective cover or wire cage for your diving computer display. Buy a roll of the clear self-adhesive masking tape used by garages when they spray-paint vehicles and stick the correct length of it over your display – the tape is hard wearing and easily replaced if necessary.

Dive Profiles

Finish all dives, whether non-decompression or decompression dives, with a five-minute safety stop at 5m (16ft). Sometimes, particularly in a swell, it can be difficult to hold to a decompression stop at 3m (10ft). It is easier to hold a decompression stop at 5m

(16ft) where you can allow a little leeway if the swell causes you to ascend a little. If you take your decompression stop a little deeper, a good computer will compensate for this by quoting longer times. Go very slowly when ascending from 5m (16ft) to the surface.

Note that different diving computer manufacturers use different algorithms. If your buddy's computer quotes different no-stop or decompression times, stick to the times given by your own. Modern diving computers also take into account your total nitrogen loading over many dives, not all of which may have been with the same buddy.

Do not dive to the computer's limits. The chances of decompression sickness increase with poor circulation, exertion, dehydration, cold, drugs (including alcohol and caffeine) and poor physical fitness. If you are making repetitive dives, reduce the limits progressively and if you are diving over several days take a day off on the fourth day to allow your body time to out-gas the nitrogen that will have accumulated.

Below: *Two examples of a diving computer – the one on the left also covers Nitrox diving.*

Disposable soft lenses are designed to be discarded after use so their loss is less of a problem; indeed some divers use disposable lenses just for diving.

There are currently two kinds of refractive surgery to permanently correct short-sightedness: Radial Keratotomy (RK) and Photo-refractive Keratectomy (PRK). If you have undergone RK surgery, ensure that during a dive your mask is fully equalized, as mask squeeze can aggravate the healing cuts. With the newer PRK, once the eye is fully healed there are no limitations on diving.

NITROX AND OTHER MIXED GAS TECHNICAL DIVING

Larger operators in Aruba, Bonaire and Curaçao can now offer Nitrox and other mixed gas technical diving training.

Nitrox, also called SafeAir, is enriched air that has more than the natural amount of oxygen and therefore less nitrogen. Normal air contains roughly 21% of oxygen, 78% nitrogen and 1% inert and other gases, whereas Nitrox air has an oxygen content of up to 32% or 36% for normal diving and up to 50% for decompression diving.

The main advantages of Nitrox diving are that it enables bottom time to be extended beyond the normal no-decompression time and shortens any necessary decompression time – when compared with breathing compressed air. Other benefits of Nitrox are a reduction in the narcotic effect of nitrogen, a lower rate of gas consumption and a reduction in the feeling of fatigue experienced by some divers after diving. However, there are also a few dangers in its use. When the partial pressure of oxygen in the breathing mix is increased, it becomes toxic at a shallower depth than normal and also repeated dives build up the chance of oxygen toxicity. It is important not to exceed the depth limits that produce oxygen toxicity or the time limits

Below: *The Arashi Airplane Wreck (Aruba, Site 2) is one of a variety of wrecks off Aruba.*
Opposite: *Excellent underwater visibility in the ABC islands attracts many photographers.*

for oxygen exposure, and to allow at least one hour on the surface breathing air between dives to clear the body of the problems caused by breathing oxygen and nitrogen under pressure.

There are special tables and diving computers that cover the use of Nitrox in diving and it is essential that you take a course to understand the problems of Nitrox before being allowed to use it. A number of necessary checks have to be made when using Nitrox air. Since oxygen has a fire risk if it comes into contact with any oil contamination, any cylinders that are used for oxygen-enriched mixtures must be carefully cleaned of all oils or greases and should be clearly marked and colour-coded with bands of green and yellow, as well as being clearly tagged. There are also special cleaning requirements for regulators and special 'O' rings that must be used when using the higher levels of oxygen mixtures. During training you are taught how to analyze the air mixture in a cylinder.

When using mixtures containing enriched oxygen you must not go deeper than 40m (130ft) on Nitrox 32% or 34m (112ft) on Nitrox 36%. Mixtures containing more than 36% are used only to increase the efficiency of out-gassing nitrogen while decompressing at shallow depths. You can increase the safety of your diving when breathing Nitrox, by not exceeding the depth limit for your gas mix, and using the decompression tables calculated for air or diving computers that are programmed for air – a good procedure to adopt if you are out of condition.

Commercial, scientific and technical divers have been using 100% oxygen for many years in conjunction with in-water decompression but recent studies suggest that 85% oxygen mixed with 15% helium is likely to be safer (though the recommended total single oxygen exposure time may still be reached quite quickly). Taking breaks to use air are also beneficial. However, if oxygen is not actually required and is just being used to increase the safety factor, then breathing SafeAir 50 (Nitrox 50%, ie. 50% oxygen) has operational and physiological advantages over 85% or 100% oxygen. This gas mixture can solve the problems of oxygen toxicity caused by long dives that approach the limits of oxygen exposure, while realizing a significant increase in the out-gassing of nitrogen when compared with air.

DIVE FLAGS

The official international flag for divers is the 'A' Flag. It is split into two colours, white nearest to the flagpole and blue beyond it; the blue part has a section shaped like a 'V' on its side cut out of it. This flag covers both professional and sport divers. When flown, the 'A' Flag signifies that a vessel has divers in the water so other vessels should keep clear and reduce speed. It is illegal to fly this flag if the vessel concerned does not have divers actually in the water.

However, dive centres all over the world – including in the ABC islands – tend to use a diffferent flag altogether. This flag is all red except for a narrow white stripe running diagonally from the top nearest the flagpole to the bottom furthest away from it (some companies add their own logo to this flag). It does not have any legal international meaning and will often be flown outside diving establishments and on vessels that do not have divers in the water. It has however, come to be universally recognized as a 'divers down' flag.

ARUBA

A merican divers voted Aruba as having the best topside attractions in the Caribbean. Of the three ABC islands, Aruba has the finest beaches; all but one of which are public and free. Also the Arubans graciously welcome tourists and even though half a million tourists 'invade' the island for their holidays each year there is no hint of resentment on the part of the locals. It is no surprise that Aruba attracts such a high ratio of repeat visitors.

Expanses of beaches and solitary coves line both sides of the island, although there are fewer on the northeast side where the sea is rough and not good for swimming. There is a plethora of non-diving watersports, especially windsurfing and yachting in the 15–20 knot trade winds. The winds are so consistent that Arubans can sail to the coast of Venezuela, about 25km (15 miles) away, in less time than it takes by ferry.

Other activities include fishing, mountain biking, horse riding, tennis and golfing. Also, for those not inclined to get wet, Aruba's marine life can be viewed from submarines, semi-submarines and glass-bottomed boats. Rock climbing is available in the east of the island.

HISTORY
The first people known to have inhabited Aruba were Arawak Indians called Caiquetios who migrated north from the Orinoco Basin in South America. Remnants of their culture can be found at a number of sites around the island including hieroglyphics still visible on granite boulders and in some caves.

It is thought that the Spanish explorer Alonso de Ojeda claimed the island for Queen Isabella in 1499, hoping to find gold there. However, the name Aruba seems to have originally derived from Arawak Indian words, either *oibubai* (which means guide), *oruba* (meaning well-placed, convenient to the mainland) or *ora* (shell) and *oubao* (island).

The Spanish found the climate too arid for cultivation and failed to find any gold, so in 1515 they exported almost the entire Indian population to Santo Domingo on Hispaniola. Here they were put to work in the cattle farms, horse farms and mines, though twelve years later some of the Indians were sent back to Aruba to help protect the Spanish Main. During

---

Opposite: *The sandy beaches lining the leeward side of Aruba include beautiful Druif Beach.*
Above: *A lasting Dutch colonial influence is evident in the design of a modern Aruban house.*

the following 150 years the island became a hiding place for pirates and buccaneers preying on ships transporting New World treasures back to Europe. Fortunately, because the Spanish considered Aruba useless, the island was spared the usual horrors of Spanish occupation and the Indian population was not exterminated.

In 1636, near to the culmination of 80 years war between them, the Dutch, who had been expelled by the Spanish from their base in St Maarten and were looking for another place to establish a colonial presence, captured Aruba, Bonaire and Curaçao from the Spanish. Curaçao became the administrative capital for the Dutch West India Company in the Netherlands Antilles, with Aruba operating as one of its main satellites. The fortress Fort Zoutman, the oldest building on the island, was built soon after. There was a short period from 1805 to 1815 when the island was captured by the British, but Aruba has remained under Dutch control ever since.

Alluvial gold was discovered at Rooi Huit in 1824, with the ruins of a 19th-century smelting plant still surviving in Balashi, northwest of Spanish Lagoon. The gold mines yielded over 1,360,000kg (3,000,000lb) before they ceased to be economic in 1916. However, black gold (oil) was then found in the Maracaibo fields in Venezuela in the 1920s and the Dutch islands presented ideal locations for refineries.

The Royal Dutch Shell refinery was built along the Eagle Beach area in 1926, and in 1929 the Pan American Petroleum Corporation built a refinery at San Nicolas. In 1934 EXXON bought this refinery (the world's largest until 1968), turning San Nicolas into a major commercial centre: Aruba was the largest refiner of petrol for the allied forces during World

ARIKOK NATIONAL PARK

Covering 17 per cent of Aruba's landmass, Arikok National Park was first designated as an area of national importance in the early 1980s. It is an area of unique scenic beauty, flora and fauna, geological formations and cultural resources. On land, the park includes the three primary geological formations that make up the island. These rocks and their microclimates play an important role in supporting indigenous plants and wildlife. The limestone formation supports the island's largest natural freshwater spring, and formed the site of the agricultural settlements of the early Europeans.

War II. The Eagle refinery was closed down in the 1950s and the EXXON refinery in 1985 because of a worldwide glut in petroleum. The emphasis then turned to tourism.

In 1991 the Coastal Oil Company of Houston, Texas reopened the San Nicolas refinery, but the island has continued to invest heavily in tourism, which has long since replaced oil as Aruba's major industry. Some light industries produce tobacco, beverages and consumer goods but it is petroleum refining and tourism that give Aruba one of the highest standards of living in the Caribbean.

STATUS APARTE

Historically, Curaçao had long been the more senior of the ABC islands, a source of some resentment among Arubans who earned their own oil money but had to give it to the Netherlands Antilles Parliament in Curaçao. In the 1940s, a separation movement began, led by Gilberto François Croes, known locally as Bertico. After continuous lobbying the Dutch Government agreed to Aruba becoming autonomous in 1986. Though still within the Kingdom of the Netherlands (and dependent on the Netherlands for defence and foreign affairs) it now has its own currency and elected parliament.

The system of government in Aruba is based on Western democratic principles. A Governor is appointed by the Dutch monarch (presently Queen Beatrix) for a term of six years and acts as the sovereign's representative on the island. The unicameral national Legislature, the Staten, consists of a 21-member parliament, elected every four years. The Council of Ministers is presided over by the Prime Minister and forms the executive power.

In 1996 the Arubans were due to take full independence but, in the light of problems faced by like-minded islands in the Caribbean, these plans have been shelved indefinitely.

Opposite: *Richly coloured architecture is a striking feature in Oranjestad, Aruba's capital.*
Below: *Soft white sand carpets the beach beside the Tamarijn Beach Resort.*

LOCAL HIGHLIGHTS

Oranjestad, named after the reigning Royal Dutch House of Orange during the nineteenth century, is the capital city. It is a bustling free port town located on the south coast. Pastel-coloured Dutch colonial architecture is a notable feature, though many of the buildings in the Antillean style are actually modern and do not date from colonial times. The downtown area and the Seaport Village are the primary shopping areas.

Restored in 1980, the 17th-century Fort Zoutman is the oldest building in the country. The Willem (William) III Tower was added to the fort around 1868, serving as both town clock and lighthouse; its kerosene lamp was first lit on the birthday of King Willem III in 1869. The fortress now houses Aruba's Historical Museum, where Caiquetio Indian artefacts are displayed beside remnants of the Dutch colonial period and other items of local interest. Other museums include the Archaeological Museum at 1 Zoutmanstraat and the Numismatic Museum at 27 Zuidstraat.

Travelling northwest along the coast from Oranjestad's town centre, you pass the commercial area and reach Eagle Beach and the resort hotel area. Where the road turns north is 'De Olde Molen' restaurant, formerly an old windmill that was built in Holland in 1804 and then shipped to Aruba and reconstructed in 1960. Further north, beyond Palm Beach, Hadicurari is one of the most popular places for fast windsurfing. Here the water is shallow and there aren't any hotels to break up the wind.

The village of Noord has the Santa Anna Church, founded in 1766, rebuilt in 1831 and again in 1886; its present stone structure was erected in 1916. The church's neo-Gothic oak altar, pulpit and communion rails were made by the Dutch craftsman, Hendrik van der Geld, and prized at the Vatican Council exhibition in 1870. Not far from Noord is the Bubali Bird Sanctuary, where two man-made lakes attract more than 80 species of migratory birds.

Near the north coast is the tiny Chapel of Alto Vista, constructed on the site of a chapel built by the Spanish missionary, Domingo Antonio Silvester in 1750. It is so small that stone pews have been built in semi-circles outside the entrance of the Chapel. The Santa Anna Church and the Chapel of Alto Vista are still in use today, so visitors should dress appropriately.

Also on the north coast are the ruins of gold mines at Bushiribana, the centre of Aruba's gold rush during the nineteenth century and operational from 1872 to 1882. Nowadays the old gold smelter is often referred to as a Pirate Castle. A poorly maintained road then leads east on to a natural bridge, the largest of eight on the island. This coral formation 8m (25 feet) high and 30m (100 feet) long has been carved out by the pounding surf.

Inland, at Casibari and Ayó, there are huge diorite boulders that have been carved into unusual shapes by the

Opposite: *A well maintained walking trail leads through the dry surroundings of Aruba's Arikok National Park.*

wind. At Casibari steps lead up to the top for a good view of the island; Ayó has no steps so you have to scramble to the top, but it's worth the effort to see the Indian inscriptions marked on the boulders. Hooiberg (Mount Haystack), 165m (541ft) high, does have steps to the top, and on a clear day you can see across to the coast of Venezuela.

East of here is Arikok National Park, featuring some of the oldest Arawak frescoes, a restored old *cunucu* house and a great many of Aruba's plants and animals. Further east are the dunes and three caves of Boca Prins; nearby Fontein cave has a large chamber at the entrance and a 100m (110yd) tunnel containing Indian paintings. Further along the coast are the Guadirikiri caves, two large sunlit chambers connected by passages. A third cave, Huliba, is next to the 'Tunnel of Love'. Walking through the tunnel takes 30 minutes with a 10-minute return walk above ground. Helmets and torches can be hired for all the caves.

The road continues south to the second largest city in Aruba, San Nicolas, which started out as a company town for an oil refinery. It is the town that put Aruba on the map, since it is the birthplace of Aruba's Carnival, reputedly the third largest in the world after the carnivals of Rio and Trinidad. On Aruba's eastern point near Seroe Colorado, Grapefield Rock has been developed by Club Active Aruba for rock climbing; there is also some caving. Near Colorado Point Lighthouse there is a picturesque natural bridge.

Heading northwest back towards Oranjestad, you pass through Savaneta, the oldest town in Aruba and the original capital. This is where the Dutch first settled after re-establishing control of the island in 1816; today it is a fishing village. The oldest house in Aruba, a *cas de torto* or mud-hut dating back some 150 years, still stands here.

Further along the coast is Spanish Lagoon, once a pirates' hideout, now a bird sanctuary. There is quicksand so it is best not to walk off marked paths. Slightly inland is Frenchman's Pass, where the French attacked the Indians in 1700. From here you can head east to

Above: *The largest of Aruba's impressive natural bridges is near Andicuri on the north coast.*

Yamanota, at 188m (617 feet) the highest point on the island, or west to Balashi, which has the ruins of another gold smelting plant from the 19th-century gold rush.

Boat trips to nearby Venezuela (which require a passport) and Curaçao are also available, and there are regular organized theme parties on boats and beaches.

DIVING IN ARUBA

The waters off Aruba offer great diving, particularly on wrecks – on the north coast lies the largest wreck in the Caribbean, the German freighter *Antilla* (Site 3). Known as the wreck capital of the Caribbean, Aruba also has plenty of watersports and other activities taking place, so it is ideal for a non-diving partner or family. There are dive sites to suit every style of diver, from novices taking a resort course to those wanting an advanced experience in the waves and currents on the northeast side. Most larger dive operators have dive shops offering a complete range of rental gear for both diving and snorkelling.

A shallow sandy plateau surrounds the island so the most convenient way to reach the offshore reefs is by boat. Aruba is not for the five-dives-per-day fanatic, and more appropriate for a two- or three-dives-per-day schedule. The current is usually slight, but when it is running it is ideal for drift-diving. Reefs on the leeward southern coast mainly slope gently from 5–18m (15–60ft) then drop off at an angle of 40–60 degrees to a sandy seabed with coral heads at 30–40m (100–130ft). The west coast is flatter and, except for Malmok Reef, ranges from 11m (35ft) to 18m (60ft). Diving operators often have their own names for some of the dive sites. The resorts' custom-built dive boats do not visit the northeast coast of the island too often, but if you are an experienced diver the resort's dive operators will organize and supply diving equipment for you to shore-dive.

The water averages 27°C (80°F) year round and teems with marine life including manta rays, barracuda, and green moray eels. Note that coral spawning occurs roughly a week after the full moon in September and October. Aruba is working to preserve the ecological health of its reefs, and a number of conservation and educational programmes are under way, including the installation of mooring buoys, the popular Perrier Reef Clean-up Programme and the establishment of a protected underwater park.

Seasoned divers would be wise to avoid the peak cruise ship months of December and January, as the most popular sites tend to be crowded. The larger diving operators place block-bookings from cruise ships years ahead; moreover, the cruise ships seldom keep to their planned schedule, so organising your own diving plan to avoid the crowds can be impossible.

As many of the hotel and resort divers are collected from their accommodation, the dive boats start relatively late in the morning. The most popular sites such as the Antilla Wreck and Arashi Airplane (Site 2) are often crowded, with several diving and snorkelling boats, the *Atlantis* submarine and the Seaworld Explorer semi-submarine all possible at the same time. Some diving operators also set time limits for how long divers may stay in the water so that those in the group who use up air quickly can move on to the next dive.

Serious divers and underwater photographers can join together as a group or club and charter one of the diving boats for themselves. In this way you can then choose your own times to dive. Note that there are no facilities for Nitrox diving on Aruba.

SPECIAL COINS

A special limited edition 25AFl coin depicting sea turtles has been issued in an effort to contribute to the survival of these unique animals.

Designed by local artist Evelino Fingal, Director of the Archaeological Museum, it is made of 925/1000 grade silver. The reverse side of the coin has a profile of the Queen of the Netherlands and the Dutch text, 'Beatrix Koningin Der Nederlanden', also used on other Aruban coins.

The turtle coin is in regular circulation and is available as a set together with the 5AFl banknote depicting turtles – which is now being removed from circulation. Either can be obtained from Aruba's commercial banks, the Centrale Bank van Aruba, or the Caribbean Mint.

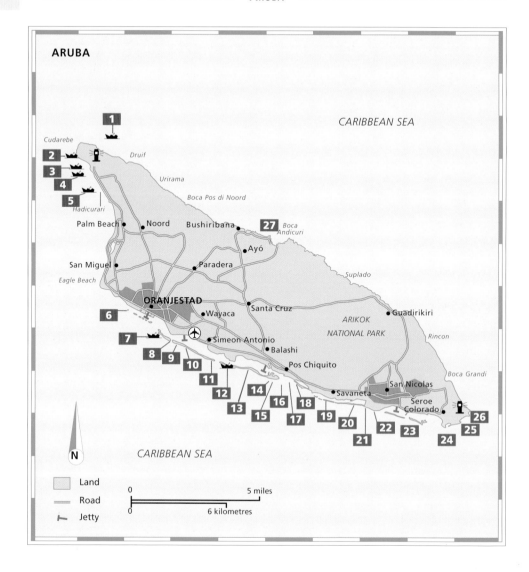

ARUBA

CARIBBEAN SEA

Cudarebe
Druif
Urirama
Boca Pos di Noord
Hadicurari
Palm Beach • Noord • Bushiribana • Boca Andicuri
• Ayó
San Miguel • • Paradera
Eagle Beach
Suplado
ORANJESTAD
• Wayaca • Santa Cruz • Guadirikiri
ARIKOK NATIONAL PARK
Rincon
• Simeon Antonio
• Balashi
• Pos Chiquito
Boca Grandi
San Nicolas
• Savaneta
Seroe Colorado
CARIBBEAN SEA

N

Land
Road
Jetty

0   5 miles
0   6 kilometres

1 CALIFORNIA WRECK
★★★

Location: North coast, to the northeast at the north end of the island
Access: By boat
Conditions: Strong currents and rough seas
Average Depth: 12m (40ft)
Maximum Depth: 14m (45ft)
Visibility: 20m (65ft)

This interesting wreck is at a good depth for underwater photography. The wreck rises to 9m (30ft) and is surrounded by large coral formations and an abundance of reef fish. However, it is located in the choppy seas and strong currents of the island's windward side and can be difficult to reach. It is therefore suitable only for advanced divers and then only during unusually calm weather. The most likely months for calm conditions on this side of the island are September and October.

The SS *California*, a wooden-hulled brig or barquentine that ran aground off the Hudishibana area on the north coast over 50 years ago, is almost 100 years old. The remains are scattered about, covered in sponges, cup corals and anemones and attract large groupers including Goliath Grouper, barracuda, lobsters and the occasional shark.

On land the area nearby is now popularly called The 'California Dunes' and there is a lighthouse known as the 'California Lighthouse'.

SS CALIFORNIA

The SS *California* (Site 1) is often mistaken for the ship that received the 'mayday' signals broadcast by the *Titanic* when it hit an iceberg in 1912, but failed to respond. That ship was the *Californian*, a 136m (447ft) Leyland liner that was torpedoed off Cape Matapan by a German U-boat on November 9th 1915, during World War I.

2 ARASHI AIRPLANE
★★★☆☆☆

Location: West coast, off Arashi Beach
Access: By boat
Conditions: Can have a strong current
Average Depth: 10m (33ft)
Maximum Depth: 15m (50ft)
Visibility: 20m (65ft)

An easy site for beginners, there used to be two aeroplanes here but the smaller one, a Lockheed LoneStar, has disintegrated beyond recognition. A twin-engined Beechcraft sits in 10m (33ft) of water – its propellers have fallen off but the basic aeroplane is still there. The passenger cabin is full of shoaling fish and the cockpit often contains a green moray eel (*Gymnothorax funebris*). Grazing fish eat the algae on the fuselage and shoals of sergeant majors, jacks, goatfish and grunts swim around the outside. Angelfish, parrotfish and pufferfish are common, and brain corals, star corals and sea fans can be found around the wreck.

There is snorkelling off the beach but the currents would put off all but the strongest snorkellers from reaching the wreck.

3 ANTILLA WRECK
★★★★☆☆☆☆☆

Location: West coast, off Malmok Beach
Access: By boat
Conditions: Calm except in strong winds
Average Depth: 17m (55ft)
Maximum Depth: 18m (60ft)
Visibility: 18m (60ft)

The largest wreck and one of the best dive sites in the Caribbean, the 120m (400ft) long *Antilla* was a German freighter that was scuttled off Malmok by the Germans on May 10th 1940. She was locally known as the 'ghost ship' because of her captain's ability to elude pursuers. When the Germans invaded Holland in World War II she was anchored off the western shore of Aruba, then a Dutch territory. The authorities suspected her of supplying a wolf pack of German U-boats and gave her captain 24 hours to surrender. The captain ordered the

---

Above: *A grouper signals for the attentions of cleaner fish at a cleaning station.*

boilers to be supercharged and then flooded her engine compartment, causing an explosion that almost ripped the ship in two. She now lies in 18m (60ft) of water, listing to her port side.

The wreck has large compartments so it is easily penetrated, and having spent more than 50 years in warm water it is covered in tube sponges, cup corals, tunicates, hydroids, corals and fan worms. The fish life includes sergeant majors, parrotfish, moray eels, trumpetfish (*Aulostoma maculatus*), snappers, queen angelfish (*Holacanthus ciliaris*), very large groupers and many species of shoaling fish. Shoals of silversides are common during spring and early summer. It is popular as a night dive.

Worth several dives, part of the wreck's starboard side is above water so seabirds use it, and pelicans can be seen diving during the day. It is common for there to be several diving and snorkelling boats moored on the wreck at the same time and there is often a strong current.

The semi-submersible *Seaworld Explorer* is often present circling over the wreck, so divers should take great care when surfacing. The safest method of ascent is for divers to go up the weighted line that is deployed by most diving boats to a buoy off their stern.

4 MALMOK REEF/BLUE REEF AND DEBBIE II
★★★

Location: West coast, off Malmok Beach
Access: By boat
Conditions: There can be a strong current
Average Depth: 22m (70ft)
Maximum Depth: 22m (70ft)
Visibility: 27m (90ft)

This bottom reef can have a strong current that carries food for a multitude of fish, including moray eels, parrotfish and trumpetfish. Malmok is known for its lobsters, stingrays, barrel sponges, leaf corals and brain corals. In 1992 the 37m (120ft) fuel barge *Debbie II* was sunk here as an artificial reef. She now sits upright on the sand with her forward holds allowing some difficult penetration dives. The wreck attracts shoaling fish including barracuda.

5 PEDERNALES WRECK
★★★★

Location: West coast, off Hadicurari Beach
Access: By boat
Conditions: Often strong current and poor visibility
Average Depth: 8m (25ft)
Maximum Depth: 11m (35ft)
Visibility: 27m (90ft) – less when current is strong

The *Pedernales* was an oil tanker torpedoed by the German submarine U-156 on February 16th 1942. The US military cut the original wreck into three pieces. The mid-section, damaged by the torpedo, was left behind, and the bow and stern were towed to America and welded together into a smaller vessel, which took part as a landing craft in the Allied invasion of Normandy on D-day.

What was left is now in several large pieces at 8m (25ft), with the tanker's pipeline system, cabins, wash basins, lavatories, etc spread out between coral formations. It is an easy dive that is delightful for its prolific fish life. The area around the wreck contains many species of groupers and angelfish and even a whale shark has been seen here. It is ideal for novices though there is often a strong current and poor visibility.

6 HARBOUR REEF/PILOT BOAT
★★★★

Location: South coast, off the Oranjestad harbour
Access: By boat
Conditions: Normally calm
Average Depth: 27m (90ft)
Maximum Depth: 30m (100ft)
Visibility: 27m (90ft)

Beginning at around 12m (40ft), the slope gradually drops past heads of large brain corals, orange, black, and blue sponges, lots of plant life and gorgonians. This is a good dive for novices. Green moray eels, French angelfish (*Pomacanthus paru*), spotted eagle rays (*Aetobatus narinari*), stingrays and seahorses have been seen, which together with the old Pilot Boat make this a good dive for photographers.

7 SONESTA AIRPLANE
★★★★★★★★

Location: South coast, northwest tip of Sonesta Island
Access: By boat
Conditions: Normally calm
Average Depth: 12m (40ft)
Maximum Depth: 30m (100ft)
Visibility: 20m (65ft)

Above: *Fish take refuge in the Arashi Airplane Wreck – formerly a twin-engined Beechcraft (Site 2).*
Below: *The engines still have their propellors attached at the Sonesta Airplane Wreck (Site 7)*

This site used to boast two aeroplanes. A Convair-400 (similar in shape to a Dakota DC-3), which was confiscated by the Aruban Government for drug smuggling, was sunk here through the collective efforts of some of Aruba's diving operators. It now sits upright in 15m (50ft) of water. The fore and aft doors and most of the interior were removed before it was sunk so the aircraft is easy to penetrate; and the propellers are still attached to the engines.

A twin-engined Beechcraft-18, which used to be in 5m (15ft) of water on top of the coral slope, has now disintegrated beyond recognition, though wreckage from both aircraft is spread around the seabed.

Straight out from Sonesta Beach Hotel's private island, the reef features elkhorn corals (*Acropora palmata*), staghorn corals (*Acropora cervicornis*), brain corals, fire corals and gorgonians. Barracuda, green moray eels and octopus are common among the fish life. The site begins around 5m (16ft) and the reef continues down to 30m (100ft).

The *Atlantis VI* submarine gets close to the aircraft so divers should keep a careful look-out when underwater. When surfacing it is safest to ascend the weighted line that is deployed by diving boats to a buoy off their stern.

8 SPONGE REEF
★★★

Location: South coast, off the south side of Sonesta Island at the western end
Access: By boat
Conditions: Normally calm
Average Depth: 12m (40ft)
Maximum Depth: 25m (80ft)
Visibility: 20m (65ft)
Often treated as a drift-dive as the current can be strong, this site begins at 5m (16ft) and has colourful orange elephant ear sponges (*Agelas clathrodes*), purple and yellow tube sponges, purple vase sponges, leaf and plate corals and gorgonians. Green moray eels, French angelfish, foureye butterflyfish and rock beauties are among the abundant fish life at this site, as well as lobsters and octopuses.

9 BARCADERA REEF
★★★★★

Location: South Coast, off the south side of the reef east of Sonesta Island
Access: By boat
Conditions: Normally calm
Average Depth: 15m (50ft)
Maximum Depth: 25m (80ft)
Visibility: 20m (65ft)

Beginning at 6m (20ft), this site is a healthy reef with elkhorn, staghorn and brain corals and large gorgonian sea fans on sand. Barracuda, mantas, wrasse, parrotfish, pufferfish and French angelfish have all been seen here.

10 KANTIL REEF
★★★

Location: South coast, off the south side of Sonesta Island, midway along (south of Bucuti Yacht Club)
Access: By boat
Conditions: Normally calm
Average Depth: 25m (80ft)
Maximum Depth: 33m (110ft)
Visibility: 25m (80ft)
There is a drop-off beginning at 12m (40ft) with large heads of brain, leaf, sheet and star coral and large gorgonian sea fans. The marine life includes manta rays, eagle rays, groupers, moray eels and the occasional sleeping nurse shark. This is a good dive for photographers.

11 SKALAHEIN
★★★

Location: South coast, off the southeast tip of Sonesta Island
Access: By boat
Conditions: Normally calm
Average Depth: 15m (50ft)
Maximum Depth: 30m+ (100ft+)
Visibility: 25m (80ft)
The reef slopes gently from 5m (15ft) to 15m (50ft), then more steeply past 30m (100ft). Known for its population of barracuda and the occasional manta ray or spotted eagle ray, it also has great coral formations and sponges. Brain and star corals dominate in shallow water and there are black corals and gorgonian sea fans below 20m (65ft). Seahorses have even been seen at this site, which is excellent for photography.

12 JANE SEA WRECK
★★★★

Location: South coast, off the south side of De Palm Island at the western end.
Access: By boat
Conditions: Normally calm, can be a very strong current
Average Depth: 25m (80ft)
Maximum Depth: 29m (95ft)
Visibility: 30m (100ft)
This spectacular wreck is a 75m (250ft) long freighter which was sunk intentionally as an artificial reef. It lies

Atlantis VI is a passenger-carrying submarine that has been taking tourists to dive sites off the coast of Aruba since 1990. US Coast Guard approved, it won the Aruba Tourism Scholarship Foundation (TOUSA) Iguana Award for the 'Most Outstanding Tourism Attraction'.

The vessel operates at normal atmospheric pressure, is air-conditioned, has 13 viewing windows, each 60cm (2ft) in diameter, and is electrically powered by DC batteries. She is 20m (65ft) long by 4m (13ft) beam and 6.4m (21ft) high, including the conning tower; displacement is 72,576kg (160,000lb). There is a crew of three and her passenger carrying capacity is 46. She has a submerged speed of 1^1/2 knots.

GRACEFUL LADY OF THE DEEP

On the submarine voyage you can see an abundance of exotic fish and marine creatures, spectacular sponge gardens and remarkable formations. *Atlantis VI* also visits a number of dive sites that have fascinating histories. One of the particularly interesting sites is that of the *Mi Dushi*, known now as the Graceful Lady of the Deep. She is a wooden-hulled sailing trawler, built in 1928 and used in the North Sea until World War II, when she served as a cargo vessel and a rescue vessel for downed Allied aircrew. After the war finished the *Mi Dushi* was used for smuggling tobacco and whisky to Scandinavia. Eventually she was bought by a couple who converted her into one of Aruba's best-known charter boats. When the boat became too old for charters, she was cleaned of all fuel and oil and sunk as an environmentally friendly artificial reef.

After finishing the voyage on the *Atlantis VI*, you receive a certificate as proof that you have been to a depth of 150 feet. All trips depart from the dock located in the harbour opposite the Sonesta Resort in downtown Oranjestad. The submarine's dive site is a 30-minute ferry ride from the dock and the dive itself lasts for one hour. You can also book a place on the trip at Palm Beach, on the DePalm Pier across the beach from the Radisson Resort; group rates or special charters are available if booked in advance.

Below: *Typical of the kind of scenery visible from the Atlantis VI is this impressive brain coral.*

Above: *The Jane Sea Wreck is ablaze with colourful cup corals and encrusting sponges.*

upright with the 2m (6ft) propeller at 29m (95ft), the deck at 18m (60ft), the aft wheelhouse at 14m (45ft) and the bow at 15m (50ft). There is plenty of colour – orange cup corals, fire coral and red and pink encrusting sponges are found on the hull, and there are some black corals on her port side. The wreck attracts shoaling fish, barracuda, lobsters and green moray eels, while brain corals and gorgonian sea fans feature here.

In poor visibility, divers can find the ship's anchor chain at the bottom of the mooring rope and follow it in an arc to the right, first up the reef where there are large coral heads, then down the reef to the bow of the wreck. The superstructure and propeller are great for photography, as are the coral heads in shallow water where you can have a safety stop. There can be a very strong current.

13 PLONCO REEF
★★★

Location: South coast, off the south side of De Palm Island, midway along.
Access: By boat
Conditions: Normally calm
Average Depth: 20m (65ft)
Maximum Depth: 30m+ (100ft+)
Visibility: 30m (100ft)

Starting shallow at 6m (20ft), this reef slopes down beyond 30m (100ft) with large, healthy brain, fire and star corals, boring and encrusting sponges and gorgonians. Lobsters are common while fish life includes barracuda, rainbow runners (*Elagatis bipunnulata*), green moray eels and many species of reef fish.

There is often enough current to turn the dive into a drift dive. It is also a good dive for normal and macro photography.

14 DE PALM SLOPE
★★★★★★★★★

Location: South coast, off the southeast end of De Palm Island
Access: Boat or shore
Conditions: Calm
Average Depth: 20m (65ft)
Maximum Depth: 36m (120ft)
Visibility: 25m (80ft)

This is a good shore dive from 5m (16ft) to deep water with fine coral formations and great snorkelling. Often done as a drift dive, there are barracuda, parrotfish, surgeonfish, yellowtail grunts and sergeant majors; spotted eagle rays are often seen.

15 THE FINGERS
★★★

Location: South coast, off the southeast end of De Palm Island
Access: By boat
Conditions: Calm, though there can be a strong current
Average Depth: 20m (65ft)
Maximum Depth: 36m (120ft)
Visibility: 25m (80ft)
Beginning at 6m (20ft), this site resembles a finger pointing into deep water. It features good coral heads, gorgonian sea fans and abundant fish life. Note that there can be a strong current.

16 MIKE'S REEF
★★★★

Location: South coast, off the southeast end of De Palm Island
Access: By boat
Conditions: Calm
Average Depth: 20m (65ft)
Maximum Depth: 27m (90ft)
Visibility: 25m (80ft)
Probably the best reef dive in Aruba, Mike's Reef is a rock garden that begins at 8m (25ft) and is dominated by brain corals, star corals and gorgonian sea fans and plenty of colourful sponges. There are lobsters under the corals and the varied fish life includes barracuda, green moray eels and rainbow runners.

THE PERRIER REEF CARE PROJECT

Impressed by the efforts of divers elsewhere with reef clean-up campaigns, Castro Perez, Ecotourism Manager of Aruba Tourism Authority (ATA), decided to instigate a similar campaign to raise awareness of the need to conserve Aruba's marine environment.

Initially helped by the American Center for Marine Conservation, he enlisted the support of Licores Aruba who persuaded Perrier Mineral Water to sponsor the project. In 1994 the 'Perrier Reef Care Project' was established. Working with marine biologist Byron Boekhoudt, Doreen Boekhoudt, local dive operators and over 200 volunteers, 2 tons of rubbish were collected from dive sites and beaches along Aruba's leeward coast.

In 1995 the clean-up was accompanied by a Marine Life Symposium and now, every year, there is a two-day Perrier Reef Care Project that attracts hundreds of volunteers. Certified divers register with a dive operator for a free dive each day and in return collect rubbish from the zone covered by that operator. Non-diving volunteers also help by collecting rubbish from the beaches.

As a result of the project, local co-operation has increased over other issues. In 1996 the Aruba Watersports Association (AWA) helped set up an island-wide mooring system. In 1997 the Minister of Tourism and Economic Affairs presented a special Iguana award to Castro Perez for his work.

---

17 MANGEL HALTO REEF
★★★★★★★★

Location: South coast, off Mangel Halto Beach
Access: Boat or shore
Conditions: Normally calm
Average Depth: 25m (80ft)
Maximum Depth: 34m (110ft)
Visibility: 25m (80ft)
This dive has a steep slope from 5m (15ft) down to 34m (110ft), with stony corals, gorgonians, sea anemones, tube sponges, vase sponges and an abundance of other marine life from octopuses to seahorses.

18 PORTO (POS) CHIQUITO/ SNAPPER CITY
★★★★★★★★

Location: South coast, south of Pieter Boer and west of Savaneta
Access: Boat or shore
Conditions: Calm
Average Depth: 20m (65ft)
Maximum Depth: 25m (80ft)
Visibility: 25m (80ft)
A pretty shore dive of great diversity, this site features large star corals together with brain corals. Once called 'Snapper City' by local divers, there is plenty of fish life and you may well also see turtles and manta rays. Easily accessible from the shore, the site is often done as a night dive. It is also popular for those wishing to observe coral spawning in September and October.

19 ISLA DI ORO REEF
★★★★★★★

Location: South coast, off Savaneta
Access: By boat
Conditions: Normally calm
Average Depth: 20m (65ft)
Maximum Depth: 27m (90ft)
Visibility: 30m (100ft)
This site is very similar to nearby Mangel Halto (Site 17) but there can be a current that can make this a challenging dive. It starts with brain, staghorn, leaf and star corals, while deeper down there are gorgonian sea fans, sea rods and sea whips. Lobsters, parrotfish, Spanish hogfish (*Bodianus rufus*), French angelfish, coral crabs and shoals of snappers are usually seen. At depth the corals form caves that shelter moray eels. In parts the reef drops below 37m (120ft).

20 COMMANDEURS REEF
★★★★

Location: South coast, off the south side of Commandeurs Bay.
Access: By boat
Conditions: Normally calm
Average Depth: 20m (65ft)
Maximum Depth: 27m (90ft)
Visibility: 30m (100ft)
Sloping from 12m (40ft) into the deep, this site consists of leaf and sheet coral and a rich fish life including barracuda, rainbow runners, jacks, groupers, grunts, French and queen angelfish and snappers.

21 LAGO REEF
★★★★

Location: South coast, off southeast edge of Commandeurs Bay
Access: By boat
Conditions: Normally calm
Average Depth: 30m (100ft)
Maximum Depth: 37m (120ft)
Visibility: 30m (100ft)

This is one of Aruba's deepest dive sites, with beautiful coral formations, gorgonian sea fans, sponges, sea anemones and abundant crustacean and fish life including many large species.

22 INDIAN HEAD
★★★★

Location: South coast, off southeast edge of Commandeurs Bay
Access: By boat
Conditions: Normally calm
Average Depth: 25m (80ft)
Maximum Depth: 37m (120ft)
Visibility: 27m (90ft)
So named because of a large coral formation that resembles a head, this site features good brain and star corals and abundant fish life.

23 THE CROSS
★★★★

Location: South coast, off San Nicolas
Access: By boat
Conditions: Normally calm
Average Depth: 12m (40ft)
Maximum Depth: 18m (60ft)
Visibility: 25m (80ft)
Often treated as a drift dive, this site has a 3m (10ft) memorial to San Nicolas embedded in the sea floor on the side of the reef. The reef itself has good coral heads, an assortment of gorgonian sea rods, sea whips and sea fans and bountiful fish life.

24 BABY BEACH REEF
★★★☆☆☆

Location: South coast, off Baby Beach
Access: Shore or boat
Conditions: Normally calm
Average Depth: 12m (40ft)
Maximum Depth: 18m (60ft)
Visibility: 25m (80ft)
Probably the best shore dive on Aruba, the site slopes into the open sea. Large formations of elkhorn coral and sheet coral make good hiding places for crabs, lobsters and octopuses. Beginning at 6m (20ft) this site is great for experienced snorkellers, but can be very choppy outside of the breakwater and lacks interest inside it. Angelfish, butterflyfish, parrotfish, Spanish hogfish, trumpetfish, surgeonfish and snappers are common and occasionally barracuda and rainbow runners are found in deeper water.

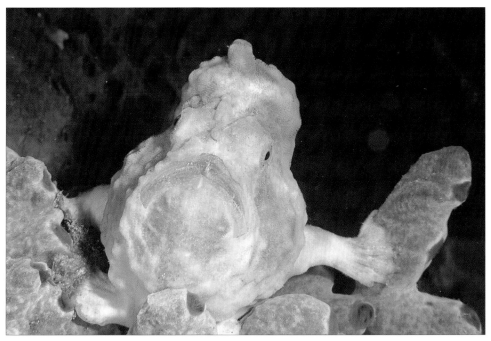

Above: *The beguiling longlure frogfish lies in wait of any unsuspecting passing prey.*
Opposite: *An azure vase sponge makes a fine photographic subject.*

25 SANTANA DI CACHO REEF
★★★

Location: South coast, east of Baby Beach Reef
Access: Shore or boat
Conditions: Rough entry
Average Depth: 12m (40ft)
Maximum Depth: 15m (50ft)
Visibility: 20m (65ft)
The entry is rough, but this reef offers the same attractions as Baby Beach Reef (Site 24): elkhorn and staghorn corals and an abundance of marine life. This dive is often treated as a drift dive finishing at Baby Beach Reef.

26 CABEZ REEF
★★★

Location: South coast, south of Colorado Point Lighthouse
Access: Shore
Conditions: Rough seas and strong currents
Average Depth: 12m (40ft)
Maximum Depth: 15m (50ft)
Visibility: 18m (60ft)

Rough seas with strong currents make this a dive for experienced divers only. After an exciting shore entry, you find shoals of amberjack, barracuda and rainbow runners attracted by the current as well as stingrays and many species of reef fish.

27 NATURAL BRIDGE
★★★

Location: North coast, at the western end of Boca Andicuri
Access: Shore or boat
Conditions: Rough seas and extremely strong currents
Average Depth: 30m (100ft)
Maximum Depth: 33m (110ft)
Visibility: 20m (65ft)
Another site for advanced divers and then only during unusually calm weather on this side of the island due to rough waters and extremely strong currents. The best months for this site are September and October. It features huge boulders and large formations of brain and star coral as well as plenty of fire coral, black coral, gorgonian sea fans, sea rods and sea whips. Large barrel sponges are found on the seabed.

GETTING THERE

The Queen Beatrix International Airport (Aeropuerto Internacional Reina Beatrix) is on the south coast of Aruba, at the southeast end of Oranjestad Marina.

If travelling by air from Europe, KLM has non-stop flights from Amsterdam, or you can fly from other European cities via Curaçao. Some KLM flights connect via Caracas and others continue to Lima.

Various American airlines have regular flights from New York's J.F.K. International Airport, Atlanta, Baltimore, Houston, Miami, Newark, Tampa, Port of Spain, Bogotá, Baranquilla, Medellín, Cali, Caracas, Brazil, Sint Martin, Dominican Republic, Puerto Rico, Bonaire and Curaçao. There are also many charter flights from Boston, Chicago, Cleveland, Detroit, Hartford, Philadelphia, Los Angeles, Minneapolis, Philadelphia, Pittsburgh, and Houston, mainly in the winter season.

From Canada there are scheduled services from Montreal and Toronto via Miami as well as charter flights.

Aerorepublica, Avensa, Avianca, Aserca, SAM, Servivensa, VASP and other airlines connect with South America.

On departure, if flying out to the USA, you clear US customs and immigration in Aruba, saving time at the other end. Airport departure tax is now included in the price of your ticket.

Aruba's cruise ship terminal is also located on the south coast, at the northwest end of Oranjestad Marina.

WHERE TO STAY

Aruba has a considerable number of accommodations and restaurants, often with gourmet dining. Along Druif Bay and Eagle and Palm Beaches a cluster of glittering luxury hotels has sprung up. Some hotels add a US$3–5 per day energy surcharge as well as service charges and taxes. The accommodation listed here is a small selection of what is available.

EXPENSIVE
Most of the imposing and luxurious so-called high-rise hotels are along Palm Beach.

Aruba Palm Beach Resort & Casino
79 J.E. Irausquin Boulevard, Palm Beach; tel 297 863900; fax 297 861941
Located on Palm Beach, Aruba Palm Beach Resort is a typical multistorey hotel with all facilities while maintaining a cosy atmosphere. With large rooms it has its own casino, nightly entertainment, conference rooms and two restaurants with cuisine to suit all tastes.

Hyatt Regency Aruba Beach Resort & Casino
85 J.E. Irausquin Boulevard, Palm Beach; tel 297 586 1234; fax 297 586 1682; e-mail: adventur@hyatt.com
Situated on Palm Beach, this is a large multistorey hotel with 360 rooms, casino,

sports facilities, four restaurants, and conference and banqueting facilities. The Hyatt Group owns the Red Sail Sports chain.

Playa Linda Beach Resort
87 J.E. Irausquin Boulevard, Palm Beach; tel 297 586 1000; fax 297 586 3479; e-mail: genmgr@playalinda.com; www.playalinda.com
There are 194 luxury suites, each with its own balcony and kitchen. The two restaurants can satisfy most tastes.

Wyndham Aruba Beach Resort & Casino
77 J.E. Irausquin Boulevard, Palm Beach; tel 297 586 4466; fax 297 586 8217; e-mail: info@arubaresortspa.com; www.arubaresortspa.com
There are 444 large rooms, each with private balconies and ocean views. Also four restaurants, a casino and meeting and banqueting facilities.

MID-RANGE
Less imposing but cheaper and found on equally good beaches are lower-rise hotels.

Best Western Manchebo Beach Resort
55 J.E. Irausquin Boulevard, Manchebo; tel 297 582 3444; fax 297 583 2446; e-mail: info@manchebo.com
Set on Eagle Beach, the largest beach in Aruba. There are 71 rooms with either patios or balconies, and the Alhambra Casino and shopping bazaar is next door. The beachside restaurant is a popular meeting place.

Divi Aruba Beach Resort
45 J.E. Irausquin Boulevard, Druif Beach, tel 207 594 7888; e-mail: info@diviaruba.com
This is a mid-range resort, with a relaxed atmosphere.

Tamarijn Aruba Beach Resort
41 J.E. Irausquin Boulevard, Punta Brabo Beach; tel 207 594 7888; e-mail: info@tamarijnaruba.com
All inclusive, popular with American, South American and European visitors.

INEXPENSIVE
A number of much cheaper guest houses in the US$30–60 bracket, usually away from the beaches, may be found.

Aulga's Place
31 Seroe Blanco; tel 297 822717
Inexpensive, but if you have not already hired a vehicle to shore dive then you will also have the cost of transport to a boat jetty.

Cactus Arpartments
5 Matadera, Noord; tel 297 582 2903; fax 297 582 0433; e-mail: cactus.apts@setarnet.aw
Conveniently situated in Noord, not far from Palm Beach. Some operators will pick you up from here, otherwise you will have to arrange your own transport.

Pauline's Apartments
22 Keito, Palm Beach; tel 297 582 5337; fax 297 583 2542
Conveniently situated near Palm Beach. Either arrange for the operators to pick you up from here or hire your own transport.

WHERE TO EAT

More than a hundred restaurants are available, with cuisine from many different countries. Most of the hotels have several restaurants ranging from up-market venues (that include dress codes) to coffee shops; some require prior reservations. There are also plenty of fast food outlets to choose from.

ARUBAN, CARIBBEAN & INTERNATIONAL
Boonoonoonoos
18A Wilhelminastraat; tel 297 831888; fax 297 827015
International dishes are available, though the owner specializes in Caribbean cuisine. Friendly with good service, and tasty and attractive food.

Brisas Del Mar
222A Savaneta; tel 297 847718
This open-air restaurant offers seafood and local cuisine while giving a romantic view of the Caribbean Sea.

Charlie's Bar & Restaurant
56 Zeppenfeldtstraat, San Nicolas; tel 297 584 5086
A meeting place for the locals since 1941 and a mini-gallery for artists, writers and musicians, Charlie's Bar has become an Aruban tradition. An archive of local history and memorabilia, it is also known for good service.

Mi Cushina
La Quinta Beach Resort; tel 297 848335
Meaning 'My Kitchen', Mi Cushina specializes in local cuisine and a selection of international dishes. Its decor reflects the Caribbean atmosphere, including a ceiling made of coffee bags, light fittings made from old wagon wheels and a small museum covering the early processing of Aloe Vera.

Papiamento International Cuisine & Grill
61 Washington; tel 297 586 4544
Seafood and grilled specialities that can be eaten either on a poolside terrace or indoors.

Pega Pega Grill and Bar
Best Western Manchebo Beach Resort, 55 J.E. Irausquin Boulevard, Manchebo; tel 297 582 3444; fax 297 583 2446
Popular with the locals, divers and yacht crews.

The Pelican Nest Bar & Seafood Grill
On Pelican Tours & Watersports' Pier, off the beach between the Holiday Inn and the Playa Linda Resort; tel 297 582 3444; fax 297 583 2446
Popular with divers and lovers of seafood.

The Mill (De Olde Mollen)
330 L.G. Smith Boulevard; tel 297 586 2060
Formerly an old windmill that was first built
in Holland in 1804 and then shipped to
Aruba and reconstructed in 1960. The
cuisine is a mixture of international and
Caribbean.

CHINESE
Kowloon Restaurant
11 Emmastraat; tel 297 582 4950
Serves a mixture of favourite oriental dishes,
with some more untraditional Chinese dishes.

FRENCH
Chez Mathilde
23 Havenstraat; tel 297 583 4968
Known as Aruba's most distinguished French
restaurant. A 19th-century house kept in its
original state, it has a reputation for seafood.

La Bouillabaisse
69 Bubali; tel 297 871408
Known for growing its own herbs.
Specializes in traditional and authentic
seafood, Caribbean and French cuisine.

DIVE FACILITIES

The Aruba Tourism Authority recommends
the dive operators listed below that are
marked with an asterisk.

Atlantis Submarine - see Red Sail Sports

Dax Divers*
7 Kibaima, Santa Cruz; tel 297 585 1270;
fax 297 586 7271
A small operator specializing in small groups
for both boat and shore diving, with
instruction up to Assistant Instructor level
offered in Dutch, English and Spanish.

De Palm Watersports
tel 297 582 4400; fax 297 582 3012
A small operator specializing in small groups
for both boat and shore diving.

Dive Aruba*
8 Williamsstraat, Oranjestad; tel 297 582
7337; fax 297 582 1817; e-mail:
dbrand@centuryinter.net
A small operator offering boat dives for
small groups and instruction up to PADI
Divemaster in Dutch, English and Spanish.

Native Divers*
Washington 19, Noord, Aruba; tel 297 586
4763; fax 297 586 8515; e-mail:
nativedivers@setarnet.aw
A small operator that has been taking small
groups diving for over twelve years. Boat and
shore diving and instruction up to PADI
Divemaster level in Dutch, English and Spanish.

Pelican Watersports*
Irausquin Boulevard 232, Oranjestad, Aruba;
tel 297 587 2302; fax 297 587 2315; e-mail:
pelican-aruba@setarnet.aw;
www.pelicanaruba.com
A PADI 5-Star Gold Palm Resort.

Pro Dive*
Ponton 90 Aruba; tel 297 582 5520; fax 297
587 7722; e-mail: dive@arubaprodive.com;
www.arubaprodive.com
A small operator specializing in small groups.
Boat and shore diving and instruction up to
PADI Advanced Open Water level offered in
Dutch, English and Spanish.

Red Sail Sports*
83 J.E. Irausquin Boulevard, Palm Beach;
tel 297 586 1603; fax 297 586 6657; e-mail:
info@redsailaruba.com
This is the largest watersports/diving
organization on Aruba and it was the first
Aruban diving operator to achieve the PADI
5-Star Dive Centre and Instructor
Development Centre rating. It is based at
the Hyatt Regency Aruba Resort with
connections at Allegro, Sonesta Resorts,
Aruba Marriott Resort, Stauffer Hotel and
Stellaris Casino. Red Sail Sports is well
equipped to handle disabled divers, and also
offers kayak diving. Instruction is offered in
Dutch, English, German, Portuguese,
Spanish and Swedish.

S.E.A. Aruba Fly 'n Dive
L.G. Smith Boulevard 1-A; tel 297 588 1150;
fax 297 585 2023; e-mail:
searaba.fly.n.dive@setarnet.aw;
www.searaba.com
A small operator specializing in small groups
for both boat and shore diving.

Unique Watersports of Aruba*
Radisson Resort, J.E. Irausquin Boulevard No.
81, Oranjestad; tel/fax 297 586 0096
A PADI 5-Star Gold Palm Resort.
Unique Watersports is the third largest
watersports/diving organization in Aruba,
with connections at Aruba Palm Beach and
The Mill. Instruction up to Divemaster level
offered in Dutch, English, German,
Portuguese and Spanish.

EMERGENCIES

There is no recompression chamber on the
island. The nearest chamber is on Curaçao,
and patients who require hyperbaric
treatment are transferred there by low-flying
aircraft.

Hotels have doctors and dentists on call. The
Dr Horacio Oduber Hospital has reputable
medical staff and is equipped with up-to-
date equipment. The hospital is located
across from Eagle Beach on L.G. Smith
Boulevard, near to the vicinity of the main
hotel area. Services such as oxygen and
haemodialysis are available at the hospital.
To obtain more information contact the
following:

Dr Horacio Oduber Hospital
Sasakiweg, Aruba; tel 297 587 4300; fax
297 587 3348

Aruba Emergency Telephone Numbers:
All Emergencies	911
Police	911
Fire	911
Ambulance Oranjestad	582 1234
Ambulance San Nicolas	584 5050

USEFUL CONTACTS

www.arubatourism.com
www.aruba.com

ATA – Aruba and Caribbean
PO Box 1019, 172 L.G. Smith Boulevard,
Orangestad, Aruba; tel 297 582 3777; fax
297 583 4702; e-mail:
ata.aruba@aruba.com

Aruba Tourism Authority (ATA) – Europe
1 Schimmelpennincklaan, 2517 JN, The Haag,
Holland; tel 31 70 3 566220; fax 31 70 3
604877; e-mail: ata.holland@aruba.com

ATA – Chicago
6811 W. Higgins Ave., Chicago, Illinois
60656; tel 773 467 8170; fax 773 202
7293; e-mail: ata.chicago@aruba.com

ATA – Florida
6811 W. Higgins Ave., Chicago, Illinois
60656; tel 773 467 8170; fax 773 202
9293; e-mail: ata.chicago@aruba.com

ATA – Canada
5875 Highway No. 7, Suite 201,
Woodbridge, Ontario, Canada L4L 1T9;
tel 905 264 3434; fax 905 264 3437;
e-mail: ata.canada@aruba.com

Dirección de Turismo de Aruba – Venezuela
Centro Ciudad Comercial Tamanaco, Torre
C. Piso 8, Oficina C-805, Chuao, Caracas,
Venezuela; tel 0602 959 9166; fax 0602
959 6346; e-mail: ata.venezuela@aruba.com

BONAIRE

Over the last thirty years, Bonaire has developed a reputation as one of the best diving and snorkelling destinations in the Caribbean, mainly as a result of the island's conservation of its marine resources with the creation of a national marine park. The license plates proclaiming 'Diver's Paradise' are a testament to how important diving is to the locals. There are also many other activities to enjoy, including mountain biking, horseback riding, windsurfing, sea kayaking, deep-sea fishing and caving – over the last ten years more than 40 caves have been discovered. You can charter a yacht, take a trip on a glass-bottomed boat, go bird watching, see Indian frescoes, gamble at a casino or enjoy a day trip to Venezuela.

Bonaire is not known for its beaches since the sand tends to be full of broken coral and hard on the feet. The beaches on the leeward coast are narrow, though those in front of some hotels have been improved with extra sand. However, they do offer tranquillity and there are no hawkers. There are no high rise hotels or traffic lights on Bonaire, and jet skis are supposed to be banned (though you may see them racing about at dusk).

HISTORY
Bonaire's earliest known inhabitants were the Caiquetios, who came from Venezuela around 1000 AD. The Arawak Indian name for the island, Bo-nah, means low country, and later became 'Boynay' in the local dialect.

Alonso de Ojeda and Amerigo Vespucci claimed Bonaire for Spain in 1499 and named it Isla de Brazil, which means Island of Dyewood, since the dye the Caiquetios used in their cave paintings came from the dyewood tree. As Bonaire had neither gold nor enough rainfall for large-scale agricultural use, the Spanish saw no reason to develop the colony. They forced the native Caiquetios into slavery and deported them to work on the plantations and mines of Hispaniola. As a result the native population was almost eradicated by 1515.

In 1526, Juan de Ampues, the governor of Aruba, Bonaire, and Curaçao, began cattle ranching on the island. Using Caiquetios and other Indians from Venezuela as labourers, he soon had cows, sheep, goats, pigs, donkeys and horses being raised. The animals' hides were

Opposite: *The varied scenery of Washington-Slagbaai National Park includes limestone headlands.*
Above: *On mainland Bonaire most dive sites are clearly marked from the shore.*

WASHINGTON-SLAGBAAI NATIONAL PARK

Over a century ago, two plantations, or *kunukus* in Papiamento, called Washington and Slagbaai, occupied the site of this national park. They exported cattle, goats, aloe, charcoal and salt, each plantation from its own harbour. A park was first established in 1969 from the land that had been Washington plantation. Then in 1979 Slagbaai (the name means slaughter because cattle were slaughtered here) was added to form the present-day park. You can still discern the fence that separated the two properties.

The 5463ha (13,500-acre) Washington-Slagbaai National Park presents a cross-section of the landscape, flora and fauna of the island. Covering nearly one-fifth of Bonaire, it offers arid desert scenery, salt pans, hills and beaches. The animal life includes iguanas, wild donkeys and goats. There are two rugged but driveable dirt roads through the park, though four-wheel drive vehicles are recommended.

The park is open daily from 0800 to 1700 except on official holidays, though no entry is permitted after 15:00. Entry is US$5 per person.

worth more than their meat, so they required little tending and were generally let loose to wander freely. Today the island has abundant feral populations of donkeys and goats.

For the next three centuries, few of the island's inhabitants arrived willingly. There was an inland settlement at Rincon, away from pirate raids, but development was not encouraged. Bonaire's immigrants were mostly convicts from Spanish colonies in South America. The Dutch admiral Boudewijn Hendricksz landed Spanish and Portuguese prisoners to establish the town of Antriol and for most of the next 300 years, Bonaire remained a penal colony.

In 1633, the Dutch captured the ABC islands. Curaçao became a naval base in their war with Spain, while Bonaire became a plantation of the Dutch West India Company. The remaining convicts, Indians and a few African slaves were put to work cultivating dyewood and maize and, from 1639, collecting salt dried by the sun. Slave quarters, no taller than 1.2m (4ft) and built of stone, can still be found around Rincon and along the saltpans as a grim reminder of Bonaire's history.

When the Dutch West India Company collapsed in 1791, the Dutch government confiscated its property. The slaves, now owned by the Kingdom of the Netherlands, came to be known as 'government slaves'. The slaves were allowed to grow and sell their own produce, and sometimes even to

Above: *Steps in the foreground provide safe entry and exit when diving Bonaire's Town Pier.*
Opposite: *Obelisks were built beside slave huts in the south of the island to guide merchant ships in.*

buy their own freedom. However, living conditions on Bonaire worsened, and in 1835 a rebellion began amongst the slaves. The Dutch transferred the remaining slaves to the stronghold of Tera Cora, but the end of slavery had begun. Slavery was finally abolished in 1862.

At the beginning of the 19th century the Dutch were harassed by British and French privateers. Twice, once during 1800–1803 and again during 1807–1815, the British gained control of Bonaire, which they leased to the North American shipping magnate Joseph Foulke to exploit for lumber. The ABC islands were later returned to the Netherlands under the Treaty of Paris in 1816, and Fort Oranje was built to ward off further attacks.

Bonaire lacked the resources that made many other Caribbean colonies rich but did have an abundance of salt, a necessary preservative for meat and fish in the days before the invention of refrigeration. Over the following two centuries Bonaire's salt industry was expanded, first under the Dutch West India Company and later under direct government control. However, the salt industry fell into sharp decline in the middle of the 19th century when the abolition of slavery and increased international competition

SOLAR SALT PRODUCTION

At the Cargill Salt Bonaire N.V., wind and sun evaporate seawater in salt pans. The seawater is fed into the Pekelmeer (Pickle Lake) then on through locks to 'condenser basins' where it becomes brine. Just before full saturation is reached, the brine is pumped into 'crystallizer basins' where the salt crystals form. These crystallizers are flooded periodically to maintain a constant level.

The solar salt crystals are collected once a year and transported by truck to a washing plant where they are slurried with brine and cascaded over curved gratings to remove impurities. After washing it is windrowed for several months to drain and dry and stored in large white mounds. Finally the salt is loaded onto ships by conveyor belt and exported to other Caribbean islands and the United States for industrial use, water softening and ice control.

Above: *A local dance troupe puts on a colourful performance at a Bonaire resort.*

reduced its profitability. Bonaire's nine salt pans were purchased from the government by E.B.F. Hellmund in 1870, though nowadays they are operated by Cargill Salt and remain important to the economy.

When the discovery of oil in Venezuela led to the development of refineries on Aruba and Curaçao, Bonaire also benefited from the prosperity. Roads were asphalted, the harbour rebuilt, electricity installed and telephone connections established. Fort Oranje's old lighthouse was replaced by a stone beacon in 1932 and an airport was built in 1936.

Bonaire's male population was given the right to vote in 1936 and political parties emerged over the next decade. After World War II the islanders began to press for greater autonomy and in 1954 Queen Juliana of the Netherlands granted self-rule to all the Antilles (though they remained a Dutch protectorate). With independence came tourism. On Playa de Lechi, the Bonaire Beach Hotel was opened in 1962, while Bonaire's Flamingo Airport, was expanded to handle the increase in traffic in 1972. Later Bonaire's Marine Park and Washington-Slagbaai Park were established to ensure the survival of its natural attractions.

Bonaire has never had the wealth of Aruba and Curaçao but is now more prosperous than ever before. The salt industry has been revived and modernized and there is income from radio transmitting stations. The greatest income comes from the 65,000 tourists who visit Bonaire per year, most coming for the diving.

LOCAL HIGHLIGHTS

Located on the island's west coast, Kralendijk (meaning 'coral dyke' but called 'Playa' by the locals), is Bonaire's capital. Its Dutch colonial houses, the Museo Boneriano and Fort Oranje offer an insight into the island's history. Pink Beach, past the Salt Pier and beside the salt pans, is the best beach on Bonaire with fine sand and shallow water that is good for swimming; there are some pink corals and at sunset the sand glows pink. Opposite White Slave and again further south near Red Slave, 9m (30ft) obelisks, built to direct merchant ships to their anchorage, tower above neat rows of tiny slave huts. The slaves who had to live in them led a miserable existence, six to a hut and only allowed to visit their families on Sundays – some 25km (15 miles) walk away. Further south is Willemstoren lighthouse, which was first lit in 1838.

Lac Bay, on Bonaire's windward side, is the centre of the island's windsurfing. It is also one of two wetland sites on Bonaire listed under the Ramsar Convention (an inter-governmental treaty governing the conservation of wetlands of international importance) – the other being Klein Bonaire.

North of Kralendijk is Rincon, Bonaire's oldest town, built inland to avoid sea-borne raiders. East of the town the limestone caves at Fontein and Onima were a refuge for the island's Caiquetio Indians many centuries ago. Rock paintings and petroglyphs made with the dye of the dyewood tree can be seen at Onima and also in the caves at Spelonk, Ceru Pungi, and Ceru Crita-Cabai.

> **SUBI BRANDARIS**
>
> In the centre of Washington-Slagbaai National Park there is a walking track up Bonaire's highest hill, Subi Brandaris, 240m (784ft) high. The track leads up a ridge from the car park and is marked with yellow circles on the rocks. From the top, hikers have a panoramic view of the park, with Kralendijk and the Salt Company's mounds of salt in the distance. On clear days, Curaçao can be seen on the western horizon and Venezuela is visible. The round trip takes about three hours.

Washington-Slagbaai National Park offers all the landscape, animals and most of the birds to be encountered on Bonaire. Boca Slagbaai was the harbour for the Slagbaai plantation, and is popular with tourist boats for snorkelling. The fine sand is good for sunbathing and there are buildings dating back to 1868, including the house of the manager of Slagbaai plantation, a customs office and a warehouse (*magasina*), once used for storing salt. Nearby, Gotomeer and Saliña Slagbaai are home to flocks of flamingos, Bonaire's national symbol. Nukove, roughly 3km (2 miles) west of Gotomeer, has good beaches for swimming, hidden caves, and some of the island's best snorkelling. In the northeast Playa Chiquito is good for sunbathing but dangerous for swimming due to strong surf.

DIVING IN BONAIRE

With over 30,000 diving enthusiasts visiting each year, Bonaire is the number one destination in the Caribbean for shore diving and vies with Grand Cayman and Cozumel as the overall top Caribbean diving destination for American divers. Nowadays Bonaire's largest industry is diving and almost every hotel, resort or apartment complex has a dive operation attached to it. What sets Bonaire apart from most other diving destinations is that a system of well marked roads makes driving around the island very simple and the marine park has placed yellow-painted rocks along the roads to mark the easiest access points for dive sites. The ease of shore entry is especially attractive to underwater photographers who can pick their dive site and dive at a time of day when the sun is in the best position, not having to worry about getting back to a boat at a particular time. Boat dives are also organised several times a day to all the popular sites.

> **BONAIRE NATURE ALLIANCE**
>
> Of the conservation organizations in Bonaire, one notable grouping is the Bonaire Nature Alliance, comprising:
>
> **Tene Boneiru Limpi** (Keep Bonaire Clean)
> **BONHATA** (Bonaire Hotel and Tourism Association)
> **CURO** (Council of Underwater Resort Operators)
> **Amigu di Tera** (Friends of the Earth)
> **Foundation for the Preservation of Klein Bonaire**
> **Tourism Corporation Bonaire**

All operators can organize suitable vehicles for shore diving and some either have their own or can arrange a 10 per cent discount. Double-cab pick-up trucks are the preferred vehicles – remember only to take what you need in the water and do not leave valuables in an unattended vehicle while diving. For many shore entries you often have to cross sharp coral so booties are recommended.

The least developed and least populated of the ABC islands, Bonaire is also a leader in the movement for preservation of underwater resources. The whole area is a protected marine park. Two localities have been designated marine reserves (where no diving is allowed): north from Boca Kayon to Boca Slagbaai, and west of Karpata. Lac Bay is also a protected area because of its mangroves and sea-grass beds. Free advanced buoyancy courses are provided to limit fin damage to the coral and wearing gloves is forbidden unless you are diving on a wreck or ascending or descending a shotline. Light (Xylem) sticks are also prohibited on night dives.

Any diver who has not dived on Bonaire within the last calendar year must attend a diver orientation session dealing with Bonaire Marine Park regulations. These orientation sessions are usually held the morning after you arrive on Bonaire, ruling out diving on your day of arrival. On completion of the orientation session you receive a Marine Park tag. This tag is not transferable, lasts for one year and is charged for to cover the park's maintenance costs. The tag must be displayed so that it can be easily seen, in order to dive legally in Bonaire's waters. While the same requirement does not technically apply to snorkellers, they are encouraged to attend the orientation and obtain a park tag.

There are several distinct diving areas in Bonaire. In general, the drop-off is slightly further offshore in the south than in the north. One distinctive areas is between Punt Vierkant and Salt Pier, with a reef system known as the 'Alice in Wonderland' double-reef complex. The reef slope is at a shallow angle and descends to a sandy channel at 20–30m (65–100ft), where there is then a second reef. Another distinct area is on the leeward coast of Klein Bonaire, where buttresses and steep reef slopes dominate the diving. Different again is an area in the northern part of the island, from the edge of the hotel and housing development to the Karpata Ecological Centre. On the east side of the island there is a shelf and then a drop-off about 12m (40ft) from the shore, descending to a coral shelf at 30m (100ft) and then dropping down to the ocean floor; the sea here is rough for most of the year but often calms down in October or November.

There are over 85 recognized dive sites (including wreck sites as well as reefs) and heavily dived sites are closed off sporadically to allow them to recover. One of the most popular dives on Bonaire is a day or night dive under the town pier in Kralendijk. It is a credit to the Government and the Marine Park that divers are allowed to dive here – a mooring point for large ships and cruise liners, it remains one of the best night dives in the world.

A guided snorkel programme is available, and dive boats regularly take snorkellers along when dive sites are close to shore. Playa Bengé is considered to be the best snorkelling site on Bonaire. Most dive operators offer full diver training, diving and snorkelling equipment for rent and boat dives in the morning, late morning, and early afternoon – sign-up the day before for boat dives, by location. On a diving package, you will usually get unlimited shore dives, so normally you can just pick up the equipment and go diving anywhere from the shore.

Opposite: *The datu candle cacti* (Lemaireocereus griseus) *has thorn-bearing fruit.*

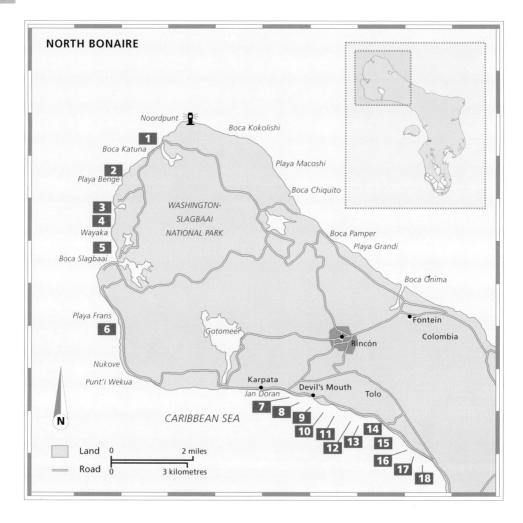

North Bonaire

1 BOCA BARTOL
★★★★

Location: Northwest coast, the northernmost site of the marine park
Access: By boat or shore
Conditions: Currents can be strong
Average Depth: 20m (65ft)
Maximum Depth: 40m (130ft)
Visibility: 30m (100ft)
This dive site can have large swells and currents coming from the windward side of the island. It features a classic spur-and-groove formation with elkhorn corals, star corals and gorgonian sea fans; many of the larger fish species are found here. There is a chance to see black durgon (*Melichthys niger*), bigeyes, soldierfish, squirrelfish and ocean triggerfish while rays and garden eels are found on the sandy bottom. The drop-off is a long swim from the shore so shore diving is not recommended.

2 PLAYA BENGÉ
★★★★★★★★

Location: Northwest coast, off Playa Bengé
Access: By boat or shore
Conditions: Strong currents
Average Depth: 20m (65ft)
Maximum Depth: 40m (130ft)
Visibility: 30m (100ft)

Along the northwest coast of Washington-Slagbaai Park, Playa Bengé has strong currents so it is recommended only for advanced divers. Another classic example of spur-and-groove formations, the shallows have star and staghorn corals, blade fire coral (*Millepora complanata*) and large gorgonian sea fans. The drop-off is a long swim out and has sponges, tiger groupers (*Mycteroperca tigris*), mahogany snappers and stingrays.

3 PLAYA FUNCHI

★★★★☆☆☆☆☆

Location: Northwest coast, off Playa Funchi
Access: From the shore
Conditions: Moderate to strong currents
Average Depth: 20m (65ft)
Maximum Depth: 40m (130ft)
Visibility: 30m (100ft)

Playa Funchi is for advanced divers due to the moderate to strong currents. The presence of elkhorn and staghorn corals close to the beach means that this site is popular with snorkellers. In depths of 4.5–30m (15–100ft), angelfish, grunts, parrotfish, bigeyes, soldierfish, groupers and bar jacks (*Caranx ruber*) are found and horse-eye jacks (*Caranx latus*) can be seen out in blue water. The shallow shelf continues a long way across sand and staghorn coral to the drop-off where the current is stronger and stingrays are found on the sand below.

4 BISÉ MORTO

★★★★☆☆☆☆☆

Location: Northwest coast, between Playa Funchi and Wayaka
Access: By boat or shore
Conditions: Moderate to strong currents
Average Depth: 20m (65ft)
Maximum Depth: 40m (130ft)
Visibility: 30m (100ft)

The name translates as 'dead deer', a reference to the elkhorn and staghorn corals found in the shallow water. The deeper water can surprise you with larger species, and whale sharks and manta rays have been seen.

5 BOCA SLAGBAAI

★★★★☆☆☆☆☆

Location: Northwest coast, off Wayaka
Access: By boat or shore
Conditions: Moderate to strong currents
Average Depth: 20m (65ft)
Maximum Depth: 40m (130ft)
Visibility: 30m (100ft)

Just north of the no diving reserve, Boca Slagbaai is popular for beach outings, with non-divers snorkelling off the beach entry point. For divers there are moderate to strong currents. There are six concrete replicas of cannons which were buried for the film *Shark Treasure*. Barracuda, tarpon, whitespotted filefish and shoals of palometa (*Trachinotus goodei*) can be seen. You may also see mantas or smaller rays. At the south end of the cove, there are two real cannons in just 3m (10ft) of water.

The drop-off begins at 12m (40ft) and features horse-eye jacks, grunts, tiger groupers and schoolmaster snappers (*Lutjanus apodus*). Occasionally one may spot a hawksbill turtle.

6 NUKOVE

★★★★☆☆☆☆☆

Location: Northwest coast, just south of Playa Frans
Access: From the shore
Conditions: Mild to strong currents
Average Depth: 20m (65ft)
Maximum Depth: 30m (100ft)
Visibility: 30m (100ft)

Below: *An anchor lies embedded in coral on the drop-off at Karpata (Site 7).*

This shore dive is a bit hard to find. It ranges from 6–30m (20–100ft) and has mild to strong currents. Divers will find a channel through the elkhorn coral in the shallows, with anemones, shrimps, parrotfish, bigeyes, soldierfish, squirrelfish, shoals of algae-grazing reef fish and many juveniles present. To the south, sponges, crinoids, black coral, filefish, wrasse and black durgon are evident and the drop-off has large coral heads that sometimes shelter nurse sharks.

7 KARPATA
★★★★

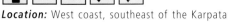

Location: West coast, southeast of the Karpata Ecological Centre
Access: By boat or shore
Conditions: Light to moderate currents
Average Depth: 20m (65ft)
Maximum Depth: 40m (130ft)
Visibility: 40m (130ft)
One of Bonaire's most popular dives, Karpata has spur-and-groove formations from 10m (33ft) down to sand at 30m (100ft). To the west is a prohibited area, so head to the east and explore the drop-off where you will find several large anchors, one of which is embedded in the coral at 10m (33ft). Staghorn corals, large gorgonian sea fans and sea rods feature here, as well as French angelfish, goatfish, groupers, grunts, trunkfish, wrasse, snappers, parrotfish and sometimes hawksbill turtles.

8 LA DANIA'S LEAP
★★★★

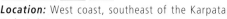

Location: West coast, southeast of the Karpata Ecological Centre
Access: By boat
Conditions: Light currents
Average Depth: 20m (65ft)
Maximum Depth: 40m (130ft)
Visibility: 30m (100ft)
In the early days of Bonaire diving, boats were hard to come by, so Captain Don Stewart led dives that involved having to 'leap' off the shore and then drift-dive to Karpata before exiting the water. La Dania was an early student who impressed Captain Don in 1966. With light currents and depths of 5–30m (15–100ft), La Dania's Leap is one of Bonaire's few vertical walls, with numerous canyons and sand shoots.

The wall has various sponges and black corals and in the shallow water there are grunts, parrotfish, snappers, whitespotted filefish (*Cantherhines macroceros*) and trumpetfish.

9 RAPPEL
★★★★

Location: West coast, off Devil's Mouth southeast of the Karpata Ecological Centre
Access: By boat
Conditions: Moderate currents
Average Depth: 20m (65ft)
Maximum Depth: 40m (139ft)
Visibility: 30m (100ft)
This is another site named by Captain Don Stewart, who used to get divers to rappel (abseil) down the cliff. Now it is reached by boat or by swimming from Karpata.

One of the best dives on Bonaire, Rappel features large gorgonian sea fans, sea rods and star corals and an abundance of nudibranchs in the shallows. *Tubastrea* coral grows in the shade of ledges and 73m (80yd) south of the mooring there is a cave sheltering large groupers. The rich marine life also includes banded coral shrimps, spiny lobsters and squid.

10 BLOODLET
★★★★

Location: West coast, east of Devil's Mouth and southeast of the Karpata Ecological Centre
Access: Preferably by boat, but can be dived from the shore by swimming from Karpata
Conditions: Moderate currents
Average Depth: 20m (65ft)
Maximum Depth: 30m (100ft)
Visibility: 30m (100ft)
A difficult shore entry means that Bloodlet is usually dived by boat. Moderate currents have given rise to a

rich reef that harbours shoals of algae-grazing blue tangs. Yellow and green tube sponges are common and turtles are often sighted.

11 OL' BLUE
★★★★★★★★★

Location: West coast, off Boca di Toto
Access: By boat or shore
Conditions: Light to moderate currents
Average Depth: 20m (65ft)
Maximum Depth: 45m (150ft)
Visibility: 30m (100ft)

Ol' Blue is named after the rich blue colour of the sea that is found over the site's shallows. The dive is similar to Weber's Joy (Site 15), but has even more fish. A shelf at 6m (20ft) extends seaward for 90m (100yd), covered with staghorn coral, gorgonian sea fans, sea plumes and sea rods, star coral, sponges and a rich fish life. The drop-off starts at 10m (33ft) and descends to sand. At the eastern end, various fish shelter around several large boulders including bigeyes, French angelfish, grunts, tiger groupers, mahogany snappers, scorpionfish, barracuda and shoals of horse-eye jacks.

12 COUNTRY GARDEN
★★★★

Location: West coast, off the southeast of Boca di Toto
Access: By boat
Conditions: Moderate currents
Average Depth: 20m (65ft)
Maximum Depth: 40m (130ft)
Visibility: 30m (100ft)

At this site, large boulders that have fallen from the cliffs provide shelter for schoolmaster snappers, grunts, bigeyes, soldierfish, squirrelfish and goatfish.

13 BON BINI NA CAS
★★★★

Location: West coast, west of 1000 Steps
Access: By boat or by shore by swimming from 1000 Steps
Conditions: Normally calm
Average Depth: 20m (65ft)
Maximum Depth: 40m (130ft)
Visibility: 30m (100ft)

Below: *The conspicuous markings of the flamingo tongue are instantly recognisable.*

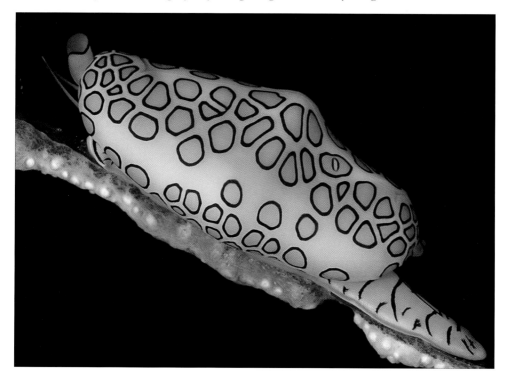

Above: *A diver explores the reef, with its light covering of encrusting sponges and cup corals.*
Below: *Healthy staghorn coral is a common sight on Bonaire's reefs.*

'Welcome to my home' in Papiamento, Bon Bini Na Cas lies up against the cliff just next to 1000 Steps. It features a gentle sandy slope down to 12m (40ft) with stony corals, gorgonian sea fans, sea rods and sea plumes, sponges, scrawled filefish (*Aluterus scriptus*), French angelfish, groupers, blue tangs, Creole wrasse (*Clepictus parrai*) and trumpetfish. There is then a steeper drop-off where there are vase and tube sponges, lobsters, green moray eels, barracuda and jacks.

14 1000 STEPS
★★★★★☆☆☆☆

Location: West coast, between Boca di Toto and Barkadera Lont, in front of the southernmost of the Radio Netherlands transmitter pylons
Access: By shore or boat
Conditions: Normally calm
Average Depth: 20m (65ft)
Maximum Depth: 40m (130ft)
Visibility: 30m (100ft)
Soon after the 67 steps down to the shore here were constructed in 1968, one of Captain Don's clients remarked that they can seem like 1000 steps when carrying heavy scuba equipment back up. The site was then aptly named 1000 Steps.

There is a gentle slope to 10m (33ft) with brain and staghorn coral, large star corals and many gorgonian sea rods, sea whips and sea plumes. A steeper but less interesting drop-off then descends to 40m (130ft) with occasional shoals of schoolmaster snappers and blue tangs (*Acanthurus coeruleus*). Keep an eye on the open water as almost anything can pass by – hawksbill turtles, manta rays, dolphins and a whale shark have all been seen here.

15 WEBER'S JOY/WITCHES HUT
★★★★☆☆☆☆

Location: West coast, off Barkadera Lont
Access: By boat or shore
Conditions: Normally calm
Average Depth: 20m (65ft)
Maximum Depth: 40m (130ft)
Visibility: 30m (100ft)
Originally called Witches Hut (after the local name for a hut on the shore) when it was only a shore dive, Weber's Joy is a favourite with underwater photographers. The shallow shelf has elkhorn, staghorn and blade fire coral, angelfish, butterflyfish and many other reef fish. The drop-off descends from 13m (40ft) to sand at 40m (130ft) with gorgonians and undercut star corals encrusted with *Tubastrea* cup corals. Various sponges make this site particularly

colourful and there are cleaning stations that are popular with groupers. Manta rays often cruise by.

16 JEFF DAVIS MEMORIAL
★★★★

Location: West coast, off the southeastern end of Barkadera Lont
Access: By boat or shore
Conditions: Normally calm
Average Depth: 20m (65ft)
Maximum Depth: 40m (130ft)
Visibility: 30m (100ft)
A good site for beginners, with light to moderate currents. The shallows feature gorgonian sea fans, sea rods, sea whips and sea plumes and you may spot a turtle. Over the drop-off, stony coral forms chutes that lead to a sandy bottom.

17 OIL SLICK LEAP
★★★★

Location: West coast, off the southeastern end of Barkadera Lont
Access: Preferably by boat but can be dived from the shore
Conditions: Normally calm
Average Depth: 20m (65ft)
Maximum Depth: 40m (130ft)
Visibility: 30m (100ft)
Originally the site for a proposed oil storage terminal (hence the name Oil Slick Leap), it is recommended that you treat this site as a boat dive – though if you want to make it a shore dive, strong divers will find a steel ladder leading to the water. As well as the ubiquitous gorgonians and stony corals, large numbers of barracuda are seen here.

18 BARCADERA
★★★★

Location: West coast, opposite Bonaire Marine Park Headquarters
Access: By boat
Conditions: Normally calm
Average Depth: 20m (65ft)
Maximum Depth: 40m (130ft)
Visibility: 30m (100ft)
A good dive for novices, where the shallows are covered with elkhorn coral and gorgonians. Fish life that feature here include Spanish hogfish, trumpetfish, whitespotted filefish, grunts, snappers, trunkfish, bigeyes, soldierfish, squirrelfish and shoals of blue tangs, jacks and Creole wrasse.

The Bonaire Marine Park surrounds the islands of Bonaire and Klein Bonaire, extending from the high water mark to the 60m (200ft) depth contour and covering an estimated 2700ha (6672 acres). It is used mainly for recreational diving and snorkelling, though there is some subsistence fishing by locals and other watersports take place.

The park took shape over a number of years. In 1961, legislation was passed to protect marine turtle eggs and nests; ten years later spear fishing was banned. In 1975 new legislation made it illegal to damage coral or remove it from the sea, and finally in 1979, with financial support from the World Wildlife Fund of Holland, the government of Bonaire created the Bonaire Marine Park.

Due to financial difficulties the park was not actively managed from 1984 to 1991 – after which it received Dutch Government funding. In 1987, Captain Don Stewart and other enthusiasts began establishing fixed moorings for all dive sites, which were monitored by the dive operators. The sites were also closed occasionally to give them time to recover from diver pressure.

The park is managed by STINAPA, which also manages Washington-Slagbaai National Park and the Karpata Ecological Centre. The park's six staff run shore and boat patrols daily to ensure that the marine park is unharmed. They look after over 70 fixed moorings and insist on the use of these moorings to avoid anchor damage. The marine park staff are also actively involved in promoting public understanding of the park and in providing information to the park's 60,000 annual visitors. Videos and slide shows about the park are laid on; check with your nearest dive shop on Bonaire for times of these shows.

RESEARCH

Marine parks are excellent locations for scientists to collect data on the changes to a natural environment over time. Recently there have been a number of scientific programmes at Bonaire's Marine Park. In 1993 a long term monitoring programme was set up to assess changes in the reef benthos, using a technique of photographing five permanent one square metre quadrants at sites at 9m (30ft). These have been monitored yearly to study the change in coral cover and diversity. Every two years the park also monitors 15 sites along the coast at 9m (30ft) and 18m (60ft) to characterize the coral community over the whole area.

In order to study the diver-carrying capacity of the park, baseline data have also been collected on heavily dived and little dived reefs. Observations have been made on the negative effects of nutrient enrichment and anchor damage on the reefs. The results show that large areas are degrading as a result of diver damage, and studies suggest that the carrying capacity of Bonaire's reefs have been reached. Although the park's authorities wish to repeat these studies before deciding to limit visitor numbers, it is obvious that great care must be taken when diving on the reefs.

There have been various other studies on the biology of the marine park. CEDAM (Conservation, Ecology, Diving, Archaeology, Museums) sent volunteers to study cleaner shrimps and carry out fish censuses, while the Netherlands Institute for Sea Research has ongoing studies of the parrotfish population. Dedicated volunteers from Bonaire have also been involved in research investigating the temporal and spatial distribution of the colonial ascidian *Trididemnum solidum,* between 6 and 40m (20 and 130ft). *Trididemnum solidum* easily overgrows living corals, has little predation and has a high rate of reproduction so it is known for causing problems to reefs. The authorities on Bonaire have also carried out their own fish census and, after an initiative set up by Manfred van Veghel, of Reef Care Curaçao, coral spawning at night during September and October has been studied every year since 1992.

DIVING IN THE PARK

Bonaire's Marine Park charges US$10 per person per annum to anyone wishing to dive or snorkel off Bonaire. Tickets and tags can be bought from any of the island's dive operators or from the park headquarters at Barcadera. All divers must be briefed on the

Above: *Marker stones clearly indicate the route down to the beach at 1000 Steps (Site 14).*

park's rules before their first dive and all dive operators give free Buoyancy Control Courses. Your dive tags must be with you whenever you go diving or snorkelling in the park and produced when requested.

PARK RULES

It is vital that you always follow the park rules and report any infringements to the park staff.

Anchoring is prohibited everywhere, irrespective of the type of seabed, except between the customs dock and the marina. Public moorings may be used by any vessel up to 12m (38ft) on a first-come-first-served basis for up to two hours. You must put out a scope line, which is at least as long as the vessel and can only tie on by the bow. Only one rigid-hulled boat is permitted on a mooring at any one time, but up to three inflatables can share a mooring if each is less than 4m (12ft) long.

Spear fishing is completely prohibited. Also, do not take anything, living or dead (e.g. corals, sea fans, shells or the like), out of the water, except garbage. Conchs are internationally protected, so taking back one shell may cost you dearly. Equally, do not throw anything overboard from boats; garbage containers are available onshore. Take all of your garbage home with you – Bonaire's motto is 'Tene Boneiru Limpi', or 'keep Bonaire clean'.

Boat crew should always keep a look-out for divers, their bubbles and snorkellers. Boats must pass to seaward of dive moorings.

Divers and snorkellers should make as little contact with the reefs as possible. Do not sit on, stand on, or hold on to coral. Divers should make sure that they are neutrally buoyant, that all consoles and gauges are secured where they cannot drag along the bottom, and that they do not wear gloves.

Note that turtles are on the list of endangered species and completely protected internationally. Do not buy turtle shells or other turtle by-products or you will be heavily fined!

Remember, 'Take only pictures, leave only bubbles'. Further information about the park can be obtained from: Bonaire Marine Park, PO Box 368, Bonaire; tel/fax 00 599 78444

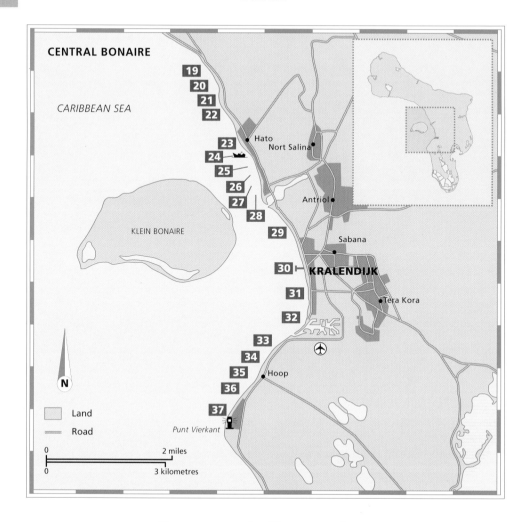

CENTRAL BONAIRE

CARIBBEAN SEA

19
20
21
22

23
24
25
26
27
28
29

30   **KRALENDIJK**

31

32

33
34
35
36

37

Hato
Nort Salina

Antriol

Sabana

Tera Kora

Hoop

Punt Vierkant

KLEIN BONAIRE

N

 Land

 Road

0   2 miles
0   3 kilometres

Central Bonaire

19 ANDREA II
★★★★☆☆☆☆☆

Location: West coast, just north past the desalination plant at Santa Barbara
Access: By boat or shore
Conditions: Normally calm
Average Depth: 20m (65ft)
Maximum Depth: 35m (115ft)
Visibility: 30m (100ft)
This site is ideal for novices, as the currents are mostly light. The shallow water has staghorn and fire corals and there are lots of parrotfish. There are also many anemones and gorgonians offering camouflage to hungry trumpetfish and slender filefish. The drop-off

starts at 15m (50ft) with gorgonians, star and sheet corals and sponges descending to sand. Banded coral shrimps (*Stenopus hispidus*), grunts and snappers are common and there is a good chance of seeing seahorses.

20 ANDREA I
★★★★☆☆☆☆☆

Location: West coast, southeast of Andrea II
Access: By boat or shore
Conditions: Normally calm
Average Depth: 20m (65ft)
Maximum Depth: 35m (115ft)
Visibility: 30m (100ft)

The profile of this site is similar to that of Andrea II (Site 19), with a gentle slope to 15m (50ft) then a drop-off.

21 PETRIE'S PILLAR
★★★★

Location: West coast, southeast of Andrea I
Access: By boat or shore
Conditions: Normally calm
Average Depth: 20m (65ft)
Maximum Depth: 35m (115ft)
Visibility: 30m (100ft)

Petrie's Pillar is a dive for novices. It is named after a friend of Captain Don Stewart and the pillar coral that grows on the reef. The terrain is similar to that of Andrea I and II (sites 19-20). The shallows also host shoals of blue tangs.

22 SMALL WALL
★★★★★★★★

Location: West coast, opposite the Black Durgon Inn.
Access: By boat or shore; permission is needed to cross the private property for shore entry.
Conditions: Normally calm
Average Depth: 20m (65ft)
Maximum Depth: 40m (120ft)
Visibility: 30m (100ft)

A shallow, well-protected wall dive that is ideal for beginners and night dives. The top of the reef has elkhorn and brain coral and lots of branching gorgonians that seahorses attach themselves to. Parrotfish, bigeyes, soldierfish, squirrelfish, grunts and French angelfish abound. A small wall starts 30m (100ft) out from the shore and drops from 12m (40ft) to 22m (70ft). A cave can be found at 18m (60ft), and there is a possibility of seeing a sleeping nurse shark or green moray eels. Below the cave, large elephant ear sponges make this a good site for underwater photography. Lobsters can be found on night dives.

23 CLIFF
★★★★★★★★

Location: West coast, opposite the Hamlet Villas north of Captain Don's Habitat.
Access: By boat or shore
Conditions: Normally calm
Average Depth: 20m (65ft)
Maximum Depth: 40m (130ft)
Visibility: 30m (100ft)

A channel runs through elkhorn coral into a shelf with gorgonians and stony corals. The drop-off descends as a short wall from 9m (30ft) to 22m (70ft) with a ledge of sand 2m (6ft) wide then slopes to sand at 40m (130ft). The wall has orange and tube sponges, gorgonian sea whips and abundant fish life. There is supposed to be an underwater stone memorial from Captain Don to 'divers who have gone before us', marked with a plaque and dive flag, but I didn't ever come across it!

24 LA MACHACA
★★★★★★★★

Location: West coast, off Captain Don's Habitat
Access: From the shore
Conditions: Normally calm
Average Depth: 14m (45ft)
Maximum Depth: 40m (130ft)
Visibility: 30m (100ft)

Captain Don's Habitat's house reef, this site is named after the wreck of a local 14m (45ft) fishing boat *La Machaca*, 30m (100ft) from the shore in 14m (45ft) of water. Ideal for training divers, snorkelling, night diving and general fish photography, most of the reef fish encountered on Bonaire can be found here. Because of the popularity of this site much of the marine life has become so used to divers that you can find yourself being aproached by fish (it seems that only drums are shy). Lizardfish and peacock flounders (*Bothus lunatus*) are common and spotted moray eels can even be found swimming freely during daylight.

A rope stretched along the seabed from the shore-entry jetty (Baby Dock) goes directly out 15m (50ft) to the drop-off and then down the slope to another deeper wreck. Divers returning to the jetty can easily

---

BONAIRE GUIDED SNORKELLING PROGRAM

A group of expert snorkellers and underwater photographers together with the marine park authorities and local operators researched the leeward coast of the main island and the coast of Klein Bonaire to set up the Bonaire Guided Snorkelling Program.

There are 12 sites in the program, each selected to offer distinct experiences. However, remember that many other excellent snorkelling sites may also be found, especially immediately adjacent to those listed. Where a site is marked with an asterisk, the snorkel site lies inshore of the dive site.

Bonaire sites	Klein Bonaire sites
Playa Funchi	No Name*
Nukove	Leonora's Reef
1000 Steps	Jerry's Jam*
Cliff	Munk's Haven*
Windsock	Just A Nice Dive*
Invisibles	
Mangroves	

locate this rope to find their way back without straying into the path of boats leaving from or returning to the separate boat jetty (Papa Dock).

There are elkhorn coral, palometa and flounders in the shallow water by the entry jetty, brain and star coral, gorgonians, orange elephant ear and tube sponges over the drop-off, and the wrecks attract tarpon, jacks, grunts, snappers, sergeant majors and groupers.

25 REEF SCIENTIFICO

Location: West coast, southeast of Captain Don's Habitat
Access: From the shore
Conditions: Normally calm
Average Depth: 12m (40ft)
Maximum Depth: 40m (130ft)
Visibility: 30m (100ft)
South of La Machaca (Site 24), a transect (grid system) has been set out in 12m (40ft) of water to monitor algal growth on the reef. The site is much the same as La Machaca but fewer divers have been here so the fish are not as tame.

26 BUDDY'S REEF

Location: West coast, in front of Buddy Dive Resort
Access: From the shore
Conditions: normally calm
Average Depth: 20m (65ft)
Maximum Depth: 40m (130ft)
Visibility: 30m (100ft)
This shore dive is great for beginners and snorkellers, with mild currents. Black crinoids perch on coral heads in the shallows; night divers often encounter a shoal of tarpon.

27 BARI REEF

Location: West coast, in front of Sand Dollar Condominium Resort
Access: From the shore
Conditions: Moderate currents
Average Depth: 20m (65ft)
Maximum Depth: 37m (120ft)
Visibility: 30m (100ft)

Above: *Kralendijk's Town Pier (Site 30) is the best known of Bonaire's dive sites.*
Opposite: *An adult stoplight parrotfish grazes on algae using its large parrot-like beak.*

Sand Dollar Resort's house reef, this site is ideal for snorkelling and training novice divers though it is showing signs of wear. There is usually some current, so start your dive by heading into it. A flat, sandy plateau continues out 91m (100yd) from the service deck to the drop-off, which varies in depth from 6m (20ft) to 12m (40ft). The plateau and the drop-off have star corals, gorgonians and sponges, and attract French angelfish, foureye butterflyfish, trunkfish, peacock flounders, scorpionfish, bigeyes, soldierfish, squirrelfish and goatfish. Night divers regularly encounter tarpon (*Megalops atlanticus*).

28 FRONT PORCH
★★★★☆☆☆☆☆

Location: West coast, in front of the Sunset Beach Resort
Access: From the shore
Conditions: Light to moderate currents
Average Depth: 20m (65ft)
Maximum Depth: 30m (100ft)
Visibility: 30m (100ft)

Accessed from either the dive jetty or the beach, Front Porch is an easy dive ideal for diver training or snorkelling. Beginning at 5m (16ft) under the pier, the slope continues down to beyond 25m (80ft), where a small wreck of a tugboat lies upside down. The wreck is covered in orange *Tubastrea* cup coral and harbours a profuse fish life.

29 SOMETHING SPECIAL
★★★☆☆☆☆

Location: West coast, just south of Kralendijk Marina entrance
Access: By boat or shore
Conditions: Mild currents
Average Depth: 20m (65ft)
Maximum Depth: 40m (130ft)
Visibility: 20m (65ft)

This is an area where sailing boats are allowed to anchor. There is very little coral growth here but there is abundant fish life; rays can often be seen at the sandy bottom. Good for night diving.

DECEPTIVE CORALS

Many divers are surprised when they first see black coral underwater, since it is not in fact black at all. The polyps of most black corals are translucent with pigments that make the colony appear brown, green or grey – although in wire corals they are a brighter red or yellow-green. As in stony corals, black coral polyps have six tentacles but ,unlike stony corals, they are not retractable.

It is only the skeleton of black coral that is black. This material is laid down in concentric layers; if the skeleton is cut crosswise it looks like the yearly growth rings of trees. In deep water some black corals grow very large, and it is the branches of these that are collected so that the skeleton can be fashioned into jewellery.

The scientific name for black coral, antipatharian, means anti-disease, a reference to a historical belief in its medicinal properties. Due to their collection for jewellery some black coral forests have disappeared from the Caribbean – you can protect the remaining black coral trees by not purchasing products made from them.

Black corals are protected under the Convention in International Trade in Endangered Species (CITES) – they cannot be exported or imported except under licence.

30 TOWN PIER
★★★★

Location: West coast, off the Town (North) Pier, next to the customs office in Kralendijk
Access: By boat or shore (with permission)
Conditions: Normally calm
Average Depth: 5m (16ft)
Maximum Depth: 9m (30ft)
Visibility: 20m (65ft)

This is the best known dive site on Bonaire and one of the best night dive sites in the world. In 9m (30ft) of water, the pier's stanchions are home to a rich world of small invertebrate life and lots of other marine creatures seeking shelter or food. There are usually a couple of large tugboats coming and going, and permission should first be obtained from the harbour master to be sure that no large ships are expected that could pose a danger to divers (also the visibility can be lowered to just a few metres by the movement of large ships). You should be accompanied by a local dive guide and must be careful about where you surface, or you could become trapped between the pier and any boats docking against it. At night, aim for your dive boat's location beacon.

Boat diving is almost always done at night with one of the island's dive operators. When shore diving you should enter and exit the water by the steps down to the small beach that is immediately south of the pier. Walk the few metres to the pier and you can then duck safely under it in water that is too shallow for large boats.

The pier begins at a right angle from the shore and then turns north at a right angle. Its stanchions are covered in sponges of many colours including orange, yellow, green and purple. The site is a macro photographer's paradise, featuring orange *Tubastrea* cup corals, seahorses, Christmas tree worms, arrow and decorator crabs and various shrimps. The shelter of the pier acts as a nursery for juvenile fish including frogfish, French angelfish, foureye and banded butterflyfish, trunkfish, pufferfish, moray eels and shoals of bluestriped and smallmouth grunts (*Haemulon scirius* and *H. chrysargyreum*). It is well worth searching among the tyres and other rubbish strewn around the seafloor as many juveniles (including lobsters, octopuses, chain moray eels [*Gymnothorax moringa*], drums and soapfish) find shelter there.

31 CALABAS REEF
★★★★★★★★

Location: West coast, in front of Dive Bonaire at the Divi Flamingo Resort and the Carib Inn.
Access: Any of Dive Bonaire's jetties or the Carib Inn jetty
Conditions: Mild currents
Average Depth: 30m (65ft)
Maximum Depth: 27m (90ft)
Visibility: 30m (100ft)

This site is fine for snorkellers and all levels of divers, from novice to advanced. It begins as a shallow sandy shelf with some staghorn and star coral, anemones and sponges and many reef fish including French angelfish, parrotfish, snappers, bigeyes, soldierfish, squirrelfish Creole wrasse and Spanish hogfish.

The drop-off starts at 9m (30ft) and slopes down to 27m (90ft) and includes orange sponges, purple tube sponges, star coral, most species of reef fish and the occasional turtle or ray. Off the Calabas Restaurant jetty there is an anchor at 9m (25ft) and just below this there is an old lifeboat.

32 EIGHTEEN PALMS
★★★★★★★★

Location: West coast, opposite The Lieutenant Governor's House
Access: By boat or shore
Conditions: Mild currents
Average Depth: 20m (65ft)
Maximum Depth: 30m (100ft)
Visibility: 30m (100ft)

Opposite: *Sponges, like this orange rope sponge, are supported by a skeleton of spicules and fibres.*

Named after the 18 palm trees in the front garden of the Lieutenant Governor's house, this is an ideal site for novices and snorkellers. Southern and eagle rays are often seen on the sandy bottom.

Above: *Sponges of all kinds are responsible for much of the colour on Caribbean reefs.*

33 WINDSOCK STEEP

★★★★☆☆☆☆☆

Location: West coast, off the small beach that is opposite the Flamingo Airport runway
Access: By boat or shore
Conditions: Mild currents
Average Depth: 20m (65ft)
Maximum Depth: 30m (100ft)
Visibility: 30m (100ft)
Named after the windsock that flies from a pole on the airport runway, this dive site is known for excellent snorkelling. The sandy bottom has lots of fire coral in the shallows and there are many angelfish, sergeant majors, barracuda, snappers and trumpetfish. Divers often see turtles and rays.

34 NORTH BELNEM/DICK'S PLACE

★★★★☆☆☆☆☆

Location: West coast, just at the southern end of the small beach that is opposite the Flamingo Airport runway
Access: By boat or shore
Conditions: Mild currents
Average Depth: 20m (65ft)
Maximum Depth: 30m (100ft)
Visibility: 30m (100ft)
The shallows here feature branching and blade fire coral, staghorn coral and some elkhorn coral. The drop-off begins at 10m (33ft) with star corals, gorgonians, orange and purple tube sponges, trunkfish, filefish, cowfish, black durgon, trumpetfish, parrotfish, bigeyes, soldierfish, squirrelfish and shoals of blue tang.

35 BACHELOR'S BEACH

★★★★☆☆☆☆

Location: West coast, opposite the Hoop
Access: By boat or shore
Conditions: Mild currents
Average Depth: 20m (65ft)
Maximum Depth: 30m (100ft)
Visibility: 30m (100ft)
This makes a good boat dive, though novices will find it easily accessible from the shore and the currents are light. In the shallows there are fire, staghorn and elkhorn corals and lots of gorgonians. The deeper water has purple tube sponges, angelfish, butterflyfish, filefish, pufferfish, parrotfish, trumpetfish and surgeonfish. There is also the possibility of seeing turtles.

36 CHEZ HINES/SOUTH BELNEM

★★★★☆☆☆☆

Location: West coast, opposite the Great Escape, Belnem
Access: By boat or shore
Conditions: Mild currents
Average Depth: 20m (65ft)
Maximum Depth: 30m (100ft)
Visibility: 30m (100ft)
Sometimes called South Belnem, Chez Hines is similar to North Belnem, and is another site where turtles are often seen. There are star corals, gorgonians and tube sponges, while fish life includes trumpetfish, whitespotted filefish, parrotfish, French angelfish, rock beauties and blue tangs.

37 LIGHTHOUSE POINT

★★★★☆☆☆☆

Location: West coast, off Punt Vierkant Lighthouse
Access: By boat or shore
Conditions: Mild currents
Average Depth: 20m (65ft)
Maximum Depth: 30m (100ft)
Visibility: 30m (100ft)
This site has a sandy sloping bottom rather than a drop-off. There are lots of gorgonian sea rods, sea whips and sea plumes, as well as staghorn and star corals. The fish life is good, including French and queen angelfish, rock beauties, foureye, banded and spotfin butterflyfish, whitespotted filefish, parrotfish, trunkfish, snappers, grunts and Creole wrasse.

Below: *The beautiful queen angelfish is notable for its brilliant colouration.*

Anyone who regularly read diving magazines in the 1970s could not fail to come across the name of Captain Don Stewart. The winner of numerous diving awards, Don Stewart has played an enormous part in putting Bonaire on the world map of diving. While known as the father of Bonaire's dive-tourism industry, Don Stewart has also been instrumental in the success of Bonaire's programme of conservation. In 1982, in celebration of his 20th year on the island, he was issued a Certificate of Appreciation 'in recognition of his valuable contribution to the island of Bonaire and its people'.

Born in California in 1925, Don Stewart joined the American navy medical corps during World War II at the age of 17. After the war he became a successful inventor and businessman owning three factories, but he grew restless and decided to take a year off to raft down the Mississippi. In 1959 he bought a wooden hulled, two-masted, gaff-rigged 21m (70ft) schooner, *Valerie Queen,* and set out to run sailing charters and adventure tours. These trips were to lead him to the ABC islands, and on May 21st 1962 Captain Don made his first visit to Bonaire.

BONAIRE'S FIRST DIVE OPERATION

Initially he caught small tropical fish for the marine aquarium trade. He then moved on to become manager of the Flamingo Beach Club Hotel, the wooden barracks of a World War II internment camp that had been converted into Bonaire's first hotel. Here Captain Don set up the island's first dive operation. The only air cylinders he could use were the six that he had brought with him, and he had to use compressed air ferried across from Curaçao. Without any depth gauges, Don devised a system of using red ribbons to give the depth reading. This simple but effective

Below: *The world-famous Captain Don's Habitat was opened in 1976.*
Opposite: *Captain Don Stewart has played an important part in placing Bonaire on the diving map.*

system relied on the fact that red is the first colour of light to be filtered out by water with depth; when the red ribbons appeared to look black the divers knew that they were diving too deep.

In 1972 Captain Don set up Aquaventure, one of the first dedicated diving companies in the Caribbean. It was not until 1976, however, that he opened Captain Don's Habitat. In these early days, not only was Captain Don the dive guide and resort manager, but also the head cook, bottle washer, plumber, electrician and gardener! A large part of the Habitat was used as a nursery for local plants, as Captain Don was keen to promote not just marine conservation but also conservation on land. The ethos behind the Habitat was to encourage 'total diving freedom' – and to learn and care for all ecological systems.

CONSERVATION TO THE FORE

Even in these early days of diving, Captain Don realised that diving and spear fishing were causing a great deal of harm to Bonaire's reef system. If the reef system were to have a future it had to have a programme of conservation. Captain Don therefore lobbied hard to preserve Bonaire's underwater resources, and became instrumental in setting up the Bonaire Marine Park. One of Captain Don's ideas was to initiate the permanent mooring programme, where permanent moorings marked by buoys are set up to protect the delicate reef system. He also put forward the plan to temporarily close certain busy dive sites every now and then to allow them to 'rest' and regain their natural splendour.

Captain Don was keen to spread the idea of conservation and encouraged other Caribbean islands to follow the example Bonaire had set in preserving its reef system. In 1977 he co-founded the Caribbean Underwater Resort Operators (CURO), which brought together the operators of 18 Caribbean islands to encourage marine conservation throughout the Caribbean.

In 1987 Captain Don sold the Habitat, becoming a minority shareholder. Still very active, he now has a farm growing local plants, Island Grower N.V., and a landscape gardening business. Captain Don has been showered with recognition for his contributions to diving, to conservation and to Bonaire. On January 30th 1998, at DEMA (the Diving Equipment and Marketing Association's annual trade show), Captain Don was presented with the 'DEMA Reaching Out Award', one of the highest honours in the diving industry. This award puts Captain Don in the hall of fame with previous winners that include Captain Jacques-Yves Cousteau, Hans Hass, Jean-Michel Cousteau, Dr Eugenie Clark, Stan Waterman and Sylvia Earle.

When Captain Don started out on his pioneering road to conservation, his efforts were often regarded as rather controversial and somewhat unorthodox. Now he and Bonaire are considered to be world leaders in the modern drive towards preserving the environment for future generations to enjoy. As he says, 'Bonaire is to reef ecology as Greenwich is to time.'

South Bonaire

38 PUNT VIERKANT
★★★★

Location: West coast, south of Punk Vierkant lighthouse, north of the Transworld Radio transmitting pylons
Access: By boat or shore
Conditions: Mild currents
Average Depth: 20m (65ft)
Maximum Depth: 30m (100ft)
Visibility: 30m (100ft)
This site marks the start of the double-reef system, part of the 'Alice in Wonderland' complex (see Site 42). Staghorn coral and gorgonians can be seen in the shallows, while the reef slope has large brain and star corals, sponges and gorgonians down to a channel of

sand between the two reefs at 22–30m (70–100ft). There are scrawled filefish, Spanish hogfish, trunkfish, bigeyes, soldierfish, squirrelfish and rock beauties. The outer reef attracts barracuda, snappers, jacks, groupers and rays.

39 THE LAKE
★★★★

Location: West coast, southwest of the Transworld Radio transmitting pylons
Access: By boat or shore
Conditions: Mild currents
Average Depth: 20m (65ft)
Maximum Depth: 30m (100ft)
Visibility: 30m (100ft)

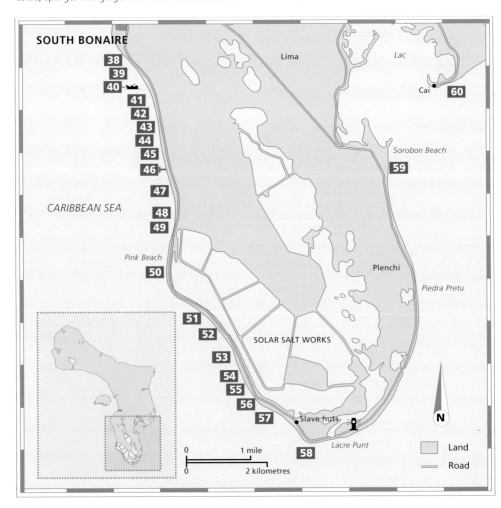

This is another double-reef dive, part of the 'Alice in Wonderland' complex. The Lake features gorgonian sea rods, sea whips and sea plumes, purple tube sponges, stony corals and a profusion of reef fish, including filefish, Spanish hogfish, trunkfish, bigeyes, soldierfish, squirrelfish and rock beauties. The seaward side of the outer reef has barracuda, snappers, jacks and groupers.

40 HILMA HOOKER
★★★

Location: West coast, south of The Lake (Site 39)
Access: By boat or shore
Conditions: Strong currents
Average Depth: 25m (80ft)
Maximum Depth: 30m (100ft)
Visibility: 20m (65ft)

The 72m (235ft), 1043-tonne (1027-ton) Korean freighter *Hilma Hooker* docked at the Town Pier for urgent repairs but alert Customs officers found marijuana hidden on board so the ship was confiscated and the drug burnt. As she was slowly sinking, on September 12th 1984 Bonaire's dive operators towed her out to the sand between the double-reef system and deliberately sunk her.

Unfortunately the anti-fouling wasn't removed so marine organisms have been slow to establish themselves on the structure. However, it is now being colonized by sponges and is shelter to tiger and black groupers, black margates (*Anisotremus surilnamensis*), mahogany snappers and yellowtail snappers *(Ocyurus chrysurus)*. Large horse-eye jacks cruise the open water beyond the wreck and midnight parrotfish can be seen grazing on the hull. Except where there are large open compartments in the central section, penetration of the wreck is not advised.

A cluster of dive-buoys along the wreck now marks the site. The ship rests on her starboard side at the bottom of the reef slope – the highest point of the vessel is at 18m (60ft).

41 ANGEL CITY
★★★★

Location: West coast, south of the Hilma Hooker (Site 40)
Access: By boat or shore
Conditions: Moderate currents
Average Depth: 25m (80ft)
Maximum Depth: 30m (100ft)
Visibility: 20m (65ft)

Another double-reef dive, this site is named after its friendly angelfish, which approach divers. There is a 'swim-through' coral arch near to the mooring, which provides a frame for photography. The outer reef has large boulders and large heads of star coral.

42 ALICE IN WONDERLAND
★★★★

Location: West coast, south of Angel City (Site 41)
Access: By boat or shore
Conditions: Moderate currents
Average Depth: 25m (80ft)
Maximum Depth: 30m (100ft)
Visibility: 20m (67ft)

This site lies roughly midway along the double-reef system (which also includes sites 38–49). The two distinct reefs are separated by a sand channel where garden eels and stingrays can be seen. There are staghorn corals and gorgonians in the shallows as well as French angelfish and parrotfish. The slope drops from 12m (40ft) to the sand at 25–30m (80–100ft) and the swim across the sand to the second reef is about 20m (65ft). This second reef rises to within 15m (50ft) of the surface and then drops off again into deep water where there is brain and star coral and shoals of black margate and schoolmaster snappers.

43 AQUARIUS
★★★★

Location: West coast, south of Alice in Wonderland (Site 42)
Access: By boat or shore
Conditions: Moderate currents
Average Depth: 25m (80ft)
Maximum Depth: 30m (100ft)
Visibility: 20m (65ft)

An easy dive that is part of the double reef system. Parrotfish, angelfish, surgeonfish and butterflyfish can be found between the two reefs. There are staghorn corals and gorgonians, jacks, grunts, trunkfish, bigeyes, soldierfish, squirrelfish and groupers. You may also spot rays or turtles in the shallows. On the seaward side of the outer reef you will encounter barracuda and large groupers.

Above: *A diver is dwarfed by the imposing stern section of the Hilma Hooker (Site 40).*
Opposite: *Salt Pier (Site 46) is home to a wide variety of fish, including French angelfish.*

44 LARRY'S LAIR
★★★★

Location: West coast, south of Aquarius (Site 43), the second dive site north of Salt Pier
Access: By boat or shore
Conditions: Moderate currents
Average Depth: 25m (80ft)
Maximum Depth: 30m (100ft)
Visibility: 20m (65ft)
The shore entry is over sharp rocks so hard-soled booties are recommended; this and the current make shore entry more difficult than that by boat. Still part of the double reef system, the topography is similar to that of Aquarius. Staghorn and star corals, gorgonians, Spanish hogfish, trunkfish, bigeyes, soldierfish, squirrelfish and rock beauties are found in the shallow water, while the outer reef attracts barracuda, snappers, jacks and groupers.

45 JEANNE'S GLORY
★★★★

Location: West coast, north of Salt Pier (Site 46)
Access: By boat or shore
Conditions: Moderate currents
Average Depth: 25m (80ft)
Maximum Depth: 30m (100ft)
Visibility: 20m (65ft)
Some operators and maps refer to this site as Jeannie's Glory. Still part of the double reef system with similar topography, this is another easy dive with lots of gorgonians in the shallows and sandy bottom for rays. Staghorn and star corals, angelfish, butterflyfish, trumpetfish, goatfish, snappers, Spanish hogfish, trunkfish, bigeyes, soldierfish and squirrelfish are common in the shallow water, while the outer reef has barracuda, snappers, jacks and groupers. Turtles are often seen along these southern dive sites.

46 SALT PIER
★★★★

Location: West coast, opposite the salt loading pier at the end of the overhead conveyor belt of the Salt Works
Access: From the shore
Conditions: Light currents
Average Depth: 15m (50ft)
Maximum Depth: 15m (50ft)
Visibility: 20m (65ft)
This site should not be attempted when a ship is loading its cargo or arriving or departing from the pier. As with the Town Pier (Site 30), the stanchions are covered with coral and sponge growth and act as shelter for juvenile fish. The stanchions near to the shore are in 6m (20ft) of water while those further out are in 15m (50ft). The drop-off slopes into deep water but it is the area directly beneath the pier that is more interesting. The pier itself is T-shaped; the stem of the 'T' runs west at right angles to the shore and the top of the 'T' runs north–south.

Tubastrea cup corals are a blaze of colour at night and there are tiny crabs, shrimps and fish among the growth on the stanchions. Surgeonfish graze the algae and French and queen angelfish, drums, soapfish, pufferfish, snappers, grunts, moray eels, groupers and shoals of goatfish and Creole wrasse are abundant. A great dive for photography.

47 SALT CITY
★★★★

Location: West coast, south of the salt loading pier of the Salt Works
Access: By boat or shore
Conditions: Moderate currents
Average Depth: 25m (80ft)
Maximum Depth: 30m (100ft)
Visibility: 20m (65ft)
Part of the double-reef system, Salt City features elkhorn, fire, staghorn and star corals, French angelfish, palometa, groupers, snappers, sand tilefish, garden eels, and occasionally eagle rays and turtles.

48 TORI'S REEF
★★★★★★★★

Location: West coast, by the outflow from the Salt Works
Access: By boat or shore
Conditions: Moderate currents
Average Depth: 25m (80ft)
Maximum Depth: 30m (100ft)
Visibility: 25m (80ft)

Still within the double reef system, there are large stands of elkhorn coral here and smaller ones of fire coral in the shallow water, while star corals, sponges and gorgonian sea plumes, sea rods and sea whips are found in deeper water. Rays inhabit the sandy sea floor while shoals of black margate and schoolmaster snappers, barracuda, jacks and groupers are found off the seaward reef. Scrawled filefish, Spanish hogfish, pufferfish, bigeyes, soldierfish, squirrelfish, surgeonfish, scorpionfish, goatfish and rock beauties can all be encountered.

49 THE INVISIBLES
★★★★★★★★★

Location: West coast, north of Pink Beach (Site 50)
Access: By boat or shore
Conditions: Moderate currents
Average Depth: 25m (80ft)
Maximum Depth: 30m (100ft)
Visibility: 20m (65ft)

One of the last of the double-reef dives, this is a site where divers can see garden eels in the sand in shallow water between the reefs. All the expected reef inhabitants are found, including elkhorn and fire coral in shallow water, and brain and star corals, sponges and gorgonian sea plumes, sea rods and sea whips in deeper water. Fish life includes angelfish, butterflyfish, pufferfish, surgeonfish, scrawled filefish, Spanish hogfish, soldierfish, squirrelfish, goatfish, peacock flounders, barracuda, snappers, jacks, groupers and rays.

50 PINK BEACH
★★★★★★★★

Location: West coast, off Pink Beach
Access: By boat or shore
Conditions: Can have strong currents
Average Depth: 25m (80ft)
Maximum Depth: 30m (100ft)
Visibility: 20m (65ft)

This site lies off one of Bonaire's most famous beaches, Pink Beach, from where it is a long swim – about 90m (100yd) – out to the drop-off. The shallows consist mainly of sand with staghorn coral, gorgonians and the smaller reef fish. The sloping drop-off starts at 9–12m (30–40ft) and features stony corals, gorgonians, anemones, arrow crabs, purple vase sponges, scorpionfish, peacock flounders, bigeyes, squirrelfish and shoals of goatfish. In deeper water there are shoals of horse-eye jacks and you can often see stingrays on the sandy bottom.

Opposite: *The stanchions of Salt Pier (Site 46) are covered in coral and sponge growth.*

51 WHITE SLAVE
★★★★

Location: West coast, by the white obelisk and the northerly group of slave huts
Access: By boat or shore
Conditions: Currents can be moderate to strong
Average Depth: 20m (65ft)
Maximum Depth: 30m (100ft)
Visibility: 20m (65ft)

Named after the white obelisk and the slave huts that stand on the shore opposite the mooring. The shallows have staghorn coral, gorgonians and most of the smaller reef fish, while the deeper water has jacks and barracuda. Turtles are regularly seen at this site.

52 MARGATE BAY
★★★★

Location: West coast, to the south of White Slave (Site 51)
Access: By boat or shore
Conditions: Mild to moderate currents
Average Depth: 20m (65ft)
Maximum Depth: 30m (100ft)
Visibility: 20m (65ft)

As at White Slave, turtles are regularly seen here. Good stony corals and gorgonians abound while shoals of black margate can be seen on top of the reef.

TOUCH THE SEA

Leading naturalist and environmentalist Dee Scarr established her unique 'Touch The Sea' programme in 1982 and since then has introduced thousands of people to the joys of interacting with the marine environment. Dee has spent hundreds of dives at particular sites where she has hand-fed various animals, so that now when Dee turns up with divers they recognize her and come out of their holes in the hope of getting something to eat. Her association with the marine creatures that she has befriended imparts new recognition of the coral reef ecosystem.

Before her organized dives she gives a 45-minute talk on Bonaire's aquatic life, so guests are likely see more on the reef than ever before. From feeding anemones, tickling fish and being cleaned by coral shrimps, to meeting frogfish, moray eels, octopuses or scorpionfish, Dee's understanding of reef creatures is wide-ranging. Under her leadership, participants of any level of diving experience can learn to enjoy the marine environment.

Dee Scarr, **TOUCH THE SEA**, PO BOX 369, 133 Kaya Gobernador Debrot, Bonaire; tel 599 717 8529; or TOUCH THE SEA, PO BOX 369, Conifer, CO 80433, USA; website: http://www.touchthesea.com

53 RED BERYL
★★★★

Location: West coast, the second dive site south of White Slave (Site 51)
Access: By boat or shore
Conditions: Moderate or strong currents
Average Depth: 20m (65ft)
Maximum Depth: 30m (100ft)
Visibility: 20m (65ft)
Star corals, sponges and gorgonian sea plumes, sea rods and sea whips can all be encountered here while the fish life includes angelfish, rock beauties, pufferfish, surgeonfish, black durgon, Spanish hogfish, goatfish, peacock flounders, barracuda, snappers, jacks and groupers. Turtles, rays, and large shoals of small fish feeding near to the surface are often found.

54 ATLANTIS
★★★★

  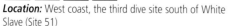

Location: West coast, the third dive site south of White Slave (Site 51)
Access: By boat or shore
Conditions: Moderate or strong currents
Average Depth: 20m (65ft)
Maximum Depth: 30m (100ft)
Visibility: 20m (65ft)
The sites at this end of the island catch some of the currents blown round from the windward eastern side, so some of the larger species of fish are seen here as well as turtles and rays. Healthy brain and star corals are common, as are gorgonian sea fans, sea plumes, sea rods and sea whips. Fish life includes French angelfish, rock beauties, pufferfish, trumpetfish, surgeonfish, black durgon, Spanish hogfish, goatfish, peacock flounders, schoolmaster snappers, grunts and the smaller groupers. Those fish partly associated with the open sea include palometa, horse-eye jacks, large barracuda, black groupers, and tiger groupers.

55 VISTA BLUE
★★★★

Location: West coast, the second dive site north of Red Slave (Site 57)
Access: By boat or shore
Conditions: Moderate or strong currents
Average Depth: 20m (65ft)
Maximum Depth: 30m (100ft)
Visibility: 20m (65ft)

As with Atlantis (Site 54), the currents blown round from the windward eastern side bring some of the larger species of fish, as well as turtles. Healthy brain and star corals are common, as are gorgonian sea fans, sea plumes, sea rods and sea whips. Reef fish include angelfish, butterflyfish, pufferfish, trumpetfish, tangs, black durgon, Spanish hogfish, goatfish, peacock flounders, schoolmaster snappers, wrasse, grunts and the smaller groupers. Other fish more associated with the open sea include palometa, horse-eye jacks, barracuda, larger groupers. Turtles and rays are often encountered.

56 SWEET DREAMS
★★★★

Location: West coast, opposite Pekelmeer Flamingo Sanctuary, just north of Red Slave (Site 57)
Access: By boat or shore
Conditions: Strong currents
Average Depth: 20m (65ft)
Maximum Depth: 30m (100ft)
Visibility: 20m (65ft)
The strong currents produce rich stony corals and gorgonian sea fans, sea plumes, sea rods and sea whips in the shallows, with larger formations of brain and star corals in the depths. The shallow waters attract sergeant majors and other damselfish, tangs, angelfish, butterflyfish, peacock groupers, black durgon, goatfish, parrotfish, snappers, trunkfish, trumpetfish, filefish, cowfish, wrasse and green moray eels. In the open water you are likely to find palometa, barracuda and jacks.

57 RED SLAVE
★★★★

Location: West coast, off the southerly group of slave huts and the red obelisk
Access: By boat or shore
Conditions: Strong currents
Average Depth: 20m (65ft)
Maximum Depth: 27m (90ft)
Visibility: 30m (100ft)
The most southerly site on the lee coast, this dive site often has stronger currents and rougher seas than most, so it is recommended only for advanced divers. The current usually runs from north to south. Shore-divers should begin their dive by swimming into the current, so that they will then return with the current. Drift-diving is best done by boat, as there is a danger that, when shore diving, if you were swept around the corner you would experience heavy seas and a difficult exit.

Above: *A peppermint shrimp and brittle star share space inside a sponge.*

Red Slave has abundant fish life and there is a good chance of seeing large reef fish. Along the drop-off, which is around 8m (25ft), there is prolific growth of gorgonian sea fans, sea whips, sea rods, sea plumes and sponges. Shoals of horse-eye jacks, black margate, midnight parrotfish (*Scarus coelestinus*), southern sennet and snappers may also be encountered, along with yellowfin mojarras, rosy razorfish (*Xyrichtys martinicensis*) and very large black, yellowfin and tiger groupers and turtles. Nassau groupers (*Epinephelus striatus*), which are not common on Bonaire, may also be found.

Before the nearby lighthouse was built, a number of boats sunk in these parts. Black corals and featherstars can now be found growing on parts of wrecks on the southern slope; these include anchors and ballast stones from HMS *Barham*, which sank in 1829.

58 WILLEMSTOREN LIGHTHOUSE
★★★

Location: The southern tip of the island, by the Willemstoren lighthouse.
Access: From the shore
Conditions: Strong currents, surf and surge can cause a rough entry.
Average Depth: 20mm (65ft)
Maximum Depth: 30m (100ft)
Visibility: 20m (65ft)
This site is recommended only for advanced divers – and then only when the sea is very calm. There are large gorgonian sea fans in the shallows, along with

Above: *A common sight throughout the ABC islands is the distinctive tube sponge.*

parrotfish, snappers, grunts, bigeyes, soldierfish, squirrelfish and turtles and spectacular stony coral and gorgonian growth along the drop-off, which slopes down to sand at 25m (80ft). The fish species in the deeper water include tarpons, jacks, barracuda and tiger groupers.

A few hundred metres east of the lighthouse are the remains of a ship that went aground here before the lighthouse was opened in 1838.

ANCIENT TREASURE-TROVE OFF VENEZUELA

On May 3rd 1678, just off the Venezuelan coast, a fleet of 35 French ships were sailing past the Ilas Les Aves in heavy seas. Their intention was to attack Curaçao, but the Dutch managed to lure half of them onto a coral reef. The French flagship, *Le Terrible*, hit the reef and fired shots to warn the others, but the signal was thought to mean an attack and several ships sailed on and hit the reef.

Some 30 years ago the Venezuelan explorer Charles Brewer Carías found some of the wreckage, including a French seal, on part of the reef. Local conch fishermen had often fished the reef but the coral-encrusted, pipe-like objects on the seabed at first held no meaning for them. In 1998 a full expedition was mounted to the site of two of the ships and all was revealed. In just 4m (13ft) of water the seabed was littered with bronze, buttons, jars, pottery and cannons, one sitting on a coral head as if it was ready for action.

At least three buccaneer vessels had been hired for the French venture, so it is anticipated that the finds will include a pirate vessel. Any retrieved objects are likely to be displayed in the museum constructed on Venezuala's Isla Margarita.

---

59 BLUE HOLE/WHITE HOLE
★★★

Location: East coast, off the southern end of Lac Bay
Access: From the shore
Conditions: Strong currents; should only be dived when the sea is calm.
Average Depth: 20m (65ft)
Maximum Depth: 30m (100ft)
Visibility: 20m (65ft)
This dive is for advanced divers only. It requires a long walk in shallow water to the drop-off. The dive begins in 5m (15ft) and slopes down to 30m (100ft). This site features tarpon and stingrays and there is a chance of spotting nurse sharks (*Ginglymostoma cirratum*) and the Caribbean reef shark (*Carcharhinus perezi*).

60 CONCH SHELLS/CAI
★★★

Location: East coast, off the northern mouth of Lac Bay
Access: From the shore
Conditions: Strong and unpredictable currents
Average Depth: 20m (65ft)
Maximum Depth: 30m (100ft)
Visibility: 20m (65ft)
This site is for experienced divers who are strong swimmers. It is rarely calm enough to be boat-dived, so requires a long walk in shallow water and in full diving gear followed by a long swim to reach it. If there is any white water at all (ie. breaking waves) it is not advisable to dive this site. As this is open sea and too rough for fishermen, there will be large fish.

Fundashon Tene Boneiru Limpi (TBL) is an organization that was founded in 1991 to co-ordinate the cleaning up of Bonaire's environment. In Papiamento, *tene* means 'keep' and *limpi* means 'clean'.

Although Bonaire has led the world in reef protection since the 1960s, Tene Boneiru Limpi has adopted a policy that there is always more that can be done to protect the environment. Through education and community action plans Tene Boneiru Limpi has participated in programmes such as 'International World Clean Up' and the Centre for Marine Conservation's 'International Coastal Clean Up'. Each year Tene Boneiru Limpi has involved over 25 per cent of the island's population in ecological projects – one of the highest rates of community participation for such events in the world.

TARGETED ACTION

In particular years Tene Boneiru Limpi has focused on one specific item of concern. In 1995 it targeted the growing pollution from plastic bags, which were suffocating cactus spines and blocking the digestive systems of marine life. Tene Boneiru Limpi persuaded grocery stores and markets to have a 'Week Without Plastic Bags', donating canvas bags to all stores that took part in the clean up. The effect was so successful that most of the stores agreed to permanently switch to paper bags or cardboard boxes, even though they were more expensive. More canvas shopping bags have since been provided and the shops have agreed to charge 25 Antillean cents for grocery bags as an incentive to rid the island of as much waste as possible.

Following on from their success Tene Boneiru Limpi carried out a survey into what made up waste both on land and underwater. The results of this research showed that beverage containers made up approximately one third of all the litter collected. So in 1996 Tene Boneiru Limpi focussed on the removal of beer and soft drink can and bottle waste. On further investigation, they found that none of the waste cans or bottles were of the Amstel brand. They discovered this was because Amstel's Antillean brewery were recycling their bottles and charging a 25 Antillean Cent deposit per bottle; thus these bottles were not being thrown away. Thereupon Tene Boneiru Limpi presented the Governor and all the local politicians with a draft for a proposed 'deposit law', backed up by a petition carrying 2500 signatures, almost 17 per cent of island's residents. A final draft for the law has been submitted to the government.

Above: *An Amstel flag flies above piles of conch shells – now protected – at Lac Cai.*

Klein Bonaire

While all of Klein Bonaire's sites are normally treated as boat dives, many can also be dived from the shore if you are already on the island. They are listed anticlockwise starting from the north. Most sites are equally good for snorkelling near the shore (see box on page 85).

61 SAMPLER

★★★★☆☆☆☆

Location: The most northerly dive of Klein Bonaire
Access: By boat
Conditions: Light currents
Average Depth: 20m (65ft)
Maximum Depth: 40m (130ft)
Visibility: 30m (100ft)

This is one of Bonaire's most popular dive sites. In the past the fish have been fed here, so you might find that the fish and eels approach divers looking for food. The shallows are mostly sand with patches of finger, brain and mustard hill (*Porites astreoides*) corals, and parrotfish, French angelfish and snappers. Under the mooring the drop-off begins at 12m (40ft) where there are gorgonians, sponges, stony coral, spotted moray eels, trumpetfish, cowfish, whitespotted filefish, bigeyes, soldierfish, squirrelfish and jacks.

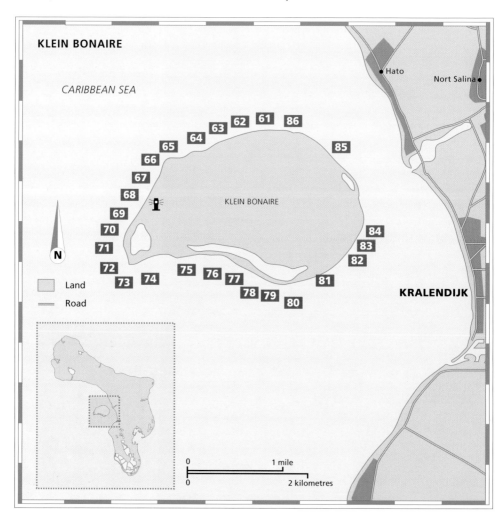

62 KNIFE

★★★★★★★★★

Location: North coast of Klein Bonaire, west of Sampler (Site 61)
Access: By boat
Conditions: Light currents
Average Depth: 20m (65ft)
Maximum Depth: 40m (130ft)
Visibility: 30m (100ft)
In the shallows, elkhorn corals fence off a mini 'lagoon' with heads of star coral, gorgonians and a multitude of fish including parrotfish, snappers, yellowfin mojarras, Bermuda chubs, peacock flounders, lizardfish and yellowhead jawfish. Due to reef slides, the drop-off has fairly limited marine life, although gorgonians, fire coral and yellow pencil coral (*Madracis mirabilis*) do occur here.

63 LEONORA'S REEF

★★★★★★★★★

Location: North coast of Klein Bonaire, west of Knife (Site 62)
Access: By boat
Conditions: Light currents
Average Depth: 20m (65ft)
Maximum Depth: 45m (150ft)
Visibility: 30m (100ft)
The shallows feature elkhorn, staghorn, fire, brain, pillar and star coral, though not as many gorgonians as there are further west. Parrotfish, yellowtail snappers, whitespotted filefish, banded and foureye butterflyfish and shoals of goatfish are common. Near the mooring, at 12m (40ft) there are black corals, gorgonians and a large star coral that has a small tunnel through. The coral is also undercut so the overhang is encrusted with *Tubastrea* cup corals on the underside. The drop-off descends beyond 40m (130ft). Star coral predominates at intermediate depths, as does plate coral at greater depth. Tube and finger sponges make good subjects for photography, while tiger and other groupers are seen in deeper water.

64 EBO'S SPECIAL

★★★★★★★★★

Location: North coast of Klein Bonaire, southwest of Leonora's Reef (Site 63)
Access: By boat
Conditions: Medium currents
Average Depth: 20m (65ft)
Maximum Depth: 45m (150ft)
Visibility: 30m (100ft)
Ebo's Special is named after Ebo Domacassé, the first native of Bonaire to become a certified diver. This site is a

microcosm of all that is good in Bonaire's diving. The drop-off begins at 8m (25ft) and slopes down to the deep. Appearing overgrown, there are thick bushes of gorgonians, orange elephant ear sponges – often with black feather stars perched on top – purple tube sponges and black corals. The abundant fish life includes parrotfish, Creole wrasse, angelfish, grunts, Spanish hogfish, Bermuda chubs (*Kyphosus sectatrix*), chromis, banded and foureye butterflyfish, snappers and groupers.

65 CARL'S HILL

★★★★★★★★★

Location: The northwest tip of Klein Bonaire
Access: By boat
Conditions: Medium currents
Average Depth: 20m (65ft)
Maximum Depth: 45m (150ft)
Visibility: 30m (100ft)
Named after underwater photographer and diving celebrity Carl Roessler. The main feature of this dive is a wall that begins 18m (60ft) offshore and drops to a sandy bottom at 22m (70ft), before sloping off to 45m (150ft). The shallows have elkhorn and pillar coral, parrotfish, French angelfish, sergeant majors, butterflyfish, bigeyes, soldierfish, squirrelfish and shoals of blue tangs. Groupers also attend cleaning stations in the shallows. The face of the wall is covered with encrusting and tube sponges, *Tubastrea* coral and gorgonians, with many small creatures to delight macro photographers. Barracuda and bar jacks (*Caranx ruber*) are seen in the open water.

66 CARL'S HILL ANNEX/YELLOW MAN
★★★★☆☆☆☆

Location: West coast of Klein Bonaire, southwest of Carl's Hill (Site 65)
Access: By boat
Conditions: Medium currents
Average Depth: 20m (65ft)
Maximum Depth: 45m (150ft)
Visibility: 30m (100ft)
This dive is another reference to Carl Roessler (though it is also called Yellow Man) and is similar to Carl's Hill. There is a profusion of gorgonians in the shallows. Seahorses may be found close to the mooring barrels and barracuda, groupers and jacks are found in the deeper areas.

67 MI DUSHI
★★★★☆☆☆☆

Location: West coast of Klein Bonaire, southwest of Carl's Hill Annex (Site 66)
Access: By boat
Conditions: Medium currents
Average Depth: 20m (65ft)
Maximum Depth: 45m (150ft)
Visibility: 30m (100ft)

Above: *A diver watches a shimmering shoal of smallmouth grunts.*

Mi Dushi means 'my sweetheart' in Papiamento. The shallows are filled with elkhorn, staghorn and yellow pencil coral and along the top of the drop-off the area is overgrown with gorgonians. Anemones are found at the top of the slope, which continues to 40m (130ft), then continues out as sand. The abundant fish life includes many smaller species of reef fish, snappers, lone barracuda and jacks.

68 VALERIE'S HILL
★★★★☆☆☆☆

Location: West coast of Klein Bonaire, southwest of Mi Dushi (Site 67) near to the lighthouse
Access: By boat
Conditions: Medium currents
Average Depth: 20m (65ft)
Maximum Depth: 45m (150ft)
Visibility: 30m (100ft)
This site was named after Captain Don Stewart's wife by local dive masters. There are numerous sponges and plentiful black coral. Scrawled and whitespotted filefish, bigeyes, soldierfish, squirrelfish and parrotfish also feature.

69 SHARON'S SERENITY
★★★★☆☆☆☆☆

Location: West coast of Klein Bonaire, southwest of Valerie's Hill (Site 68), near the lighthouse
Access: By boat
Conditions: Medium currents
Average Depth: 20m (65ft)
Maximum Depth: 40m (130ft)
Visibility: 30m (100ft)

The currents here can be a problem but are not as strong as those at Munks Haven or Southwest Corner (sites 71–72). Elkhorn, staghorn and star corals and prolific growth of gorgonian sea fans, sea rods, sea whips and sea plumes mark the shallow shelf, which extends offshore for 45m (150ft). Beginning at 12m (40ft), the drop-off descends into deep water. Equally rich in growth, the drop-off has undercut star corals forming a mushroom-like effect. Harbouring many species of fish, there are large Goliath Grouper, while barracuda and groupers are seen at cleaning stations. whitespotted filefish, parrotfish, black durgon, French angelfish, banded and foureye butterflyfish, cowfish and trumpetfish are regularly sighted. Basket stars are found on this side of Klein Bonaire on night dives.

70 TWIXT
★★★★☆☆☆☆☆

Location: West coast of Klein Bonaire, southwest of Sharon's Serenity (Site 69)
Access: By boat
Conditions: Medium currents
Average Depth: 20m (65ft)
Maximum Depth: 40m (130ft)
Visibility: 30m (100ft)

The dive sites around the southwest corner of Klein Bonaire are among the best in the Caribbean. Similar to Munk's Haven (Site 71), Twixt features large basket sponges, gorgonian sea fans, sea rods and sea whips, black coral, tube sponges, star corals and cleaning stations. The coral wall slopes down to a sandy bottom.

Below: *A nocturnal predator, the schoolmaster snapper may hang around singly by day.*

71 MUNK'S HAVEN
★★★★

Location: Southwest coast of Klein Bonaire, north of Southwest Corner (Site 72)
Access: By boat
Conditions: Moderate to strong currents
Average Depth: 20m (65ft)
Maximum Depth: 40m (130ft)
Visibility: 30m (100ft)

Named after Illinois dive shop-owner Elmer Munk, who was a regular visitor, Munk's Haven is one of the best dives in the Caribbean. There are copious quantities of staghorn and star coral interspersed with lush gorgonian growth in the shallows. The drop-off slopes steeply from 12m (40ft), where there are large sculptured coral heads, down to sand at 37m (120ft). Vase and orange elephant ear sponges, brain and star corals are common on the face of the slope, and there is a multitude of fish species including large groupers at cleaning stations.

72 SOUTHWEST CORNER
★★★★

Location: The southwest corner of Klein Bonaire
Access: By boat
Conditions: Moderate to strong currents
Average Depth: 20m (65ft)
Maximum Depth: 37m (120ft)
Visibility: 40m (130ft)

Another of the best dives in the Caribbean, this is a particular favourite with those who teach underwater photography. Southwest Corner has great visibility and appears to have thicker staghorn corals in the shallows and taller star corals and gorgonians along the drop-off than elsewhere. Large tiger and yellowmouth groupers (*Mycteroperca tigris* and *M. interstitialis*) are found at cleaning stations, black durgons; golden coneys (*Cephalopholis fulvus*), scrawled and whitespotted filefish, French and queen angelfish, sergeant majors, grunts, pufferfish, bigeyes, soldierfish, squirrelfish and yellowtail snappers are common, and shoals of blue tangs graze the algae. As is typical off Bonaire, there are smaller fish and invertebrates such as banded coral shrimps and other cleaner shrimps, all of which are popular macro subjects.

The drop-off begins at 12m (40ft) and descends steeply to sand at 37m (120ft) with colourful purple vase sponges, orange elephant ear sponges and both green and purple tube sponges.

73 FOREST
★★★★

Location: Southeast of Southwest Corner (Site 72)
Access: By boat
Conditions: Medium to strong currents
Average Depth: 20m (65ft)
Maximum Depth: 40m (130ft)
Visibility: 30m (100ft)

Named after its forests of black coral, this is another of the best dive sites in the Caribbean. It is best dived in calm weather. Above the drop-off, the shallow water has elkhorn corals and prolific growth of gorgonian sea fans, sea rods and sea whips. The drop-off itself begins at 12m (40ft) and has large star corals and impressive gorgonians. The wall drops vertically to sand, covered in black coral, sponges and gorgonians, while below 15m (50ft), large orange elephant ear sponges are great for photography. Fish action is prolific, with big groupers, mahogany snappers, large horse-eye jacks, French and queen angelfish, black durgons, scrawled and whitespotted filefish, porcupine pufferfish, shoals of bluestriped grunts and innumerable small fish making this a memorable dive.

74 HANDS OFF
★★★★

Location: South coast of Klein Bonaire, east of Forest (Site 73)
Access: By boat
Conditions: Mild currents
Average Depth: 20m (65ft)
Maximum Depth: 40m (130ft)
Visibility: 30m (100ft)

Hands Off was originally established in 1981 as a site that was not to be dived by photographers, videographers, novice divers or those who were undergoing resort courses. The site was in effect a control for comparison with reefs where unlimited access was allowed. The intention was to assess the impact that inexperienced divers and camera-carrying divers were having on reefs.

The shallow water over the drop-off has elkhorn corals, gorgonian sea fans, sea rods and sea whips. The drop-off begins at 12m (40ft) and has large star corals and prolific gorgonian growth. The wall drops vertically to sand, covered in black coral, sponges and gorgonians, while below 15m (50ft) there are large orange elephant ear sponges. There are big groupers, mahogany and schoolmaster snappers, horse-eye jacks, French and queen angelfish, black durgons, scrawled and whitespotted filefish, porcupine pufferfish, peacock flounders and shoals of bluestriped grunts.

Above: *A marvellous sponge-encrusted cleaning station attracts the presence of a grouper.*
Below: *Brightly coloured cup corals adorn a sponge.*

75 SOUTH BAY
★★★★

Location: South coast of Klein Bonaire, northeast of Hands Off (Site 74)
Access: By boat
Conditions: Mild to moderate currents
Average Depth: 20m (65ft)
Maximum Depth: 40m (130ft)
Visibility: 30m (100ft)
Staghorn coral and gorgonian growth on sand dominate the shallows here, while the drop-off begins at 10m (33ft) with lots of orange elephant ear sponges. Fish life includes parrotfish, groupers, snappers, grunts, French angelfish, banded and foureye butterflyfish, whitespotted filefish, black durgon, peacock flounders and shoals of horse-eye jacks. Lobsters are often seen in daylight.

76 CAPTAIN DON'S REEF
★★★★

Location: South coast of Klein Bonaire, east of South Bay (Site 75)
Access: By boat
Conditions: Mild currents
Average Depth: 20m (65ft)
Maximum Depth: 40m (130ft)
Visibility: 30m (100ft)

Located at the mooring is a plaque dedicated to Captain Don Stewart, the pioneer of Bonaire's diving, for his role in the preservation of Bonaire's reefs. The dive site is similar to South Bay.

77 JOANNE'S SUNCHI
★★★★

Location: South coast of Klein Bonaire, east of Captain Don's Reef (Site 76)
Access: By boat
Conditions: Moderate currents
Average Depth: 20m (65ft)
Maximum Depth: 37m (120ft)
Visibility: 30m (100ft)
Sunchi is the Papiamento word for 'kiss'. The shallow water has elkhorn corals and gorgonian sea fans, sea rods and sea whips. Sand chutes descend to gently sloping sand, while the areas between these chutes have large tube sponges and gorgonians. There is good fish action, including groupers, mahogany snappers, horse-eye jacks, French and queen angelfish, black durgons, scrawled and whitespotted filefish, porcupine pufferfish, shoals of bluestriped grunts, wrasse and peacock flounders.

Below: *Like all angelfish, the French angelfish has a short spike extending from the gill cover.*

78 ROCK PILE

★★★★

Location: South coast of Klein Bonaire, east of Joanne's Sunchi (Site 77); the mooring buoy is directly offshore from a pile of rocks
Access: By boat
Conditions: Mild to moderate currents
Average Depth: 20m (65ft)
Maximum Depth: 30m (100ft)
Visibility: 30m (100ft)
Staghorn coral and gorgonian growth on sand dominate the shallows and fish life is again prolific, including parrotfish, groupers, snappers, grunts, French angelfish, banded and foureye butterflyfish, whitespotted filefish, black durgon and peacock flounders.

79 MONTE'S DIVI

★★★★

Location: South coast of Klein Bonaire, southeast of Rock Pile (Site 78), opposite a divi-divi tree
Access: By boat
Conditions: Mild currents
Average Depth: 20m (65ft)
Maximum Depth: 30m (100ft)
Visibility: 30m (100ft)
Fish life is abundant here, including parrotfish, groupers, snappers, grunts, French angelfish, banded and foureye butterflyfish, whitespotted filefish, black durgon, bigeyes, squirrelfish, soldierfish and peacock flounders.

80 BONAVENTURE

★★★★ ☆ ☆ ☆ ☆

Location: South coast of Klein Bonaire, east of Monte's Divi (Site 79)
Access: By boat
Conditions: moderate to strong currents
Average Depth: 20m (65ft)
Maximum Depth: 40m (130ft)
Visibility: 30m (100ft)
Staghorn coral and a lush growth of gorgonians are found on the sand in the shallows, while the profuse fish life includes parrotfish, groupers, snappers, grunts, French angelfish, banded and foureye butterflyfish, whitespotted filefish, black durgon, peacock flounders and shoals of horse-eye jacks. Both lined and longsnout seahorses (*Hippocampus erectus* and *H. reidi*) are found hiding deep in crevices.

81 KEEPSAKE

★★★★

Location: South coast of Klein Bonaire, northeast of Bonaventure
Access: By boat
Conditions: Mild to moderate currents
Average Depth: 20m (65ft)
Maximum Depth: 40m (130ft)
Visibility: 30m (100ft)
In the shallows, staghorn corals and gorgonians are found on the sand and the fish life is prolific, including parrotfish, groupers, snappers, grunts, French angelfish, banded and foureye butterflyfish, whitespotted filefish, black durgon, peacock flounders, bigeyes, soldierfish and squirrelfish.

82 NEAREST POINT

★★★★

Location: East coast of Klein Bonaire, northeast of Keepsafe
Access: By boat
Conditions: Mild to moderate currents
Average Depth: 20m (65ft)
Maximum Depth: 30m (100ft)
Visibility: 30m (100ft)
There is lush gorgonian growth on the sand while the drop-off begins at 13m (40ft) with large stony corals, orange elephant ear and purple tube sponges. The fish life includes parrotfish, groupers, mahogany snappers, grunts, French angelfish, banded and foureye butterflyfish, whitespotted filefish, black durgon and peacock flounders. Black corals are found in deeper water.

83 JUST A NICE DIVE
★★★★

Location: East coast of Klein Bonaire, north of Nearest Point (Site 82)
Access: By boat
Conditions: Mild to moderate currents
Average Depth: 20m (65ft)
Maximum Depth: 30m (100ft)
Visibility: 30m (100ft)
The area between this site and Ebo's Reef is renowned for wide-angle photography. The mooring buoy here is close to the shore but in 25m (80ft) of water. The reef begins near the shore and descends steeply to sand at 25m (80ft). The wall features yellow pencil and leaf corals and many orange elephant ear and purple tube sponges. Fish life is good with parrotfish, groupers, snappers, French angelfish, whitespotted filefish, black durgon, ocean triggerfish (*Canthidermis sufflamen*) and shoals of horse-eye jacks.

84 JERRY'S REEF
★★★★

Location: East coast of Klein Bonaire, north of Just A Nice Dive (Site 83)
Access: By boat
Conditions: Mild to moderate currents
Average Depth: 20m (65ft)
Maximum Depth: 40m+ (130ft+)
Visibility: 30m (100ft)
The drop-off hosts large stony corals, gorgonians and orange elephant ear and purple tube sponges; feather stars are common. The fish life includes parrotfish, groupers, mahogany snappers, banded and foureye butterflyfish, whitespotted filefish and black durgon. This is a popular site for wide-angle photography.

85 EBO'S REEF/JERRY'S JAM
★★★★

Location: Off the northeast coast of Klein Bonaire
Access: By boat
Conditions: Mild to moderate currents
Average Depth: 20m (65ft)
Maximum Depth: 40m+ (130ft+)
Visibility: 30m (100ft)
Like Ebo's Special (Site 64), this site is named after Ebo Domacassé (though it is also called Jerry's Jam). The narrow reef crest is covered with elkhorn coral and the steep drop-off then plunges away into the depths. The upper section has large brain and star corals, and orange elephant ear sponges with black feather stars on top of them. In deeper water there are large formations of sheet corals, providing shelter for small reef dwellers, and bushes of black coral. This is an excellent night dive, especially for the colourful orange *Tubastrea* cup corals.

The abundant fish life includes parrotfish, sergeant majors, Spanish hogfish, groupers, snappers, grunts, Creole wrasse, Bermuda chubs, queen angelfish and many juveniles.

86 NO NAME
★★★★

Location: North coast of Klein Bonaire, off No Name Beach, east of Sampler (Site 61)
Access: By boat
Conditions: Mild to moderate currents
Average Depth: 20m (65ft)
Maximum Depth: 40m (130ft)
Visibility: 30m (100ft)
There is little coral here, though plenty of fish life, including parrotfish, sergeant majors and other damselfish, Spanish hogfish, fusiliers, schoolmaster snappers, grunts, Creole wrasse, Bermuda chubs, queen angelfish, rock beauties, pufferfish, scorpionfish and many juvenile species. Rays are found on the sandy bottom.

Below: *The orange elephant ear sponge often grows in unusual forms.*

GETTING THERE

Bonaire's Flamingo International Airport is a five-minute drive south of Kralendijk. It has good air connections for such a small island.

By air from Europe, KLM has direct flights from Amsterdam, which has connections all over Europe. There are also many connections via Aruba, Curaçao and Caracas in Venezuela.

By air from the USA, ALM flies from Atlanta and Miami, and Air Aruba flies from Baltimore, Miami, Newark and Tampa. Air Jamaica and various American airlines also have services.

Various airlines connect with other Caribbean islands and South America, while smaller airlines that connect between Aruba, Bonaire and Curaçao keep merging and changing their names.

The departure tax for all international destinations is USD$32.00 per person; it is lower to Curaçao and Aruba.

WHERE TO STAY

Bonaire's hotels are mostly along the leeward coast, many of them just north of Kralendijk. There are also villas for rent, both as separate entities or attached to hotels.

EXPENSIVE
Harbour Village Beach Resort
Kaya Gobernador N. Debrot No. 71; tel 599 717 7500; fax 599 717 7507; e-mail: reservations@harbourvillage.com;
www.harbourvillage.com
Bonaire's top luxury dive resort, originally targeted at the Dutch so it has a European atmosphere. The complex, as its name suggests, is like a small village complete with a marina, 70 rooms and suites, several restaurants and most amenities.

The Plaza Resort Bonaire
80 Julio A. Abraham Boulevard, Kralendijk; tel 599 717 2500; fax 599 717 7133; e-mail: info@plazaresortbonaire.com;
www.plazaresortbonaire.com
Voted by Americans as among the top ten dive resorts in the world. There are 224 suites and villas, each with a private patio or terrace. There are three restaurants, conference facilities and a casino.

MID-RANGE
Buddy Beach and Dive Resort
Kaya Gobernador Nicholaas Debrot, Kralendijk; tel 599 717 5080; fax 599 717 8647; e-mail: buddydive@ibm.net;
www.buddydive.com
A PADI 5-Star Gold Palm Resort. It has been voted by American Divers as among the top fifteen dive resorts worldwide, and by the German diving magazine *Tauchen* as the top dive resort in the Caribbean. Aimed mostly at the diver/snorkeller, the resort has four blocks with hotel rooms and one, two or three bedroom apartments, each of which has patios or balconies.

Above: *A yellowline arrow crab is camouflaged on a tube sponge.*

Captain Don's Habitat
PO Box 88, 103 Kaya Gobernador Nicholaas Debrot; tel 599 717 8290; fax 599 717 8240; e-mail: info@habitatbonaire.com
A PADI 5-Star Instructor Development Center. Captain Don's Habitat was set up by and named after Don Stewart, the well-known pioneer of scuba diving in Bonaire. The resort is mainly sold as a diving package – your room key is on a band that can be worn on a wrist in the water – and everyone is very friendly. Popular with American and British divers. Unashamedly aimed at divers, there are 93 rooms, apartments and villas for up to 6 persons.

Divi Flamingo Beach Resort & Casino
40 Julio A. Abraham Boulevard; tel 599 717 8285; fax 599 717 8238; e-mail: comments@diviresorts.com
Bonaire's first hotel and dive facility, originally managed by Captain Don Stewart. The 145 rooms and studio rooms are being renovated and the resort boasts that it has the 'worlds first barefoot casino'; i.e. it allows casual dress!

Lac Bay Resort
PO Box 261, 64 Kamindo Sorobon; tel 599 717 5706; fax 599 717 5686; e-mail: lacbay@bonairelive.com
In a protected nature area, Lac Bay and the

jointly owned Sorobon (naturist) Beach resort are the only two resorts located on the windward coast – ideal for windsurfing. There are 11 units ranging from one-bedroom condominiums to villas and studios.

Lions Dive Hotel Bonaire
Kaya Gobernador N. Debrot No. 90, PO Box 380 Bonaire; tel 599 717 5580; fax 599 717 5680; e-mail: info@LionsDiveBonaire.com
This was formerly the Coral Regency Resort. There are 31 one- or two-bedroom suites.

Sand Dollar Condominium Resort
PO Box 262, 79 Kaya Gobernador Nicholaas Debrot; tel 599 717 8738; fax 599 717 8760; e-mail: reservations@sanddollarbonaire.com; www.sanddollarbonaire.com
Voted by Americans as the second best resort worldwide. There are 85 one- to three-bedroom condominiums; the resort runs a popular Ocean Classroom for children.

INEXPENSIVE
Avanti Bungalows
9 Punt Vierkant; tel 599 717 8405; fax 599 717 8605; e-mail: hhh@bonairelive.com
Four bungalows of one or two bedrooms, each with a kitchenette.

Bruce Bowker's Carib Inn
PO Box 68, 46 Julio A. Abraham Boulevard; tel 599 717 8819; fax 599 717 5295; e-mail: info@caribinn.com
Bruce Bowker was one of Captain Don's early students. Voted by American divers as the top value-for-money dive operator and resort, it prides itself on allowing you to relax without outside communications distracting you. It is small and intimate, but with a very well equipped dive centre. There are ten one- or two-bedroom apartments and villas.

The Great Escape
97 E.E.G. Boulevard; tel 599 717 7488; fax 599 717 7412
There are ten relatively cheap apartments, but allow for the cost of transport.

WHERE TO EAT

Bonaire has some of the top restaurants in the Caribbean. Many hotels and resorts have restaurants good enough to attract non-resident clientele and there are others to suit all tastes.

CHINESE CUISINE
China Nobo Nikiboko
Kaya Andres A. Emerenciana 4, Nikiboko; tel 599 717 8981
Chinese food.

INTERNATIONAL CUISINE
Beefeater
12 Kaya Grandi, Kralendijk; tel 599 717 7776
Moderate prices and also serves vegetarian food.

De Tuin Eetcafé
9 Kaya L. D. Gerharts, Kralendijk; tel 599 717 2999
Garden dining in a restored Bonairean home and a cyber restaurant.

Mona Lisa
15 Kaya Grandi, Kralendijk; tel 599 717 8718; fax 599 717 5498
Dutch and French cuisine served in portions large enough to satisfy the hungriest divers; reservations recommended.

Richards Waterfront Dining
60 Julio A. Abraham Boulevard, Kralendijk; tel 599 717 5263
Popular with visitors.

Rum Runners
Captain Don's Habitat, 103 Kaya Gobernador Nicholaas Debrot; tel 599 717 8290
A waterfront restaurant popular with guests staying at Captain Don's Habitat. International menu, friendly service and many themed nights where different cuisine is served.

'T Ankertje
17 Kaya C.E.B. Hellmund, Kralendijk; tel 599 717 5216; fax 599 717 2943
Known as the 'local' restaurant; small and cheap with no frills.

ITALIAN CUISINE
Croccantino
48 Kaya Grandi, Kralendijk; tel 599 717 5025
A restored historic town house with Italian cuisine. It is possible to eat out in the garden.

MEXICAN CUISINE
Captain Wook's
Harbour Village Marina, Kaya Gobernador Nicholaas Debrot; tel 599 717 7500; fax 599 717 7507
Casual dining on Mexican specialities beside the marina at Harbour Village. Not open for breakfast.

SPANISH CUISINE
Admirals Tavern
Harbour Village Marina, Kaya Gobernador Nicholaas Debrot; tel 599 717 7500; fax 599 717 7507

At the bottom of the lighthouse at Harbour Village Marina. It specializes in local and Spanish seafood. Not open for breakfast.

DIVE FACILITIES

Apart from Captain Don's Habitat, all other dive operators on Bonaire are concessionary operators attached to hotels. Most resorts have dive operators on their premises, and you can usually pre-book dive packages together with your accommodation for better deals. The larger dive operators have equipment for sale as well as hire.

Black Durgon Scuba Center
Black Durgon Inn, PO Box 200; tel 599 717 8846; fax 599 717 8846; e-mail: bkdurgon@bonairelive.com
Instruction up to Open Water Diver level offered in Dutch, English, German and Spanish.

Blue Divers
Kaya Norwega 1, Kralendijk; tel 599 717 6860; fax 599 717 6865; e-mail: info@bluedivers-bonaire.com; www.bluedivers-bonaire.com
Specialize in small groups. Instruction up to Assistant Instructor level offered in Dutch, English and German.

Bon Bini Divers Bonaire, N.V.
Lions Dive Resort (formally Coral Regency Resort), 90 Kaya Gobernador Nicholaas Debrot; tel 599 717 5425; fax 599 717 4425; e-mail: info@bonbinidivers.com; www.bonbinidivers.com
A PADI 5-Star Instructor Development Center. Instruction up to Assistant Instructor level offered in Dutch, English and German.

Bruce Bowker's Carib Inn
PO Box 68, 46 Julio A. Abraham Boulevard; tel 599 717 8819; fax 599 717 5295; e-mail: info@cariiInn.com
Voted by American divers as the best value resort in the world, it is proud to be small and has a very well-equipped dive centre.

Buddy Dive
Buddy Beach & Dive Resort, Kaya Gobernador Nicholaas Debrot, Kralendijk; tel 599 717 5080; fax 599 717 8647; e-mail: info@buddydive.com; www.buddydive.com
A PADI 5-Star Gold Palm Resort. Instruction up to Assistant Instructor level offered in Dutch, English, French and German.

Captain Don's Habitat
P.O. Box 88, 103 Kaya Gobernador Nicholaas Debrot; tel 599 717 8290; fax 599 717 8240; e-mail: info@habitatbonaire.com
A PADI 5-Star Instructor Development Center.

Voted by American divers as the second most popular diving operator and the fifth most popular resort in the world, Captain Don's Habitat was set up by and named after Captain Don Stewart, the well-known pioneer of scuba diving and reef conservation in Bonaire.

A PADI 5-Star facility, NAUI Dream Destination and SSI Referral and Instructor Development Centre, Captain Don's Habitat believes in total diving freedom; its staff are not there to dictate how you dive but to assist, teach and advise. No limits are set for your time in the water and even inexperienced divers are allowed to dive solo. Three boat dives are offered as standard each day plus unlimited shore diving; full diving cylinders are available 24 hours a day. The facility is popular with American and British divers. Your room key is on an expandable band that can be worn on a wrist in the water. Training is offered in Dutch, English, German, Papiamento and Spanish.

Dee Scarr's Touch the Sea
PO Box 369, 133 Kaya Gobernador, Nicholaas Debrot; tel 599 717 8529
A noted conservationist (see box on page 99).

Dive Inn Bonaire
Kaya C.E.B., Hellmund 27, Kralendijk; tel 599 717 8761; fax 599 717 3563; e-mail: info@diveinnbonaire.com; www.diveinnbonaire.com
Located beside the Sunset Inn, with connections to both the Bonaire Oceanfront Apartments and the Caribbean Club.

Divi Flamingo Beach Resort and Casino
A. Abraham Boulevard 40, Kralendijk; tel 599 717 8285; fax 599 717 8238; www.diviflamingo.com
Diving with Divi Dive Bonaire – A PADI Gold Palm Dive Center.

Great Adventures Bonaire
Harbour Village Beach Resort, 71 Kaya Gobernador Nicholaas Debrot, Kralendijk; tel 599 717 7500; fax 599 717 7507; e-mail: reservations@harbourvillage.com; www.harbourvillage.com
Instruction up to Divemaster level offered in Dutch, English, German, Papiamento and Spanish.

Photo Tours Divers/Dive Friends Bonaire
Three locations booked through Kaya Grandi No. 6, Kralendijk; tel 599 717 3911; e-mail: ptdretail@dive-friends-bonaire.com
A PADI Gold Palm Facility.

Plaza Resort – see Toucan Divers

Sand Dollar Dive & Photo
Sand Dollar Condominium Resort, PO Box 262, 79 Kaya Gobernador Nicholaas Debrot; tel 599 717 8738; fax 599 717 8760; e-mail: reservations@sanddollarbonaire.com

Toucan Diving
Plaza Resort Bonaire, 80 Julio A. Abraham Boulevard, Kralendijk; tel 599 717 2500; e-mail: info@toucandiving.com; www.toucandiving.com
A PADI 5-Star Gold Palm Instructor Development Center, conveniently located at Plaza Resort Bonaire and Plaza Villas.

Yellow Submarine – see Photo Tours Divers/Dive Friends Bonaire

RECOMPRESSION CHAMBER

With San Francisco (St Franciscus) Hospital, Bonaire is fully equipped for any emergency. The hospital has 60 beds and also its own hyperbaric chamber with trained medical personnel on call 24 hours a day. The recompression facility is situated beside the hospital – you have to go to the hospital first in order to gain access to it.

St Franciscus Hospital
Kaya Soeur Bartola, Kralendijk; tel 599 717 8900

EMERGENCIES

Bonaire Emergency Telephone Numbers:

Ambulance	114
Fire	114
Hospital	114
Police	114

USEFUL CONTACTS

There is no tourist office for Bonaire in the UK – contact instead the European office in Holland, or visit the main website: www.infobonaire.com

Tourism Corporation Bonaire
2 Kaya Grandi, Kralendijk, Bonaire, Netherlands Antilles; tel 599 717 8322; fax 599 717 8408; e-mail: info@tourismbonaire.com

Tourist Corporation Bonaire – Europe
Basic Communicaie B.V., Mariettahof 25–29, PO Box 472, NL-2000, Al Harlam, the Netherlands; tel 31 23 543 0705; fax 31 23 543 0730; e-mail: europe@tourismbonaire.com; www.infobonaire.com

Tourism Corporation Bonaire – USA and Canada
Adams Unlimited, 10 Rockefeller Plaza, Suite 900, New York, NY 10020; tel 1 800 BONAIRE, 1 800 266 2473, 212 956 5912; fax 212 956 5913; e-mail: usa@tourismbonaire.com

South America Tourist Corporation Bonaire
Flamingo Representaciones, Yazmin Pérez de Ramirez, Avenida Humboldt, Edificio Humboldt, Piso 1 Apt. 5, Urb Bello Monte, Caracas, Venezuela; tel 58 212 953 4653; fax 58 212 951 1625; e-mail: southamerica@tourismbonaire.com

CURAÇAO

The administrative centre of the Netherlands Antilles, Curaçao is by far the largest of the ABC islands. It is a cosmopolitan island, with residents descended from over 50 different ethnic backgrounds, and plenty of sights of interest to offer. When not diving or snorkelling you can try just about any other watersport including windsurfing, deep-sea fishing, jet skiing, sailing and sea kayaking, while non-divers can view the marine life from a glass-bottomed semi-submarine. Away from the sea, there are opportunities to go hiking, mountain biking, ride horses and play tennis, squash or golf.

There are 38 beaches on Curaçao. Some are surrounded by giant cliffs with secluded coves, while others, parts of resort complexes, have been improved by adding sand. Westpunt Beach is best known for its huge cliffs and the high divers who entertain visitors by diving from the cliffs into the ocean below. South of Westpunt is Knip (Kenepa) Bay Beach, one of the island's most photographed sites, while Playa Abao, Daaibooi Bay, Cas Abao, Barbara Beach and Blue Bay are also popular.

HISTORY

As with Aruba and Bonaire, the earliest inhabitants of the islands are believed to have been the Caiquetio branch of the Arawak Indians. After the Europeans took over, the Caiquetios continued to inhabit the island, but by the 1790s they no longer existed as a separate people.

In 1499, Spanish expeditions, led by Alonso de Ojeda and navigated by Amerigo Vespucci, landed on the island and claimed the territory for Queen Isabella. Legend has it that, while on his way to South America, Vespucci put ashore on Curaçao some sailors who were suffering from scurvy. He returned a year later and was surprised to find them alive and recovered. The Spanish officially settled on the island in the early 1500s, but finding it lacking in fresh water and mineral resources, they abandoned it and the Dutch West India Company took over in 1634, making it their administrative capital for the ABC islands. Curaçao was divided into plantations, each with its *landhuis*. Some agriculture was practised but mainly salt was produced for export.

Opposite: *Curaçao is the largest of the ABC islands, with Willemstad as its sprawling capital.*
Above: *Elaborate costumes make an appearance at various performances around the island.*

Curaçao stayed at the heart of Dutch interests in the Caribbean and soon became the centre for slave trade in the colonies of the Netherlands and Spain. As many as 14,000 African slaves would be held on the island at a time before being redistributed. Many slaves absconded, often hiding in the Hato Caves. A full-scale uprising took place in 1795, known as the 'Tula Rebellion', inspired by the French Revolution and other slave revolts in the Caribbean. However, slavery was not abolished on Curaçao until 1863.

Towards the end of the 18th century the British and the French regularly besieged Curaçao. The British ruled the island during 1800–1803 and again from 1807, but Curaçao was restored to Dutch control by the Treaty of Paris of 1815. Because of its proximity to Venezuela, Curaçao became involved in Colombia's struggle for freedom from Spanish domination in the early 19th century. Two of Bolívar's aides, Manuel Pilar and Louis Brion, came from the island.

Oil later found off the coast of Venezuela brought income via the Royal Dutch Shell Refinery and bunkering terminal that were built in Schottegast in 1915. With it came the immigration of Chinese and South American labourers. Money poured in to the island and the population rocketed. During World War II, the Waterfort Arches outside Willemstad served as an outpost for Allied forces guarding the Caribbean from Nazi submarines.

In 1954, with the movement towards colonial independence that followed the war, the Netherlands Antilles became an autonomous part of the Kingdom of the

CARMABI FOUNDATION

The Caribbean Marine Biological Institute (CARMABI Foundation) was founded in 1955, initially fully financed by Dutch development funding. In the beginning CARMABI's research covered fisheries and aquaculture but in 1969 the researchers concluded that intensifying the fisheries was not sensible and marine culture was not feasible.

In 1970 CARMABI began studying the ecology and protection of coral reefs in the Netherlands Antilles with a view to stimulating tourism. When in 1983 Dutch funding was withdrawn, the statutes were revised, dropping the purely academic marine research and redirecting it towards conservation, ecological management and terrestrial research. CARMABI has been instrumental in the establishment of nine sanctuaries and parks in the Netherlands Antilles and runs the day-to-day organization of five schemes in Curaçao. CARMABI also advises governments and educates young children.

Netherlands. The economic boom that followed brought about modernization, including a moveable pontoon bridge to link the two main districts of Willemstad, separated by one of the largest natural harbours in the western hemisphere.

The boom years collapsed when automation cut the refinery workforce from 18,500 to 4,000. Shell sold the refinery to the Netherlands Antilles Government in 1985 and they in turn leased it to an affiliate of Petroleos de Venezuela S.A. Nowadays, offshore banking is an important income though tourism forms Curaçao's second largest industry.

> ### MANSALIÑA TREES
>
> Also called manchineel, mansaliña trees provide shade on many of Curaçao's beaches and in the grounds of some hotels. Their small round yellow or green fruit is extremely poisonous. The sap of the tree can also irritate the skin and can cause a severe allergic reaction. If you experience a mild reaction, bathe the area with cold water. If you suffer a severe reaction, you will require antihistamine cream and possibly antihistamine tablets.

LOCAL HIGHLIGHTS

Willemstad, the island's capital, lies on the southern coast at Santa Anna Bay. It was formerly a fortified town of strategic importance and is noted for its Dutch colonial architecture in bright colours. Relatively small but usually very busy, walking is probably the best way to see the town.

The Queen Emma Pontoon Bridge is the largest floating pedestrian bridge in the world. The 'Lady', as it is known to the local inhabitants, was originally built in 1888 by the American Consul Leonard Burlington Smith. At 213m (700ft) long, it was regarded as a feat of engineering in its day, and a toll was charged to cross the bridge though people who were too poor to afford shoes were entitled to cross it for free; the present construction, the third,

Opposite: *The historical archives building in Willemstad used to be a merchant's house.*
Below: *The present-day Queen Emma Pontoon Bridge was constructed in 1939.*

Opposite: *Various arched limestone bridges exist along the windward side of Curaçao.*

was built in 1939. The bridge links the two shopping districts of Punda and Otrobanda, swinging open as often as thirty times a day to let ships pass into or out of the bay – the pontoons can also be seen to move constantly on the waves. Beside the Queen Emma Bridge is the Floating Market, where boats arrive from Venezuela to set up market selling fresh fish, vegetables, fruits, and spices.

The imposing Queen Juliana Bridge is for motorized traffic only and has four traffic lanes. Rising 56m (185ft) above the bay and spanning 488m (1600ft), it took 14 years and cost 15 lives to complete.

Many 17th- and 18th-century fortresses ring the harbour; originally built as defence from pirates as well as the English and French navies. At the centre of historic Willemstad, stands the mustard-coloured Fort Amsterdam, dating from 1769. The fort's church doubled as a store for provisions in case of siege and a cannonball is still embedded in the church's southwest wall; nearby is the present Governor's Residence.

Nearby Fort Waterfort (Waterfort Arches), just outside Punda, was originally constructed in 1634 and rebuilt in 1827. During World War II, Allied Forces and anti-aircraft guns were accommodated here. Opposite the harbour entrance from Fort Waterfort, Fort Riffort is an impressive structure built in 1828. In World War II a steel net was stretched across the bay between the two against enemy shipping. Once housing government departments, the ramparts have been restored and now there are two restaurants here. Fort Waakzaamheid was beseiged for 26 days by Captain Bligh of 'Mutiny On the Bounty' fame in 1804. An English cannonball is imbedded in one of its walls. Fort Nassau (Fort Orange Nassau) was built in 1797 and has been preserved in much of its original state – except for the addition of a discotheque.

Also in Willemstad, the Mikve Israel-Emanuel is the oldest synagogue in continuous use in the Americas, founded in 1732 by Sephardic Jews escaping oppression in Portugal and Spain. The floor is carpeted in sand, as in the days of the Inquisition when the Jews prayed on sand to avoid being heard. The Beth Haim cemetery goes back as far as the 17th century, and many religious articles from the original Jewish community are on display at the Jewish Historical & Cultural Museum in the synagogue compound.

The Scharloo district has imposing old wealthy merchant's houses. At 77 Scharlooweg the Central Historical Archives are kept in a mansion painted green and called 'Bolo di Bruid', Papamiento for 'Bride's Cake', by the local inhabitants. The Bolívar Museum is an eight-sided Octagon House that provided sanctuary for the sisters of Simón Bolívar when they were in exile. Other attractions include the Sea Aquarium and even an ostrich farm. Near to the airport the Hato Caves, covering 4900 sq m (5860 sq yd), include fascinating stalactite and stalagmite limestone formations, a waterfall and a colony of long-nose bats. A wooded trail leads to Caiquetio Indian frescoes.

Above: *Leisurely instruction takes place on the beach at Curaçao's Eden Roc Diving Centre.*

Outside Willemstad are various *landhuizen*, houses in which the Dutch plantation managers used to live during the time of slave labour. Over 40 remain and many are now open to the public. At the entrance to Christoffel Park, Landhuis Savonet remains private but the outbuildings are now the Natural History Museum. Landhuis Kenepa (also called Knip) has recently been restored. Landhuis Habaai, the only one remaining in the Jewish Quarter of Willemstad, is unusual in that it has two storeys. Landhuis Brievengat has an antique interior, sells antiques and crafts, and offers live music, while at Landhuis Chobolobo, Curaçao liqueur is now distilled in 100-year-old vats. Landhuis Jan Kock was originally built by the Dutch West Indies Company for the manager of the nearby salt ponds.

The *cunucu* house, Kas di Yerba (House of Thatch), is a museum representing a dwelling of slave origin based on similar houses in West Africa where they originated. The walls are constructed of wattle and daub filled with rubble stone and plastered with clay or mud. The floor was sealed with a mixture of clay and cow dung and the roof was thatched with *pal'i di maishi*, a type of sorghum grass.

On the northern windward coast, Curaçao's newest national Park, Shete Boca, begins at Boca Tabla, a cave that can be accessed from its landward side and echoes each time that it is pounded by the waves. A hiking trail winds east along the cliffs and there is a longer trail where a park guide must accompany walkers. A jeep road also runs east from Boca Tabla to the protected turtle breeding inlets of Boca Wandomi, Boca Koratlein, Boca Plate, Boca Mansaliña, Boca Djegu and Dos Boca.

DIVING IN CURAÇAO

Curaçao is much larger than Aruba and Bonaire so the diving operators outside Willemstad along the leeward coast tend only to dive on sites that are within a 15-minute boat ride of their jetties. If you wish to dive on a site not normally covered by your dive operator, you can either organize to make the dive with an operator near to the chosen site or, if it can be reached from the shore, hire a vehicle for a shore dive. Some shore dives are accessed from private property where there is a small charge for entry. Dive operators can organize suitable vehicles for shore diving – double-cab pick-up trucks are the preferred vehicles.

Curaçao was originally formed from volcanic rock, on which coral has been growing for centuries. Erosion has produced caves and on many beaches it has left the limestone with sharp edges referred to as 'ironstone'. Where the ironstone is a problem, most divers will require wet suit booties or some other footwear to cross it, though others may prefer to treat the site as a boat dive.

The reefs of the island are of the fringing type. The typical reef profile includes a shallow reef shelf or plateau in 5–12m (16–40ft) of water, a drop-off with a 45° slope or less, then sand shelving into the deep. Do not expect sheer walls, though the reef is steeper at sites in the middle and east of the island. At Klein Curaçao, the wall actually curves back into itself, forming small caves. Generally, the best shore diving is in the northwest, while in the southeast the drop-offs are steeper with depths of 40m (130ft) and are usually reached less than 150m (160yd) from shore. Coral diversity is high with some 50 hermatypic species recorded.

Curaçao is not so popular a dive destination as its sister island Bonaire, but it has similar reefs that run parallel to the coast and has less diver traffic. Some of the dive sites also have wrecks, caverns and double reefs, and there are several to rival the best dive sites in the Caribbean. The entire leeward side of the island, from Noordpunt (North Point) to Oostpunt (East Point), is one large dive site. The stretch from Westpunt to the Light Tower on Cape St Marie is named Bando Abao Underwater Park, while that from Bullen Bay to the Princess Beach Hotel is called Central Curaçao Underwater Park. These two parks are voluntary, but the remaining stretch from the Princess Beach to East Point has official status as Curaçao Underwater Park.

STINAPA

STINAPA (Stichting National Parken Nederlandse Antillen), or The Netherlands Antilles National Parks Foundation, is a non-governmental, non-profit organization run by a board of local professionals who donate their time to protect and conserve the islands' natural flora and fauna. It was founded in 1963 and has been closely related to CARMABI from the beginning. Initially it was set up for the protection of Bonaire's flamingo population from salt mining activities taking place in their nesting grounds. However, STINAPA has become the management organization for several different national parks in the Netherlands Antilles.

Conditions at the northwestern sites are calm, while the southeast has less shelter from rough seas – here the currents produce healthy corals and gorgonians. However, southeastern sites may be calmer in the early morning. Water temperatures average 27°C (80°F). The visibility varies due to currents and plankton, but is usually 18–37m (60–120ft) at leeward dive sites. There is little freshwater runoff.

With the implementation of the Diver Improvement Program (DIP), the island's major shore sites are now marked with numbered white stones, similar to the yellow ones used on Bonaire. In 1998 coral spawning (see page 136) was October 1st–3rd and October 30th–November 1st.

The larger dive operators offer full diver training, diving and snorkelling equipment for rent and boat dives in the morning, late morning, and early afternoon. Sign-up the day before for boat dives. As on Bonaire, some diving packages will give you unlimited shore dives, so you can just pick up the equipment and go diving anywhere from the shore.

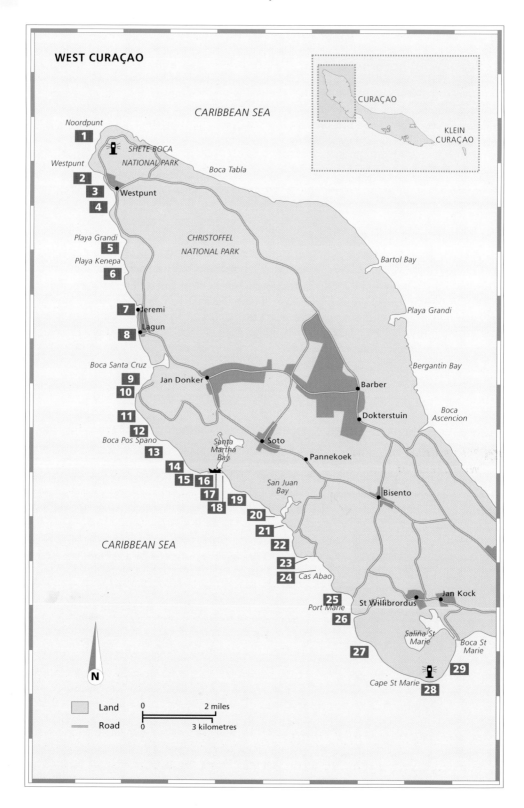

WEST CURAÇAO

CARIBBEAN SEA

CURAÇAO

KLEIN CURAÇAO

Noordpunt

1

SHETE BOCA NATIONAL PARK

Boca Tabla

Westpunt

2

3 Westpunt

4

Playa Grandi

5

Playa Kenepa

6

CHRISTOFFEL NATIONAL PARK

Bartol Bay

Playa Grandi

7 Jeremi

8 Lagun

Bergantin Bay

Boca Santa Cruz

9 Jan Donker

10

Barber

11

Dokterstuin

Boca Ascencion

12

Boca Pos Spano

13

Santa Martha Bay

Soto

Pannekoek

14

15 **16**

17 **19**

18

San Juan Bay

Bisento

20

21

22

CARIBBEAN SEA

23

24 Cas Abao

25 St Willibrordus

Jan Kock

Port Marie

26

Saliña St Marie

Boca St Marie

27

29

Cape St Marie

28

N

Land

Road

0   2 miles

0   3 kilometres

West Curaçao

1 WATAMULA
★★★★

Location: Just south of the most northerly point on the northwestern leeward side of Curaçao
Access: By boat
Conditions: Can be rough with strong currents
Average Depth: 18m (60ft)
Maximum Depth: 40m+ (130ft+)
Visibility: 30m (100ft)
This site can be subject to rough seas spreading around the north point from the windward side. However, when it is in condition, this is arguably Curaçao's finest reef dive.

Watamula is a tiny, hidden break in the cliffs between Westpunt and Noordpunt. It is similar to Mushroom Forest (Site 10) but even more lush and overgrown. The seabed is a gentle slope covered in star and brain corals, large gorgonians, anemones and vase, basket and tube sponges that shelter a multitude of fish and invertebrates. Spiny lobsters, hawksbill turtles, moray eels, spotted drums, rock beauties, whitespotted filefish, porcupine pufferfish, snappers, groupers, parrotfish, soldierfish and bluespotted cornetfish are just a few of the species found here. The sea floor is quite confusing, so either use a compass to navigate or drift with the current while your dive boat follows your bubbles.

2 PLAYA KALKI/ALICE IN WONDERLAND
★★★★★★★★★

Location: Northwest coast, off Westpunt, below Kadushi Cliffs Resort
Access: By boat or shore
Conditions: Normally calm
Average Depth: 18m (60ft)
Maximum Depth: 40m+ (130ft+)
Visibility: 30m (100ft)
Kalki translates as 'limestone' in Papiamento, referring to the cliffs. Also called Alice in Wonderland, Playa Kalki is at a well-sheltered cove, a good spot for a day on the beach. It is considered one of Curaçao's best dive sites. Shore entry is easy as there are steps descending to the beach; you then duck under the buoys on your way out down a gentle slope.

This dive offers some unusual underwater scenery. The bottom slopes gradually and from 9m (30ft) it gives the impression of rolling hills that are covered in coral. At about 18m (60ft), towards the centre of the cove, there are gorgonians and mounds of star coral. Below 30m (100ft) there are large sheets of plate coral. While there are less fish than at Watamula (Site 1), hawksbill turtles can often be seen.

3 PLAYA PISCARDÓ
★★★★

Location: Northwest coast, off Playa Piscardó
Access: By boat or shore
Conditions: Normally calm but can have strong and unpredictable currents; snorkelling is not recommended, due to boat and jet ski traffic.
Average Depth: 18m (60ft)
Maximum Depth: 40m+ (130ft+)
Visibility: 30m (100ft)
Papiamento for 'Fisherman's Beach', Playa Piscardó requires a long swim to the drop-off at 15m (50ft), so it is often dived by boat. However, it is worth the long swim or boat journey to see the lush carpets of gorgonians and large coral heads. Keep an eye out for boats and jet skis when surfacing.

4 SWEET ALICE/PLAYA FORTI
★★★★

Location: Northwest coast, below the cliffs south of Playa Piscardó
Access: By boat
Conditions: Normally calm but can have strong and unpredictable currents.
Average Depth: 18m (60ft)
Maximum Depth: 40m+ (130ft+)
Visibility: 30m (100ft)
Also called Playa Forti, Sweet Alice is similar to Playa Piscardó (Site 3) but has better coral.

CORAL BLEACHING

Coral bleaching has been observed in a variety of coral species across the Caribbean and Indo-Pacific though so far there is very little evidence of it in the ABC islands.

Coral bleaching is the whitening of coral colonies that occurs when zooxanthellae, the microscopic algae which live in symbiosis within the coral tissue, are expelled from the tissue. This loss exposes the white calcium carbonate skeletons of the coral colony. Just why corals expel the microscopic algae is unknown. It may be that when stressed, corals give the algae fewer nutrients and thus the algae desert the polyp, or the algae may produce toxins and these may affect the polyps. Corals can survive for a couple of months without their symbiotic algae, but then will usually die.

Many stresses can cause the expulsion of the algae: increased shade, salinity changes, hot water, cold water, excessive ultraviolet radiation, sedimentation or pollution. The main reason for coral bleaching is high temperatures. Corals are highly temperature-sensitive – they are stable at 25–29°C (77–84°F), depending on geographic location, but bleach if the temperature increases by as little as 2C° and remains high.

5 PLAYA GRANDI

★★★★☆☆☆☆☆

Location: Northwest coast, off Playa Grandi
Access: By boat or shore
Conditions: Normally calm but can have strong, unpredictable currents; be careful of boat/jet ski traffic.
Average Depth: 18m (60ft)
Maximum Depth: 40m+ (130ft+)
Visibility: 30m (100ft)

There is a 10-minute swim out to the reef at Playa Grandi ('Big Beach'), so ideally the reef is best dived from a boat. The drop-off is at 15m (50ft), with plenty of coral, moray eels, lobsters, hawksbill turtles, squid, lizardfish, rainbow runners, jacks, rock beauties (*Holacanthus tricolor*), blackbar soldierfish (*Myripristis jacobus*), bluespotted cornetfish, trunkfish and parrotfish among the rich marine life.

6 PLAYA KENEPA (KNIP)

★★★★☆☆☆☆☆

Location: Northwest coast, off Playa Kenepa
Access: By boat or shore
Conditions: Normally calm but can have strong and unpredictable currents, be careful of boat and jet ski traffic.
Average Depth: 18m (60ft)
Maximum Depth: 40m+ (130ft+)
Visibility: 30m (100ft)

This is a good site for a day out on the beach. However, there is a 10-minute swim out to the reef at Playa Kenepa so the reef is ideally dived from a boat. The drop-off is at 15m (50ft). The rich marine life includes lots of coral, moray eels, lobsters, hawksbill turtles, squid and lizardfish, rainbow runners, jacks, rock beauties, blackbar soldierfish, bluespotted cornetfish, trunkfish and parrotfish.

Below: *The giant anemone is the largest of the Caribbean anemones.*

Above: *Lavender stovepipe sponges inhabit deeper reefs and walls.*

7 PLAYA JEREMI

★★★★ ☆ ☆ ☆ ☆

Location: Northwest coast, off Playa Jeremi, near Landhuis Jeremi
Access: By boat or shore
Conditions: Normally calm
Average Depth: 18m (60ft)
Maximum Depth: 40m+ (130ft+)
Visibility: 30m (100ft)

Playa Jeremi is a pretty cove with a smooth beach that is protected from most of the weather. It is good for shore diving and night diving. The site is known for its flying gurnards, found on the seabed in 5m (16ft) of water.

The sandy bottom features urchins, conchs, lizardfish, goatfish and peacock flounders. To reach the coral, swim over the sand west to the mouth of the cove. The centre of the cove is deeper than its edge; the corals begin at 9–12m (30–40ft) near the edges of the cove and between 12–15m (40–50ft) in the centre. The further out you swim, the better the coral. By the north wall of the cove is a large rock sticking out of the water – the wall and this rock are covered with orange *Tubastrea* cup corals. Large trumpetfish group nearby and there are copper and glassy sweepers (*Pempheris schomburgki*) beneath the ledges.

8 PLAYA LAGUN (LAGOEN)

★★★★ ☆ ☆ ☆ ☆

Location: Northwest coast, off Playa Lagun, at the southern end of the village of Lagun
Access: By boat or shore
Conditions: Normally calm
Average Depth: 18m (60ft)
Maximum Depth: 40m+ (130ft+)
Visibility: 30m (100ft)

One of the island's top dives, Playa Lagun is a small cove enclosed by cliffs. This site is very easy to shore dive as you can almost drive up to the water. The best entry from the shore is to the southeast, where there are several small caves. To see the site's features, swim out to the drop-off at 10m (30ft). Be aware that the drop-off then drops at 45° to a second drop-off at 45m (150ft), which is beyond sport diving depths.

The first drop-off features good stony coral, gorgonian and sponge coverage, with the sponges attracting hawksbill turtles. The fish life here is profuse, including lizardfish, rainbow runners, rock beauties, blackbar soldierfish, bluespotted cornetfish and parrotfish.

9 SANTU PRETU
★★★★☆☆☆☆☆

Location: Northwest coast, off San Nicolas, just south of the inlet at Santa Cruz
Access: By boat or shore
Conditions: Normally calm
Average Depth: 18m (60ft)
Maximum Depth: 40m+ (130ft+)
Visibility: 30m (100ft)
Boca Santa Pretu is Papiamento for 'Black Sand Beach', referring to the vein of black volcanic sand found here, which illustrates the volcanic origin of the island. If shore diving, enter the water at the northwest of the beach and swim towards the centre of the cove, past the garden eels, to the drop-off at 9–12m (30–40ft). Here you will find good stony corals and extravagant gorgonian growth, sponges and rich fish life, including parrotfish, rock beauties, cero (*Scomberomorus regalis*), banded and foureye butterflyfish, blackbar soldierfish, trumpetfish and bluespotted cornetfish. The sponges also attract hawksbill turtles.

10 MUSHROOM FOREST & THE CAVE
★★★★

Location: Northwest coast, southwest of Santa Cruz, the point south of Santu Pretu, north of Sponge Forest (Site 11)
Access: By boat
Conditions: There can be a strong current.
Average Depth: 13m (43ft)
Maximum Depth: 40m+ (130ft+)
Visibility: 30m (100ft)
One of Curaçao's top dives, Mushroom Forest was so named because of the many large coral heads of mountainous star coral that have been eroded at their base to resemble mushrooms. American divers vote this site as the best in Curaçao – but do compare it with Watamula (Site 1) if you can. The sea floor is complex and the coral heads look similar and disorientating, so take your compass or a local dive guide. Although there

is a drop-off, the main area of interest is on the relatively flat, inshore shelf at 12–15m (40–50ft).

This is a diverse site, so take time to have a good look in as many cracks and crannies as you can. The 3m (10ft) coral heads are a riot of colour: anemones, flower and brain corals, lobsters, drums, moray eels, conchs, trunkfish, porcupine pufferfish, rock beauties, parrotfish, snappers, peacock flounders, trumpetfish, bluespotted cornetfish (*Fistularia tabacaria*), redspotted hawkfish (*Amblycirrhitus pinos*), Creole wrasse and turtles are just a few of the animals to be found. Sleeping nurse sharks are also regularly seen here.

There is a dive buoy that guides you to the sites. Mushroom Forest is a little beyond the buoy, while The Cave is directly inshore from it, in the cliffs at the water's edge. The Cave is only 6m (20ft) deep and with a huge entrance, so you do not need to be cave-certified to enjoy the cavern. Shoals of sweepers dash around, orange *Tubastrea* cup corals encrust the roof, while slipper lobsters crawl around the walls and lizardfish and scorpionfish hide on the bottom. Remember to bring a dive light.

11 SPONGE FOREST
★★★★☆☆☆☆

Location: West coast, off San Nicolas, northwest of Playa Hulu (Site 12)
Access: By boat
Conditions: Usually fairly calm with little current
Average Depth: 20m (65ft)
Maximum Depth: 40m+ (130ft+)
Visibility: 30m (100ft)
Protected by a point of land to the southeast of Boca Hulu, the sandy shelf by the shore here has little of interest other than small brain corals. However the slope, which begins at about 12m (40ft) and drops gradually to sand at 40m (130ft), features stony corals and gorgonians and very large basket and branched sponges in the deeper areas. There is rich fish life including damselfish, sergeant majors, chromis, rock beauties, pufferfish, trumpetfish, bluespotted cornetfish and French and queen angelfish.

12 PLAYA HULU
★★★☆☆☆

Location: West coast, off San Nicolas
Access: By boat or shore
Conditions: Usually fairly calm with little current
Average Depth: 20m (65ft)
Maximum Depth: 40m+ (130ft+)
Visibility: 30m (100ft)

If shore diving, enter the water on the southeast side of the beach and swim out to a coral-covered slope descending from 9–40m (30–130ft). The shallow waters attract Christmas tree worms and abundant fish life, while deeper down there are black corals and featherduster worms.

13 REDIHO
★★★★

Location: West coast, off San Nicolas, south of Pos Spano
Access: By boat or shore
Conditions: Choppy with strong currents
Average Depth: 20m (65ft)
Maximum Depth: 40m+ (130ft+)
Visibility: 30m (100ft)
Rediho is exposed to the open sea, so conditions are often rough, though the nutrient-rich currents produce healthy marine life. The dive and the reef profile are similar to that of the nearby Black Coral Garden (site 14). A steep drop-off begins at 12m (40ft) and descends below sport diving depths. There are most local Caribbean species here, including butterflyfish, trumpetfish, trunkfish, chromis, sergeant majors, frogfish, seahorses, moray eels, shoals of grunts, snappers, Creole wrasse and jacks. Turtles are common.

14 BLACK CORAL GARDEN
★★★★

Location: West coast, off San Nicolas, south of Pos Spano
Access: By boat or shore
Conditions: Choppy with strong currents
Average Depth: 20m (65ft)
Maximum Depth: 40m+ (130ft+)
Visibility: 30m (100ft)
There is no shelter from the open sea here, so conditions can be rough. The steep drop-off begins at 12m (40ft) and descends below sport diving depths. In deeper water the drop-off supports a colossal black coral forest. There is almost every Caribbean species present, including chromis, damselfish, sergeant majors, frogfish, seahorses, moray eels, shoals of grunts, snappers, Creole wrasse and jacks, lone barracuda, manta rays and whale sharks. Turtles are also common visitors to the area.

Below: *Spanish hogfish constantly swim about and show little fear of divers.*

Above: *A diver takes a close-up photograph of a sponge, taking care not to touch the subject.*
Below: *Hawksbill turtles are common in areas with lots of sponges.*

15 HELL'S CORNER
★★★★

Location: West coast, off the south part of San Nicolas, the corner of the reef out west from Santa Martha Bay
Access: By boat
Conditions: Sometimes calm, but usually rough with strong currents
Average Depth: 20m (65ft)
Maximum Depth: 40m+ (130ft+)
Visibility: 30m (100ft)
This site has no mooring so it is treated as a drift dive. As there is no shelter from the open sea, it is for advanced divers only. The current usually runs east to west parallel to the shore, but it can have large eddies and down-currents. If you get into trouble there is a sandy beach just to the north that is used as an emergency exit. A shallow shelf with some staghorn coral reaches the drop-off at 9m (30ft) and then falls off gradually at about 45° to sand at 40m (130ft). Large brain, pillar and star corals, gorgonians and turtles are found on the upper part of the slope and large pelagic fish as well as reef fish are often seen.

16 MAKO'S MOUNTAIN
★★★★

Location: West coast, off the south end of San Nicolas, at the point of land jutting out to sea west of the entrance to Santa Martha Bay
Access: By boat
Conditions: Choppy seas and strong currents; snorkelling is only possible on very calm days
Average Depth: 20m (65ft)
Maximum Depth: 40m+ (130ft+)
Visibility: 30m (100ft)
Similar conditions to Hells Corner (Site 15) mean that this site is only for experienced divers. The mooring buoy is in 5m (16ft) and the steep slope of the drop-off descends into the depths. The currents produce healthy marine life including sponges, gorgonian sea rods, sea plumes, sea fans and sea whips, together with most Caribbean reef fish and many pelagic species.

17 AIRPLANE WRECK
★★★★★★★★

Location: West coast, off Coral Cliff Beach
Access: By boat or shore; from the shore, enter between the two breakwaters protecting the calm lagoon
Conditions: Sheltered, usually some current and swell
Average Depth: 15m (50ft)
Maximum Depth: 40m+ (130ft+)
Visibility: 30m (100ft)

Airplane Wreck is one of several dive sites that can be reached from Coral Cliff Beach, where there are good facilities. Straight out from the breakwater, a buoy marks the remains of a Cessna aeroplane at 9m (30ft). The shallows are sand and rock rubble, but the reef descends gently into deep water where there are lots of corals, sponges and reef fish, including angelfish, peacock flounders, Creole wrasse, rock beauties, banded and foureye butterflyfish, scrawled filefish, moray eels and yellowtail snappers. This is a good site for a night dive.

18 HARRY'S HOLE/WET SUIT CITY/ CORAL CLIFF DROP-OFF
★★★★★★

Location: West coast, off Coral Cliff Beach
Access: By boat or shore
Conditions: Some chop and surge – dive only in calm conditions
Average Depth: 6m (20ft)
Maximum Depth: 40m+ (130ft+)
Visibility: 30m (100ft)
This site was previously called Wet Suit City because of the need for protection against fire coral and large bristle (fire) worms (*Hermodice carunculata*) in the surge. Enter the water at a sandy spot just to the left of the left-hand breakwater and swim out southeast to 3m (10ft) deep, turning left parallel to the shore. This is an interesting area where stands of fire coral harbour juvenile brown chromis; garden eels and scorpionfish can be found on the sand.

The drop-off used to be called Coral Cliff Drop-Off, because of the site's proximity to Coral Cliff. It begins at 12m (40ft) and slopes gently to a series of shelves at about 18m (60ft), then slopes more steeply to below 20m (100ft). There is light coral cover with large sandy

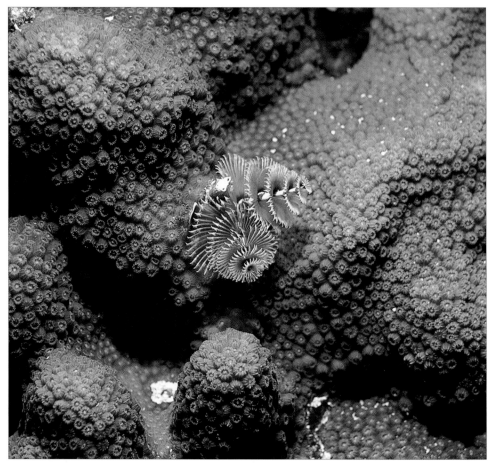

Above: *Christmas tree worms burrow into coral, leaving two fan-shaped spiral whorls protruding.*
Opposite: *A boulder star coral grows above a leathery barrel sponge.*

areas between the coral heads; some of the shelves and the area at the base of the drop-off attract garden eel colonies. In deeper water there are gorgonian sea fans and vase and basket sponges.

19 PLAYA HUNDU LOST ANCHOR
★★★

Location: West coast, south of Santa Martha Bay
Access: By boat or shore
Conditions: Can have challenging conditions, with choppy wave action and current
Average Depth: 20m (65ft)
Maximum Depth: 40m+ (130ft+)
Visibility: 30m (100ft)
Playa Hundu means 'Deep Beach' in Papiamento. The drop-off begins at 9m (30ft) and descends steeply past a

large anchor at 23m (75ft) down to sand at 40m (130ft). Most Caribbean reef fish can be found as well as gorgonians and corals.

20 BOCA GRANDI
★★★★★★

Location: West coast, just north of San Juan Bay
Access: By boat or shore
Conditions: Usually fairly calm with little current
Average Depth: 20m (65ft)
Maximum Depth: 40m+ (130ft+)
Visibility: 30m (100ft)
A compass is useful to access this site, as the drop-off is quite a long swim out northwest and very gradual. The coral cover increases with depth and at Inner San Juan Bay there are large star coral heads at 15m (50ft).

The bottom is relatively flat and slopes gently into deeper water. Eels, spotted drums and lobsters inhabit many of the nooks and crannies beneath the coral heads.

21 PLAYA MANSALIÑA

★★★ ★★★

Location: West coast, just south of San Juan Bay
Access: By boat or shore
Conditions: Usually fairly calm with little current
Average Depth: 20m (65ft)
Maximum Depth: 40m+ (130ft+)
Visibility: 30m (100ft)
The diving here is similar to that at Boca Grandi (Site 20). The coral cover increases with depth and there are large star coral heads at 15m (50ft). The bottom shelves gently into deeper water. Eels, spotted drums (*Equetus punctatus*) and lobsters may be found in many of the nooks and crannies beneath the coral heads. Be aware that the nearby beach, Playa Mansaliña, is shaded with Mansaliña (Manchineel) trees that have poisonous fruit and sap that can cause skin irritations.

The fish life here includes French and queen angelfish, peacock flounders, Creole wrasse, rock beauties, banded and foureye butterflyfish, scrawled filefish, moray eels, pufferfish, scorpionfish, trumpetfish, grunts and yellowtail snappers.

22 BIG SPONGE/MIKE'S REEF

★★★★ ★★★★

Location: West coast, north of Playa Largu (Site 23)
Access: By boat
Conditions: Choppy with some current
Average Depth: 20m (65ft)
Maximum Depth: 40m+ (130ft+)
Visibility: 30m (100ft)
The site was originally named Mike's Reef after Mike Stafford, the Dive Operations Manager at Habitat Curaçao, who was instrumental in putting this site on the map. Big Sponge is so-called because it used to have a huge sponge that was a photographer's dream. Unfortunately divers climbing into the sponge were partially responsible for its demise.

The mooring buoy is in 5m (15ft) of water and the drop-off descends to 40m (130ft), before shelving off deeper. The reef is healthy and features brain, black and star corals, gorgonian sea rods and sea whips, lobsters, stingrays and turtles. The reef fish life includes French and queen angelfish, rock beauties, banded and foureye butterflyfish, bluespotted cornetfish and pufferfish.

23 PLAYA LARGU

★★★ ★★★★

Location: West coast, off Playa Largu
Access: By boat or shore
Conditions: Usually fairly calm with little current
Average Depth: 20m (65ft)
Maximum Depth: 40m+ (130ft+)
Visibility: 30m (100ft)
This site has brain and star corals, gorgonian sea rods and sea whips. The reef fish life includes French and queen angelfish, rock beauties, banded and foureye butterflyfish, trumpetfish, parrotfish, filefish, goatfish and pufferfish.

24 LOWER HOUSE/CAS ABAO

★★★★ ★★★

Location: West coast, off Cas Abao Beach
Access: By boat or shore
Conditions: Usually fairly calm with little current
Average Depth: 20m (65ft)
Maximum Depth: 40m+ (130ft+)
Visibility: 30m (100ft)
This site features a shallow shelf near to the shore with a drop-off at about 9m (30ft), which falls off sharply to

sand below 40m (130ft). The slope is very rich in marine life, especially in crevices beneath the coral heads; you can see lobsters and often several spotted drums together under one coral head. Towards the deeper part of the slope, large orange elephant ear sponges are found.

25 THE VALLEY/PORT MARIE
★★★★★★★★

Location: West coast, off Port Marie Beach, south of Cas Abao
Access: By boat or shore
Conditions: Usually fairly calm with little current
Average Depth: 18m (60ft)
Maximum Depth: 40m+ (130ft+)
Visibility: 30m (100ft)
Also called Port Marie, The Valley is one of the island's top sites. Two healthy parallel reefs with a 'valley' in between are home to a wide variety of reef life. Often there are fish here that are rare at other sites, including small nurse sharks.

The mooring buoy in the centre of the bay is at 9m (30ft). Swimming straight out will take you over the first reef at 15m (50ft), then crossing the sandy valley leads to the second reef at about 18m (60ft). The Valley has profuse fish life including angelfish, parrotfish, groupers, brown chromis, yellowtail snapper, triggerfish, trumpetfish, bluespotted cornetfish, turtles, lobsters and stingrays. It is a good site for night diving.

26 DAAIBOOI
★★★★★★

Location: West coast, south of Port Marie beach
Access: By boat or shore
Conditions: Usually fairly calm with little current
Average Depth: 20m (65ft)
Maximum Depth: 40m+ (130ft+)
Visibility: 30m (100ft)
The swim out to the site is sheltered by high cliffs and there is no current until you reach the mouth of the bay. The shallow water has elkhorn corals and the moderate slope has brain, pillar and star corals, gorgonians and abundant reef fish. This is a pretty dive.

27 SAINT MARIE/RIF
★★★★★★★★

Location: West coast, off Habitat Curaçao
Access: By boat or shore
Conditions: Usually fairly calm with some current
Average Depth: 20m (65ft)
Maximum Depth: 40m+ (130ft+)
Visibility: 30m (100ft)

This site is Habitat Curaçao's House Reef, the best house reef on the island. As with their operation on Bonaire, Habitat Curaçao have two jetties, one for boats and one for shore diving. A yellow rope along the seabed extends the few metres out to the drop-off and then down it. It is thus easy for divers to find and make their way to and from the shore diving jetty without getting near to any boats using the boat jetty.

The shallow water features elkhorn coral, palometa (*Trachinotus goodei*), spotted moray eels swimming free, parrotfish, rock beauties, peacock flounders, lizardfish, banded and foureye butterflyfish, while over the drop-off there are also French angelfish, porcupine pufferfish, trunkfish, bluespotted cornetfish, trumpetfish, sergeant majors, grunts, snappers and shoals of goatfish. The drop-off begins at 5m (16ft) and as you get deeper the stony corals, sponges and gorgonians become denser, sheltering a multitude of invertebrates including lobsters, banded coral shrimps and Christmas tree worms.

28 LIGHT TOWER
★★★★

Location: Southwest coast, west of Cape St Marie
Access: By boat
Conditions: Rough with challenging currents
Average Depth: 20m (65ft)
Maximum Depth: 40m+ (130ft+)
Visibility: 30m (100ft)
Named after the light tower on the cape, this is a drift dive for advanced divers only. The drop-off is at 7m (23ft) from where a steep slope descends into deep water. The strong currents produce large and healthy marine life including a shoal of barracuda. Hammerhead sharks have been seen here.

29 SELDOM
★★★★

Location: Southwest coast, east of Cape St Marie
Access: By boat
Conditions: Rough seas and challenging currents
Average Depth: 20m (65ft)
Maximum Depth: 40m+ (130ft+)
Visibility: 30m (100ft)
'Seldom' dived because of the difficult conditions, this site is for advanced divers only. The drop-off begins at 7m (23ft) and descends into deep water. The wall here is about as steep as you get in Curaçao. The fish life is spectacular with many barracuda, rainbow runners and horse-eye jacks as well as reef fish and turtles.

Opposite: *A pair of banded butterflyfish swim together across the reef.*

Twice a year in the waters around Curaçao, over a few nights in September and October a week after the full moon, the corals and sponges spawn. A unique combination of the lunar cycle, water temperature and length of daylight gives rise to the right conditions for corals, brittle stars, sea urchins, sponges and worms to release their eggs and sperm smoke-like into the night's waters.

This remarkable spectacle was first observed on Australia's Great Barrier Reef in 1981. Scientists have been studying similar events around the world ever since and nowadays can get very close to pinpointing the actual nights when it will happen. This has led to a new sector in the diving market: dive packages that include night dives timed to coincide with the natural phenomenon.

As with many fish, the aim of releasing so many eggs and sperm into the water at the same time is to overwhelm predators. With food in abundance, some of the gametes will survive to have a chance of cross-fertilization. When released the buoyant gametes rise to the surface away from many of their waiting predators.

SPAWNING TIMES

All spawning occurs after sunset but different species spawn at different times on the same night. Star corals usually spawn between 22:00 and 22:30 hours. No one is sure why coral spawning occurs on one or two particular nights but the most likely explanation is that at this phase of the moon the tides are low so the gametes remain in one area for longer, rather than being swept away in a strong current.

Most reef-building corals reproduce in this way. Some are gonochoristic, which means the species has separate male or female colonies, the male colonies releasing sperm and the female colonies releasing eggs. Other species are hermaphroditic, releasing both eggs and sperm together in a single packet. In

Above: *Mixed corals and sponges are the sign of a healthy reef.*
Opposite: *The spawning of reef-building corals can be observed on all of the ABC islands.*

this case – as the aim of coral spawning is to cross-fertilize with other colonies of the same species – the eggs are often underdeveloped so they do not become fertilized accidentally within the single packet. Gametes will only fertilize another one of the same species.

Fertilized embryos develop into free-swimming planula larvae that drift with the currents and, if not eaten, may then find a suitable hard substrate in a sunny enough location to settle, build an outer shell of calcium and start a new colony. Polyps can reproduce asexually by either budding or dividing to form the colony.

SIDE EFFECTS

Coral spawning occasionally causes problems. If it happens when a tide is too low the gametes can become trapped on top of a reef where they decay quickly and, as the oxygen in the water becomes too low, much of the life beneath them dies.

Since first being noticed in the Caribbean in 1991, coral spawning events around Curaçao have been monitored systematically by marine biologists with the help of volunteer local divers. Each year the spawning is a popular event with divers and their help is co-ordinated by Dr Manfred van Veghel for Reef Care Curaçao. For information on how you can help with observing the spawning, call Reef Care Curaçao, tel/fax 599 9 7368120, or Dr Manfred van Veghel on 599 9 4613196.

Various other coral spawning events have been studied for long enough to be predicted. These occur about one week after the full moon in the following months:

Curaçao – September and October
Virgin Islands – August
Florida – August
Australia, Great Barrier Reef – November and December
Australia, Ningaloo Reef – March and April

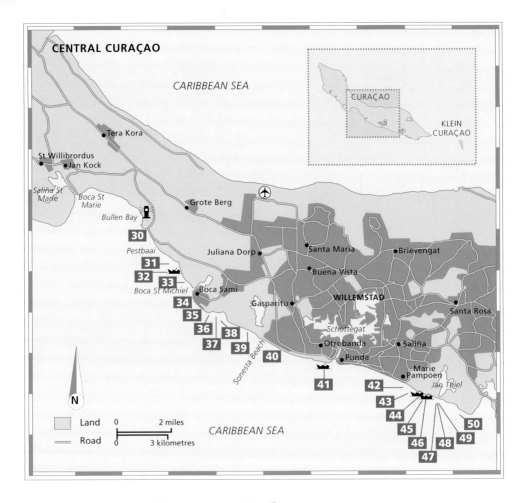

CENTRAL CURAÇAO

CARIBBEAN SEA

CARIBBEAN SEA

Central Curaçao

30 BULLEN BAY (BULLENBAAI)
★★★★★☆☆☆

Location: Southwest coast, by Bullen Bay lighthouse
Access: By boat or shore
Conditions: Choppy with some current
Average Depth: 20m (65ft)
Maximum Depth: 40m+ (130ft+)
Visibility: 30m (100ft)

This is a good dive with a protected shallow area for snorkelling and a near-vertical drop-off that is popular for deep diving. To the northwest of the buoy, the wall has lots of crevices and good coral cover, as well as lobsters, crabs and numerous reef fish, including palometa, parrotfish, rock beauties, peacock flounders, lizardfish, banded and foureye butterflyfish, French angelfish, porcupine pufferfish, trunkfish, trumpetfish, sergeant majors, and shoals of goatfish, grunts and snappers.

31 VAERSEN BAY (VAERSENBAAI)
★★★★★☆☆

Location: Southwest coast, off Vaersen Bay, south of Bullen Bay
Access: By boat or shore
Conditions: Normally calm
Average Depth: 20m (65ft)
Maximum Depth: 40m+ (130ft+)
Visibility: 30m (100ft)

This site can be dived by boat, but is also a good spot for shore diving and is popular for night diving. Enter the water from the police jetty. The drop-off begins at about 9–12m (30–40ft) and slopes down into deep water at about 45°. There are star corals, gorgonian sea plumes, sea rods and sea whips, while the fish life includes moray eels, parrotfish, rock beauties, peacock flounders, lizardfish, banded and foureye butterflyfish, angelfish, pufferfish, trunkfish, trumpetfish, damselfish, chromis, grunts, snappers and shoals of goatfish.

 CAR WRECKS
★★★★★★

Location: Southwest coast, just south of Vaersen Bay
Access: By boat or shore
Conditions: Normally calm
Average Depth: 20m (65ft)
Maximum Depth: 40m+ (130ft+)
Visibility: 30m (100ft)
This is where many old cars (and the barge that transported them) lie along the drop-off at 28m (92ft). Descending into deep water, the drop-off has profuse marine life. There are brain corals, gorgonian sea plumes, sea rods and sea whips and the fish life includes moray eels, parrotfish, rock beauties, peacock flounders, lizardfish, foureye butterflyfish, French angelfish, porcupine pufferfish, trunkfish, trumpetfish, damselfish, chromis, surgeonfish, grunts and snappers.

SEA-GRASS

Sea-grasses are the pastures of the ocean. They are found in estuaries or shallow coastal waters with mud or sand bottoms, where they stabilize the substrate, provide food and shelter and act as a breeding ground and nursery for many marine creatures.

Sea-grasses are neither true grasses nor seaweed (algae); they are in fact flowering plants with roots, stems, leaves and flowers. Their underground stems (rhizomes) and roots anchor the plants to the soft bottom and, as with land plants, the roots take up nutrients. Since the substrate where they grow is poor in oxygen it is the leaves that take up oxygen, which is transported along canals to their rhizomes and roots.

The leaves of sea-grasses also absorb sunlight for photosynthesis, so that water, carbon dioxide and other chemicals can be converted into nutrients and oxygen. One square metre (1.196 sq yd) of sea-grass produces an average of ten litres (17.6 pints) of oxygen each day and research has deduced that 100 sq m (120 sq yd) can support 500 tonnes (492 tons) of fish a year.

As with flowering land plants, sea-grasses produce pollen, which drifts with the currents, attaches itself to other flowers and fertilizes them to produce seed. Sea-grass beds mainly grow out horizontally, due to the horizontal stems that continually creep outwards along the sand.

Dugongs, green turtles, some herbivorous fish and many invertebrates feed on sea-grasses. They also slow down fast-flowing water and provide refuge for many immature fish, crabs, lobsters and prawns.

HALFWAY
★★★★★★

Location: Southwest coast, halfway between Vaersen Bay and Boca St Michiel
Access: By boat
Conditions: Normally calm
Average Depth: 20m (65ft)
Maximum Depth: 40m+ (130ft+)
Visibility: 30m (100ft)
Swim over the sandy plateau with its stingrays and garden eels to the drop-off at 9m (30ft). The drop-off descends into deep water with excellent corals, gorgonians and reef fish. There are brain and star corals, gorgonian sea plumes, sea rods and sea whips and the fish life includes spotted moray eels, parrotfish, peacock flounders, lizardfish, foureye butterflyfish, French angelfish, porcupine pufferfish, trunkfish, trumpetfish, soldierfish, sergeant majors, groupers, grunts and snappers. Frogfish and seahorses are occasional visitors.

BOCA SAMI
★★★★★★

Location: Southwest coast, off Boca St Michiel, west of Boca Sami, in front of The Wederfoort Dive Center
Access: By boat or shore
Conditions: Normally calm
Average Depth: 20m (65ft)
Maximum Depth: 40m+ (130ft+)
Visibility: 30m (100ft)
The drop-off descends from 12m (40ft) into deep water, with excellent marine life including turtles and dolphins. There are brain, star and pencil corals, gorgonian sea plumes, sea rods and sea whips, moray eels, parrotfish, peacock flounders, lizardfish, foureye butterflyfish, French and queen angelfish, porcupine pufferfish, trunkfish, trumpetfish, grunts, surgeonfish, fusiliers and snappers.

SNAKE BAY
★★★★★★

Location: Southwest coast, off Boca St Michiel, southwest of Boca Sami
Access: By boat or shore
Conditions: Normally calm
Average Depth: 20m (65ft)
Maximum Depth: 40m+ (130ft+)
Visibility: 30m (100ft)
The name refers to the moray eels seen here – the drop-off itself is the same as that of Boca Sami (Site 34). The drop-off starts at 12m (40ft) and descends into deep water. You will find brain and star corals, gorgonian sea

plumes, sea rods and sea whips, moray eels, parrotfish, peacock flounders, lizardfish, butterflyfish, French and queen angelfish, porcupine pufferfish, trunkfish, trumpetfish, grunts, fusiliers, groupers and snappers.

36 CAPE (KAAP) MAL MEEUW
★★★★

Location: Southwest coast, northwest of Blue Bay
Access: By boat or shore
Conditions: Normally calm
Average Depth: 20m (65ft)
Maximum Depth: 40m+ (130ft+)
Visibility: 30m (100ft)

This site lies off the point towards Blue Bay, where the sea can be rough but the currents produce a good wall with prolific marine life. There are brain, star and pencil corals, gorgonian sea plumes, sea rods and sea whips, moray eels, parrotfish, peacock flounders, lizardfish, foureye butterflyfish, French angelfish, trunkfish, trumpetfish, chromis, damselfish, groupers, goatfish, grunts, fusiliers and schoolmaster snappers.

37 THE WALL
★★★★★★★★

Location: Southwest coast, off the northwest corner of Blue Bay
Access: By boat
Conditions: Choppy with some current
Average Depth: 20m (65ft)
Maximum Depth: 40m+ (130ft+)
Visibility: 30m (100ft)

This is another top dive, with the drop-off beginning at about 9m (30ft) and falling off steeply into the depths. In some places the drop-off is nearly vertical but in most areas it is closer to 45°. The Wall features sheet coral, black coral, gorgonians and sponges, together with lots of reef fish, turtles and eagle rays.

38 BLUE BAY
★★★★★★★★

Location: Southwest coast, just south of The Wall (Site 37)
Access: By boat
Conditions: Choppy with some current
Average Depth: 20m (65ft)
Maximum Depth: 40m+ (130ft+)
Visibility: 30m (100ft)

Opposite: *Cup corals coat the inside of the wheelhouse of the Superior Producer (Site 41).*

Blue Bay is less dramatic than The Wall, with the drop-off beginning at 15m (50ft). There are brain, star and pencil corals, gorgonian sea fans, sea plumes, sea rods and sea whips, moray eels, parrotfish, peacock flounders, lizardfish, foureye butterflyfish, rock beauties, soldierfish, squirrelfish, black durgons, French and queen angelfish, filefish, porcupine pufferfish, trunkfish, trumpetfish, damselfish, groupers, grunts, fusiliers and snappers. Turtles and eagle rays can also be seen.

39 PISCADERA PLAYA LARGU
★★★★★★★★★

Location: Southwest coast, to the southwest of Blue Bay
Access: By boat
Conditions: Choppy with some current
Average Depth: 20m (65ft)
Maximum Depth: 40m+ (130ft+)
Visibility: 30m (100ft)

This site is a long swim from shore and is best accessed by boat. Although the beach itself is a narrow stretch of rubble, the reef's steep wall is teeming with life. As well as the smaller reef fish there are grouper, snapper, barracuda, eagle rays, turtles and sometimes dolphins. This site is a popular spot to see sponge spawning just after the full moon in September and October. Look out for boat traffic when on the surface.

40 THE CRASH
★★★

Location: Southwest coast, just off to the east of Sonesta Beach and Parasasa Beach
Access: By boat
Conditions: Choppy with some current
Average Depth: 20m (65ft)
Maximum Depth: 40m (130ft)
Visibility: 30m (100ft)

The scattered remains of an old crashed aeroplane are now mainly covered in corals and difficult to find, but the wall drops from 12m (40ft) to 35m (115ft) and features excellent corals, gorgonians, sponges and reef fish.

41 SUPERIOR PRODUCER
★★★★

Location: Southwest coast, just west of Otrobanda harbour entrance, off Holiday Beach Hotel
Access: By boat or shore but best by boat
Conditions: Exposed to wave action and currents
Average Depth: 30m (100ft)
Maximum Depth: 33m (110ft)
Visibility: 30m (100ft)

CIGUATERA FISH POISONING

Ciguatera poisoning can be caused by eating fish caught from around badly damaged or disturbed coral reefs. Blue-green algae rapidly settle on the newly exposed surfaces, and are then colonized by the dinoflagellate *Gambierdiscus toxicus*, which, as its name implies, is toxic. The dinoflagellates and algae are eaten by herbivorous fish and invertebrates, which are then consumed by carnivorous fish and so on, up the food chain. The toxin is not broken down, so it becomes concentrated in fish at the highest levels of the food chain, such as barracuda, large groupers, large jacks, moray eels, red snappers and some triggerfish.

A decrease in blood pressure distinguishes ciguatera from most other forms of food poisoning. Symptoms usually occur within three to six hours of consuming the contaminated fish and may continue for several days or longer. Studies of possible treatments for ciguatera fish poisoning are under way, but no cure has yet been found. Local hotels, resorts and fish markets will usually know which fish to avoid. It should be stressed that fish poisoning is the exception rather than the rule.

Curaçao's top wreck dive, the *Superior Producer* was outward bound when her cargo of clothes shifted and she sank outside the harbour in 1977. She now sits upright on sand at 34m (110ft) with her wheelhouse at 25m (80ft) and a mast rising to 15m (50ft). Parts of the hull and the interior of the wheelhouse are coated with *Tubastrea* cup corals and encrusting sponges. As it is a relatively deep dive, divers should swim out on the surface and descend the cable of the mooring buoy. Beware of boat traffic.

At the west end of the Holiday Beach Hotel's beach there is a double reef system. Enter the water from the concrete boat jetty, swim to the outside of the entry channel, and then pick up and follow a very thick rope over the shallow inner reef to the outside of the second reef. This second reef shelves down at a low angle with coral heads, gorgonian sea rods and sea whips, lots of reef fish, rainbow runners, horse-eye jacks and lone barracuda.

42 OSWALDO'S DROP-OFF
★★★★★★

Location: The drop-off in front of the Princess Beach Hotel
Access: By boat or shore
Conditions: Exposed, often with wave action and currents
Average Depth: 20m (65ft)
Maximum Depth: 37m (120ft)
Visibility: 30m (100ft)
Named after a local diver who was the first to record it, Oswaldo's Drop-off has a shallow shelf with elkhorn coral and thickets of staghorn corals and gorgonians. The top of the drop-off is located at 12m (40ft) and it slopes downwards at about 45° to 37m (120ft). This drop-off has brain and leaf coral and is covered with sponges.

The easiest entry and exit on the shore is at the steps by the Princess Beach Hotel's anchorage. Note the alternative exit mentioned for Car Pile (Site 43), in case the current is stronger than expected.

43 CAR PILE
★★★

Location: Southeast of Oswaldo's Drop-off (Site 42)
Access: By boat or shore
Conditions: Often a strong current
Average Depth: 25m (80ft)
Maximum Depth: 40m (130ft)
Visibility: 30m (100ft)
This site consists of a tangled mass of old cars, cables and barges on the slope of the drop-off in front of the Princess Beach Hotel. It is the remains of an experiment in artificial reef construction, and there is a danger of the pile collapsing. Use the same entry/exit as for Oswaldo's Drop-off. Swim offshore at an angle of about 45° to the west until you're over the drop-off at about 12m (40ft). Descend to 21m (70ft) and then proceed further to the west until you see cars. They begin at 18m (60ft) and continue downwards to about 40m (130ft).

To prevent being carried past the pile if the current is strong, swim straight offshore to the crest of the drop-off, descend and continue to the west along the 21m (70ft) contour to the pile. On the way back if you don't want to fight the current you can exit at a sandy beach at the west end of the Princess Beach Hotel.

44 SS ORANJE NASSAU/BOPOR KIBRA
★★★★★★

Location: South coast, offshore from the Sea Aquarium
Access: By boat or shore
Conditions: Always choppy over the wreck
Average Depth: 6m (20ft)
Maximum Depth: 30m+ (100ft+)
Visibility: 30m (100ft)
Also known as Bopor Kibra, Papiamento for 'broken ship', the SS *Oranje Nassau*, a Dutch steamer built in 1884 and owned by the Royal West India Company, ran aground here during a storm in 1906. Shore entry is best from the dive centre adjacent to the Sea Aquarium. The area is known for good corals: the shallows have elkhorn coral, then a drop-off begins at 15m (50ft) with large pillar and star corals, huge brain corals and gorgonian sea fans. The fish life includes swarms of blue chromis and Creole wrasse, French angels, rainbow runners, horse-eye jacks and barracuda. Return via the wreck, which breaks the surface.

45 ANIMAL ENCOUNTERS
★★★★★★

Location: South coast; Curaçao Sea Aquarium
Access: From the shore
Conditions: Always calm
Average Depth: 3m (10ft)
Maximum Depth: 3¹/₂m (12ft)
Visibility: Not relevant

This is not every diver's idea of a good dive, but some will consider it as their only chance to approach big fish safely. A natural tidal pool has been built near to the edge of the Sea Aquarium to house lemon and nurse sharks, stingrays and reef fish. The sharks are behind five big Plexiglas windows that have 6cm (2in) holes in them through which divers can hand-feed the animals. The sharks can be seen, photographed and filmed close up, while the divers can swim with stingrays and other fish. The stingrays have had their venomous spines removed. The proprietor of the Sea Aquarium shop will make a video of your dive on request.

46 SABA

★★★

Location: South coast, offshore from the Curaçao Sea Aquarium
Access: By boat
Conditions: Always choppy over the wreck; there can be strong currents
Average Depth: 20m (65ft)
Maximum Depth: 30m+ (100ft+)
Visibility: 30m (100ft)
Saba is a wreck about a kilometre (¹/₂ mile) southeast of the SS *Oranje Nassau*. The wreck itself is at 12m (40ft), but the wall to the southeast is worth exploring first before you out-gas on the wreck. The currents can be very strong – though because of this the corals are healthy and there is abundant fish life.

47 SANDY'S PLATEAU

★★★★★★★★

Location: South coast, out from Jan Thiel Bay
Access: By boat or shore but best by boat
Conditions: Choppy with some current
Average Depth: 20m (65ft)
Maximum Depth: 40m (130ft)
Visibility: 30m (100ft)
There are several sites to explore off Jan Thiel, and they are all top dives. Sandy's plateau is a large plateau leading out to a drop-off and a healthy wall where there are brain and star corals, gorgonians, sponges and lots of reef fish including trumpetfish, damselfish, chromis, wrasse, parrotfish, goatfish, rock beauties and sergeant majors.

48 BOCA DI SORSAKA

★★★★★★★★

Location: South coast, out from Jan Thiel Bay northwest of the beach
Access: By boat or shore but best by boat
Conditions: Choppy with some current
Average Depth: 20m (65ft)
Maximum Depth: 40m (130ft)
Visibility: 30m (100ft)

Below: *Encrusting sponges grow alongside a bright yellow branching tube sponge.*

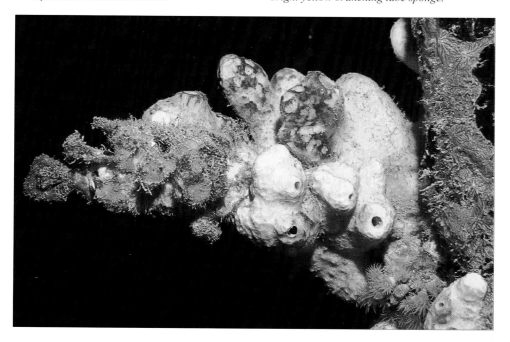

Above: *Tunicates come in numerous colours and in many cases are translucent.*

Another top dive, Boca di Sorsaka is nearer to the lagoon than Sandy's Plateau (Site 47). A similar shallow expanse of sand leads to the drop-off at 9m (30ft), with dense coral growth on an undercut ledge. Sponges and gorgonians shelter soldierfish, angelfish, trunkfish, filefish, trumpetfish, damselfish, chromis, wrasse, parrotfish, goatfish, rock beauties and sergeant majors.

49 DIVER'S LEAP
★★★★★★

Location: South coast, between Caracas Bay and Jan Thiel Bay
Access: By boat
Conditions: Choppy with strong current
Average Depth: 20m (65ft)
Maximum Depth: 40m (130ft)
Visibility: 30m (100ft)
Diver's Leap is so named because divers used to access the site by leaping from the cliffs; nowadays entry by boat is preferred. The mooring is close to the drop-off, which begins at 9–12m (30–40ft) and descends as a steep wall to depths that are deeper than the limit for sport diving. The wall is covered with gorgonians, large sponges, star coral and black coral. The fish life includes squirrelfish, soldierfish, angelfish, butterflyfish, trunkfish, filefish, trumpetfish, damselfish, chromis, wrasse, parrotfish, goatfish, grunts, snappers, barracuda, jacks and groupers.

50 PIEDRA DI SOMBRE
★★★★★★

Location: South coast, between Caracas Bay and Jan Thiel Bay
Access: By boat
Conditions: Choppy with strong current
Average Depth: 20m (65ft)
Maximum Depth: 40m (130ft)
Visibility: 30m (100ft)
Piedra di Sombre ('stone hat') is so-called because of the hat-shaped rock on the cliff that once was used to locate the site. The shallow shelf above 10m (33ft) is ideal for snorkelling and photography. There are lizardfish, many small anemones in nooks and crannies and a forest of gorgonians. Over the drop-off, the sheer wall drops to below sport diving depths, where there are a number of small caverns sheltering soldierfish, squirrelfish, black durgons, moray eels and lobsters. The wall is covered with gorgonians, large sponges, star coral and black coral. Further along the wall to the east, the slope becomes about 45° and is an equally good dive.

Thousands of years ago, masses of rock broke loose and slid into the sea to create Caracas Bay, a deep bay east of Willemstad. Royal Dutch Shell built its first oil terminal here and although it was later abandoned, the large jetties, once used by the tankers, remain with their stanchions coral-encrusted.

Established in 1983, the Curaçao Underwater Park stretches from Princess Beach Hotel to the eastern tip of the island, and includes some of Curaçao's finest reefs. Running from the high-water mark to the 60m (200ft) depth contour, the park covers a total surface area of 600ha (1483 acres) of reef and 436ha (1077 acres) of inner bays.

Past research by CARMABI indicated that coastal development, pollution, spear fishing and poaching were causing serious degeneration to the reef, fish populations were falling and black coral was becoming rare. The marine park was therefore set up with the main objective of protecting the reef and fish populations while at the same time stimulating recreational tourism activities in a sustainable manner. STINAPA obtained a grant from the World Wide Fund For Nature (WWF) to develop the Curaçao Underwater Park and is responsible for its day-to-day management.

MOORING BUOYS

Each dive site has a public mooring buoy specifically for use by visitors to the park. The buoys are anchored with a concrete block of at least one ton. The design of the mooring does not include a chain, so as to prevent a barren area developing around the mooring due to a swaying anchor chain. This means that the strength of the mooring depends entirely on the weight of the block and the length of rope paid out by the boat that ties up to it. The boat's skipper must pay out a length of at least $1^1/_2$ times the length of the boat in order to be safely moored. If properly used the mooring buoys are highly dependable and can safely secure boats of up to 12m (36ft) in length under normal weather conditions.

PARK RULES

Do not take any plants or animals, dead or alive, from the reefs other than by hook and line fishing. Collecting coral is a criminal offence.

Do not sit or step on corals, they are living animals!

Avoid any unintentional contact with corals by good buoyancy control.

Do not anchor in the coral, use the mooring buoys or select a sandy area.

Do not spear fish.

Help to keep the park clean.

Below: *A brown chromis lays its eggs in the Curaçao Underwater Park.*

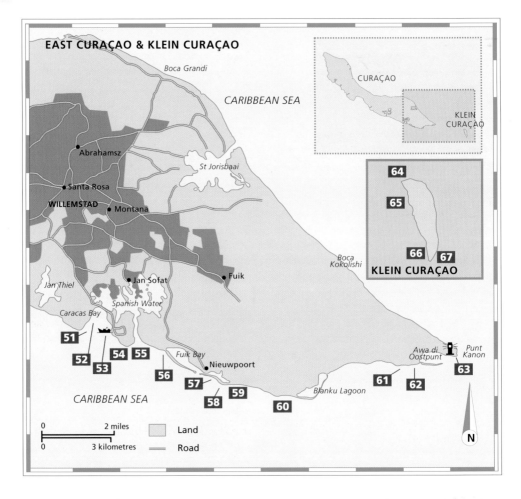

EAST CURAÇAO & KLEIN CURAÇAO

East Curaçao and Klein Curaçao

51 KABES DI BARANKA/BEACON POINT
★★★★☆☆☆☆

Location: South coast, near the entrance to Caracas Bay
Access: By boat
Conditions: Choppy with strong current
Average Depth: 20m (65ft)
Maximum Depth: 40m+ (130ft+)
Visibility: 30m (100ft)

Also called Beacon Point, Kabes di Baranka means 'head of the rock' in Papiamento. Near the mooring buoy there is a large pillar coral in the shallows, while from the drop-off at 6m (20ft) a wall descends to a ledge at 33m (110ft) before shelving into deeper water. There are healthy corals, lush gorgonians, reef fish, rainbow runners, horse-eye jacks, barracuda and occasionally sleeping nurse sharks.

52 CARACAS BAY LOST ANCHOR
★★★★☆☆☆☆

Location: South coast, along the northwest wall of Caracas Bay
Access: By boat or shore
Conditions: Choppy with strong current
Average Depth: 20m (65ft)
Maximum Depth: 40m+ (130ft+)
Visibility: 30m (100ft)

This site features a heavy anchor chain that descends to well below sport diving limits. The dive profile is similar to that of Kabes di Baranka (Site 51). The drop-off is at 6m (20ft) and drops as an apparently never-ending wall of corals, lush gorgonians, reef fish and deep water fish.

53 TUGBOAT (TOWBOAT)
★★★★ ★ ★ ★ ★

Location: South coast, off the protected southeast side of Caracas Bay
Access: By boat
Conditions: Normally calm, though around the southeast corner you are likely to hit strong and unpredictable currents
Average Depth: 5m (16ft)
Maximum Depth: 40m (130ft)
Visibility: 30m (100ft)
Another of Curaçao's top dives, this site includes a wreck that is small enough to be photographed in its entirety and a 45° sloping drop-off that begins in 9m (30ft) of water. The reef is packed with stony corals and gorgonian sea fans, sea rods and sea whips. In the shallow water, the tugboat rests upright on sand at 5m (15ft), carpeted with multi-coloured tube sponges and orange *Tubastrea* cup corals.

To the southeast of the tug the pretty, vertical wall is undercut in places and drops to about 30m (100ft) before shelving out at 45° or less. At the base of the wall there are large sheet corals. The tug attracts angelfish, trumpetfish, sergeant majors, chromis, groupers, snappers and moray eels. Along the wall, vase and basket sponges, black coral, lobsters, moray eels and scorpionfish are found. Be aware that around the southeast corner you are likely to hit strong and unpredictable currents.

54 KABAYE AND SMALL WALL
★★★★ ★ ★ ★ ★

Location: South coast, just southeast of Caracas Bay by Directors Bay
Access: By boat
Conditions: Choppy with strong current
Average Depth: 20m (65ft)
Maximum Depth: 40m+ (130ft+)
Visibility: 30m (100ft)
Kabaye and Small Wall are next to each other and share similar diving. A mooring buoy, at 5m (15ft), marks the sites. A sandy terrace leads out from the shore and features staghorn and yellow pencil corals, octopuses, seahorses, sergeant majors, butterflyfish, angelfish and trumpetfish. The drop-off features star corals and lush gorgonians though the wall descends beyond sport diving depths. Two large sandy gullies intersect this wall and there are a number of nooks and crannies where moray eels, shrimps and lobsters hide.

55 PUNT'I PIKU/BARRACUDA POINT
★★★ ★ ★ ★

Location: South coast, across from Barbara Beach, near the mouth of Spanish Water (Spaanse Water)
Access: By boat
Conditions: Choppy with strong currents
Average Depth: 20m (65ft)
Maximum Depth: 40m (130ft)
Visibility: 30m (100ft)
This area has heavy boat traffic. The shallow water east of the buoy has elkhorn, staghorn, star and fire coral, large pillar corals and good gorgonian growth.

To seaward, east of the buoy, the drop-off is over 45°, beginning at about 9m (30ft) and continuing beyond 30m (100ft). The slope features large heads of mountainous star coral around 18m (60ft). To the west of the buoy, the drop-off is a wall descending to about 18m (60ft) before shelving off more gently. It is covered with gorgonians and sponges. The fish life includes barracuda, parrotfish, rainbow runners, horse-eye jacks, surgeonfish, damselfish, sergeant majors, grunts, snappers and Creole wrasse.

56 EEL VALLEY
★★★★ ★ ★ ★

Location: South coast, northwest end of Fuik Bay
Access: By boat
Conditions: Choppy with strong currents
Average Depth: 20m (65ft)
Maximum Depth: 40m (130ft)
Visibility: 30m (100ft)
Eel Valley has the usual sandy shallow plateau leading to a drop-off at 8m (25ft). It was originally named for its unusually high number of moray eels, though the numbers of these have now returned to normal. Staghorn corals are found in the shallows while leaf and star corals and gorgonians cover the drop-off, which descends to 30m (100ft) before shelving off deeper. There is an abundance of reef fish including squirrelfish, soldierfish, angelfish, foureye butterflyfish, trunkfish,

---

TURTLES AROUND THE ABC ISLANDS

Four species of sea turtles can be found around the ABC islands. In inshore waters you will often see green turtles (*Chelonia mydas*) that are herbivores and feed on sea-grass, and hawksbill turtles (*Eretmochelys imbricata*), which mostly feed on sponges. Loggerhead Turtles (*Caretta caretta*) and the massive leatherback turtles (*Dermochelys coriacea*) are more likely to be found offshore.

All sea turtles are on the endangered species list.

filefish, trumpetfish, damselfish, chromis, wrasse, parrotfish, goatfish, grunts, rainbow runners, snappers, barracuda, jacks and groupers.

57 NEWPORT

★★★★★★★

Location: South coast, offshore of Fuik Bay
Access: By boat
Conditions: Choppy with strong currents
Average Depth: 20m (65ft)
Maximum Depth: 40m (130ft)
Visibility: 30m (100ft)

Staghorn corals are found in the shallows here, while leaf and star corals and gorgonians cover the drop-off, which descends to 30m (100ft) before shelving off deeper. There is an abundance of reef fish including soldierfish, French angelfish, butterflyfish, porcupine pufferfish, scrawled filefish, trumpetfish, fusiliers, chromis, wrasse, parrotfish, goatfish, grunts, snappers, barracuda, jacks and groupers.

58 KATHY'S PARADISE

★★★★★★★

Location: South coast, southeast end of Fuik Bay, southeast of Nieuwpoort
Access: By boat
Conditions: Choppy with strong currents
Average Depth: 20m (65ft)
Maximum Depth: 40m (130ft)
Visibility: 30m (100ft)

Kathy's Paradise is the point that juts out from Nieuwpoort and therefore catches some rough seas. The strong currents produce a healthy reef life so it is a diver's paradise. Staghorn corals are found in the shallows, while leaf and star corals and gorgonians cover the drop-off, which descends to 30m (100ft) before shelving off deeper. Reef fish life is prolific and includes squirrelfish, soldierfish, angelfish, butterflyfish, trunkfish, filefish, trumpetfish, Creole wrasse, parrotfish, groupers and shoals of goatfish, grunts, snappers, barracuda and jacks.

59 SMOKEY/PUNT'I SANCHI

★★★★★★★

Location: South coast, offshore at the far eastern side of Fuik Bay
Access: By boat
Conditions: Choppy with strong currents and surge
Average Depth: 20m (65ft)
Maximum Depth: 40m (130ft)
Visibility: 30m (100ft)

Also called Punt'i Sanchi, Smokey has a wall seaward of the mooring buoy which begins at 6m (20ft) and drops to 30m (100ft). Above and on the drop-off there is healthy coral, sponge and gorgonian growth and the profuse fish life includes filefish, groupers, snappers, grunts, stingrays and eagle rays. This is a great dive.

60 GULIAUW

★★★★★★★

Location: South coast, east of Smokey (Site 59), west of Blanku Lagoon
Access: By boat
Conditions: Exposed, very choppy with strong currents
Average Depth: 20m (65ft)
Maximum Depth: 40m (130ft)
Visibility: 30m (100ft)

A very exposed dive, this is not for those who get seasick. It is best to fully kit-up before you leave the boat jetty, as the vessel will be rocking around when over the site. Snorkelling is only possible on the calmest days. Staghorn coral grows here at the unusually deep depth of 15m (50ft). The drop-off is at 8m (25ft) – above it there are fire and elkhorn corals, gorgonian sea fans, sea rods and sea whips. On the drop-off star, brain and pillar corals dominate and reef and pelagic fish thrive, including parrotfish, snappers, grunts, groupers, filefish, triggerfish, Creole wrasse, rainbow runners and horse-eye jacks.

61 PIEDRA PRETU/BLACK ROCK

★★★★

Location: Southeast coast, east of Blanku Lagoon
Access: By boat
Conditions: Very choppy with strong currents
Average Depth: 20m (65ft)
Maximum Depth: 40m+ (130ft+)
Visibility: 30m (100ft)

This site has a spectacular vertical wall but is subject to very rough seas. As with all these eastern sites it is more likely to be calmest in the early morning.

The mooring buoy is in 6m (20ft); to seaward the drop-off begins at 8m (25ft) and descends as a wall down to about 36m (120ft), before sloping off more gradually beyond depths to which sport divers should dive. The shallow plateau is covered with staghorn and elkhorn coral, large barrel sponges and gorgonians and the wall is covered with a dense forest of black coral. Near the base of the wall there are large disks of sheet corals. At around 25–27m (80–90ft) there are crevices filled with basslets, spotted morays and large green moray eels. The reef fish that feature here include parrotfish, surgeonfish, snappers, groupers, trumpetfish, goatfish and Creole wrasse.

Above: *Although slowly breaking up, the Tugboat (Site 53) remains an unusually picturesque wreck.*

62 NO WAY
★★★★

Location: Southeast coast, off the west of the large lagoon Awa di Oostpunt
Access: By boat
Conditions: Rough with strong currents
Average Depth: 20m (65ft)
Maximum Depth: 40m+ (130ft+)
Visibility: 30m (100ft)
No Way is so-called because of the rough, difficult conditions. However, despite this, it is one of the island's top dive sites and a visit is well worth the effort – though for experienced divers only. An old Spanish cannon in about 3m (10ft) gives the area its local fishermen's name 'Punt Canon'.

The mooring buoy is at about 8m (25ft); further out to sea the drop-off wall is near vertical and descends below sport diving depths. The shallow ledge has corals, sponges, gorgonians and green moray eels among its reef fish. A cave at about 24m (80ft) often has resting nurse sharks. Deeper down among the black corals there are pelagic species including rainbow runners, horse-eye jacks and barracuda as well as a multitude of reef fish, including squirrelfish, angelfish, butterflyfish, trunkfish,

filefish, trumpetfish, damselfish, chromis, fusiliers, Creole wrasse, parrotfish, goatfish, grunts and mahogany and schoolmaster snappers.

63 BASORA
★★★★

Location: Southeast coast, off the East Point of the island, by the entrance to the large lagoon Awa di Oostpunt
Access: By boat
Conditions: Very rough with seriously strong and changing currents
Average Depth: 20m (65ft)
Maximum Depth: 40m+ (130ft+)
Visibility: 30m (100ft)
Another challenging dive that is similar in profile to Piedra Pretu and No Way (sites 61–62). Above the drop-off the shallow ledge exhibits elkhorn and staghorn corals and luxuriant growth of gorgonian sea fans, sea rods, sea whips and sea plumes. The drop-off itself also has large black, brain, pillar and star corals. The fish here include large groupers, filefish, snappers, surgeonfish, Creole wrasse, moray eels, stingrays and many pelagic species.

Klein Curaçao is a tiny uninhabited island located 1¹/₂–2 hours by boat off the southeast of Curaçao. In good weather, excursions to the island are popular for sunbathing and beach parties, although there is no shade. The lighthouse is obsolete, and there are just a few fishermen's shacks, a jetty in poor repair on the leeward side and the hulk of a tanker aground on the windward side. When conditions are calm these sites are among Curaçao's top dives.

64 NORTHWEST CORNER
★★★★

Location: Off the northwest point
Access: By boat
Conditions: Can be rough with strong currents
Average Depth: 30m (100ft)
Maximum Depth: 40m (130ft)
Visibility: 30m (100ft)
At 30m (100ft), near the bottom of a steep wall, there is a large cave where there is the possibility of seeing sleeping nurse sharks (*Ginglymostoma cirratum*). The wall itself is covered with corals and has abundant fish life including large Goliath grouper and other groupers, spotted and green moray eels, snappers, rainbow runners, jacks and barracuda. Turtles are often encountered.

Below: *A trumpetfish mimics a gorgonian sea whip for camouflage.*

65 NORTH OF THE MAIN BEACH AND

66 SOUTH OF THE MAIN BEACH
★★★★★★★★★

Location: Either side of the main beach on the leeward side of Klein Curaçao
Access: By boat or shore
Conditions: Normally calm but some current and swell
Average Depth: 20m (65ft)
Maximum Depth: 40m+ (130ft+)
Visibility: 30m (100ft)
There are two dives on the leeward (southwest) side of the island, either side of the main beach. The drop-off on this side has some sand on it, so the coral is not so rich, but there are lots of reef fish, rainbow runners and moray eels hiding under coral heads. The reef fish include soldierfish, French and queen angelfish, banded and foureye butterflyfish, rock beauties, pufferfish, scrawled filefish, trumpetfish, damselfish, chromis, wrasse, parrotfish, goatfish, grunts, snappers and groupers.

67 DRIFT DIVE STARTING ON THE WINDWARD SIDE
★★★★

Location: The windward side of Klein Curaçao
Access: By boat
Conditions: Rough with strong currents
Average Depth: 20m (65ft)
Maximum Depth: 40m+ (130ft+)
Visibility: 30m (100ft)
When conditions permit, this is a spectacular dive. Divers are dropped in the rough seas on the windward side of the island and drift round to be picked up in the calm seas of the leeward side. A pretty wall drops to 30m (100ft), and is covered with orange elephant ear sponges, purple tube sponges, black corals, huge gorgonian sea fans and massive boulder corals, before shelving out further into the depths. Nooks and crannies shelter many invertebrates and the abundant fish life includes large pelagic species, moray eels, snappers, goatfish, stingrays, eagle rays, scorpionfish and occasionally sharks. Turtles are regularly encountered.

GETTING THERE

Hato International Airport is near to the Hato Caves, 11km (7 miles) north of the capital. Air connections are very good with Europe, the Americas and many parts of the Caribbean.

From Europe, KLM have regular daily services via Amsterdam from most major and many regional airports. TAP Air Portugal connect via Lisbon and British Airways via Miami or Caracas.

Various American airlines connect with North America.

From Latin America there are regular services from Colombia, Guyana, Surinam, Venezuela and Central American countries.

Airport tax is US$23 (international) US$5.65 (domestic). Children under two years old and passengers transiting within 24 hours are exempt.

Curaçao's port is located on the south coast at the capital, Willemstad. A major port of call on the itinerary of over 200 cruises from America and Europe, the Cruise Terminal is in the Otrobanda area of Willemstad. A ferry sails regularly between Venezuela and Curaçao.

WHERE TO STAY

Curaçao has more accommodation and facilities aimed at the European market than the other two ABC islands.

Apart from Habitat Curaçao, all other dive operators on Curaçao are concessions attached to hotels. Some of them do not have their own boats, but shore dive and hire a boat when they require one.

EXPENSIVE
Curaçao Marriott Beach Resort & Emerald Casino
Piscadera Bay; tel 599 9 736 8800; fax 599 9 462 7502
There are 248 rooms, three restaurants, all facilities and a casino. Caters for the disabled.

MID-RANGE
Curaçao Caribbean Hotel and Casino
PO Box 2133, Piscadera Bay; tel 599 9 625000; fax 599 9 625846
There are 181 rooms, five restaurants with themed nights and a casino.

Habitat Curaçao
Coral Estate, Rif St Marie; tel 599 9 864 8304; fax 599 9 864 8464; e-mail: curacao@habitatdiveresorts.com
A self-contained dive resort. More remote and private than most other resorts, it embraces the 'diving freedom' concept made famous at Captain Don's Habitat on Bonaire. There is a free daytime shuttle service to Willemstad.

Holiday Beach Hotel and Casino
PO Box 2178, Patere Euwensweg; tel 599 9 462 5400, USA 800 44 5244; fax 599 9 46243979; e-mail: holbeach@cura.net; www.hol-beach.com
This hotel has 200 rooms, two restaurants with themed nights and a casino. There is also a shuttle bus that goes from the hotel to Willemstad.

Lion's Dive Hotel and Marina
Bapor Kibrá; tel 599 9 434 8888, USA 888 LIONS-DIVE; fax 599 9 434 8889; email: info@lionsdive.com; www.lionsdive.com
There are 72 rooms and three restaurants. It is located just between Princess Beach Resort and the Curaçao Sea Aquarium.

Sunset Waters Beach Resort
Santa Martha Bay; tel 599 9 864 1233; fax 599 9 864 1237; www.sunsetwaters.com

SuperClubs Breezes Curaçao
Dr Martin Luther King Boulevard; tel 599 9 736 7888; fax 599 9 461 7205; www.superclubs.com
A true mega-resort, this has everything; with 341 rooms and suites.

Van der Valk Plaza Hotel and Casino
PO Box 813, Plaza Pier, Willemstad; tel 599 9 461 2500, USA 800 766 6016; fax 599 9 461 6543; e-mail: info@plazahotelcuracao.com
A large resort with 235 rooms and 18 suites and an array of amenities including shops and a casino.

INEXPENSIVE
Airport Hotel Holland and Casino
524 Franklin D. Rooseveltweg; tel 599 9 868 8044; fax 599 9 868 8114
There are 46 rooms and a casino. It is convenient for the airport.

All West Apartments
Westpoint Beach; tel 599 9 864 0102; fax 599 9 461 2315; e-mail: info@allwestcuracao.com
There are six apartments with kitchens or studios with kitchenettes.

Trupial Inn
5 Groot Davelaarweg; tel 599 9 737 8200; fax 599 9 737 1545; www.trupialinn.com
This is a cosy family hotel in a residential district. There are 74 rooms or suites all with kitchenettes. There is also a sauna.

WHERE TO EAT

The restaurants in hotels or resorts are likely to be top class, but if you wish to try somewhere different the influence of so many different nationalities has meant that Curaçao offers a large choice of cuisine.

CARIBBEAN
Asia de Cuba Restaurant
Zuikertuintjeweg z/n; tel 599 9 747 9009; www.asiadecubacuracao.com

Golden Star
2 Socratesstraat; tel 599 9 465 4795
A typical West Indian restaurant that is located on the corner of Dr Maalweg and Hugenholtzweg. Provides everything from meat, fish and hamburgers to egg-and-bacon sandwiches.

Oasis
79 Savonet, Banda Abou; tel 599 9 864 0085
Local cuisine: goat stew, creole and seafood dishes.

Parrotz Restaurant
Trupial Inn, 5 Groot Davelaarweg; tel 599 9 737 8200
Local and international cuisine served in a 'Curaçao of the 1920s' setting.

CHINESE
Chindy's Restaurant
Nieuwe Paeraweg 16A; tel 599 9 465 7444; www.chindys.nl

Lam Yuen
25 Fokkerweg; tel 599 9 461 5540
A restaurant serving healthy quantities of Chinese food.

Rose Garden
56 Oude Caracasbaaiweg; tel 599 9 461 4574
Large helpings of Chinese food are available here.

FRENCH
Larousse
5 Penstraat; tel 599 9 465 5418
European-style restaurant for relaxed dining where French cuisine is served in the ambience of an 18th-century house. The restaurant has fresh supplies flown in from Holland.

INDIAN

Jaipur Indian Restaurant
Langestraat 8 (Kura Hulanda), Otrobanda; tel 599 9 434 7631

INDONESIAN
Caribbean Hotel; tel 599 9 625000
The restaurant serves Indonesian cuisine that is popular with the Dutch due to their past connections with Indonesia.

Rijsttafel Indonesia
13 Mercuriusstraat; tel 599 9 461 2606
Serves Javanese specialities. The speciality of the house is a 16- or 25-dish rice table, served buffet style.

INTERNATIONAL
Bistro Le Clochard
Riffortbogen, Otrobanda; tel 599 9 462 5666; e-mail: clochard@attglobal.net

De Taverne
Landhuise Groot Devalaar; tel 599 9 737 0669
An old Curaçaon *landhuis*, furnished with antiques and lit with candles. Serves fish or large steak. It is very popular so reservations are requested.

El Toro Saloon-Steakhouse
De Rouvilleweg, Otrobanda; tel 599 9 462 9400; www.eltorosteakhouse.com

Fort Nassau
tel 599 9 461 3450
Local and international cuisine served in the pleasant ambience of an 18th-century fort. Good food and a fine view over St Anna Bay.

Fort Waakzaamheid
Berg Domi; tel 599 9 462 8588
Local and international cuisine served in the ambience of an old fort that was captured by Bligh (the English captain of *The Bounty*). This restaurant is known for its value for money and has a good view over the town and harbour.

Grill King
Waterfortbogen 2–3, Punda; tel 599 9 461 6870

Grillin' Joe's Bar and Restaurant
S.B.N. van Staverenweg 6; tel 599 9 737 1600; www.grillinjoes.com

Restaurant Landhuis Daniel
Weg naar Westpunt z/n; tel 599 9 864 8400; www.landhuisdaniel.com

Oceans Bar and Restaurant
Habitat Curaçao, Coral Estate, Rif Santa Marie; tel 599 9 864 8800
Popular with divers, and local expatriates. Serves good local and international cuisine and there is a friendly service. Some nights are themed and/or have entertainment.

Rancho El Sobrino Resort
Weg naar Kniphaf z/n; tel 599 9 888 8822; www.ranchoelsobrino.com

Restaurant and Café Gouveneur de Rouville
de Rouvilleweg 9F-G, Otrobanda; tel 599 9 462 5700; www.de-gouverneur.com

Rodeo Ranch
Curaçao Sea Aquarium; tel 599 9 461 5757
This restaurant is popular among divers as a meeting place. It serves an international cuisine.

Rumours
Lions Dive Hotel & Marina, Bapor Kibrà; tel 599 9 461 7555
Another restaurant that is popular as a meeting place for divers. It serves international cuisine, including meat and the fish catch of the day.

'T Kokkeltje
Airport Hotel Holland & Casino, 524 Franklin D. Rooseveltweg; tel 599 9 868 8044
This restarant has a Dutch atmosphere and serves more than 15 types of fish or shellfish, as well as steaks. Both local seafood and fish are flown in from Holland. There is a view over the airport runway from the restaurant.

Restaurant Villa Elisabeth
Dr Martin Luther King Boulevard 125; tel 599 9 465 6417; www.villaelisabeth.com

Zambezi Restaurant
The Ostrich Farm, Groot St Joris; tel 599 9 747 2777; www.ostrichfarm.net

ITALIAN
Il Barile da Mario
Hanchi Snoa; tel 599 9 461 3025
A bar and ristorante serving pasta, minestrone, seafood and fine wines. The restaurant is located opposite the synagogue.

La Pergola
12 Waterfort Arches; tel 599 9 461 3482
Restaurant serving fine Italian cuisine in the heart of town with good views. It is expensive.

MEXICAN
Margarita
Winkelcentrum Brievengate; tel 599 9 737 2155
Authentic Mexican cuisine with a big 'Mariachi Night' on Fridays. Closed on Tuesdays.

SUSHI
Chopstick – Sushi and Raw Bar
Santa Rosa Weg 33C; tel 599 9 738 4846; e-mail: info@chop-stix.com

THAI
Sawasdee Thai Restaurant
Mercuriusstraat 13; tel 599 9 461 2606; www.sawasdeecuracao.com

DIVE FACILITIES

Apart from Habitat Curaçao, all the other dive operators on Curaçao are concessionary operators attached to hotels. Some of the operators do not have their own boats but will hire one if required.

All West Diving & Adventures Curaçao
West Point Beach; tel 599 9 864 0102; fax 599 9 461 2315; e-mail: diveshop@allwestcuracao.com
Training up to Open Water Diver level is offered in Dutch, English and German.

Atlantis Diving
6 Drielstraat; tel 599 9 465 8288; fax 599 9 465 8288; e-mail: info@atlantisdiving.com; www.atlantisdiving.com
Training up to Instructor level offered in Dutch, English, German, Papiamento, Portuguese and Spanish.

Caribbean Sea Sports N.V.
Marriott Hotel, John F. Kennedy Boulevard, Piscadera Bay; tel 599 9 462 2620; fax 599 9 462 6933; e-mail: css@cura.net; www.caribseasports.com
PADI instruction in conjunction with the Sonesta Hotel.

Curaçao Seascape
Hilton Curaçao Hotel, John F. Kennedy Boulevard; tel 599 9 462 5000; fax 599 9 462 5905; email: info@seascapecuracao.com; www.seascapecuracao.com
A PADI 5-Star Gold Palm operation. The facility has been established for 30 years, and was originally called Piscadera. Courses up to Divemaster level offered in four languages.

Diving School Wederfoort/Sami Scuba Center
93 Bocaweg; tel 599 9 868 4414; fax 599 9 869 2062; e-mail:

info@divewederfoort.com;
www.divewederfoort.com
This is a long-established facility that is associated with several hotels and apartments. Courses offered up to Assistant Instructor level.

Easy Divers Curaçao – now at Habitat Curaçao

Habitat Curaçao Dive Resort
Coral Estate, Rif Santa Marie; tel 599 9 864 8304, USA 800 327 6790;
fax 599 9 864 8464; e-mail:
curacao@habitatdiveresorts.com
A PADI 5-Star Instructor Development Center that teaches in Dutch, English, German, Papiamento and Spanish. The facility has been voted by American divers as among the top fifteen dive resorts worldwide and tied third as the best dive operator in the Caribbean.
Habitat Curaçao believes in total diving freedom. The staff at the facility are not there to dictate how you dive but to assist and advise. Three boat dives are offered as standard each day, plus unlimited shore diving; full diving cylinders are available 24 hours a day.

Lions Dive – see Ocean Encounters

Ocean Encounters
Bapor Kibra z/n, Willemstad; tel 599 9 461 8131; fax 599 9 465 5756; e-mail:
info@oceanencounters.com;
www.oceanencounters.com
A PADI 5-Star Gold Palm and IANTD Technical Dive Center, this operation is located at the Seaquarium complex and has its main facility at the grounds of the Lions Dive Beach Resort. Additional facilities are provided at Superclubs Breezes, Toucan Diving at Kontiki Beach, and Ocean Encounters West at Playa Kalki.

S.A.F.E. Diving Discover Diving Curaçao
Playa Lagun Naast 51; tel 599 9 864 1652;
fax 599 9 864 1652; e-mail:
info@DiscoverDiving.nl;
www.safediving.com

Scuba Do Dive Center
Jan Thiel Beach & Sports Resort; tel 599 9 767 9300; fax 599 9 767 9300; email:
info@divecenterscubado.com;
www.divecenterscubado.com
Training up to Assistant Instructor level is offered in five languages.

Silent Immersion N.V.
6 Drielstraat; tel 599 9 4651575;
fax 599 9 465 8288; e-mail:
info@silentimmersion.com;

www.silentimmersion.com
This operation offers deep exploration of various dive sites, as well as Nitrox, Rebreather and Trimix technical diving instruction.

Toucan Diving – see Ocean Encounters

RECOMPRESSION CHAMBER

The 750-bed St Elisabeth Hospital (St Elisabeth Gasthuis) is one of the largest and most up to date in the Caribbean. It is located in Willemstad's Otrobanda district and contains the island's two hyperbaric chambers.

St Elizabeth Hospital, tel 599 9 462 5100/462 4900
Recompression Chamber, tel 599 9 463 7457/463 7288

EMERGENCIES

Curaçao Emergency Telephone Numbers:

Ambulance	112
Fire Department	114
Hospital	110
Police	911
Tourism Security Assistance	4617991

USEFUL CONTACTS

Visit Curaçao's main websites:
www.curacao-tourism.com;
www.ctb.an

Curaçao Tourism Development Bureau Curaçao
19 Pietermaai, PO Box 3266, Willemstad, Curaçao, Netherlands Antilles; tel 599 9 434 8200; fax 599 9 461 2305; e-mail:
ctdbcur@ctb.net

Curaçao Tourism Development Bureau UK
Axis Sales & Marketing Ltd., 421a Finchley Road, London NW3 6HJ; tel 020 7431 4045; fax 020 7431 7920; e-mail:
destinations@axissm.com

Curaçao Tourist Bureau Europe
82–84 Vastland, 3011 BP Rotterdam, Holland; tel 010 414 2639; e-mail:
info@ctbe.nl

The Curaçao Tourist Board – Miami
330 Biscayne Boulevard, Suite 808, Miami, FL 33132; tel 305 3745811; 800 445 8266; fax 305 3746741; e-mail: ctbmia@gate.net

The Curaçao Tourist Board – New York
475 Park Avenue South, Suite 2000, New York, NY 10016; tel: 212 683 7660; 800

Curaçao; fax: 212 683 9337; e-mail:
ctdbny@ctdb.com

South America – Venezuela
Avenida Abraham Lincoln, entreC/Negrin y Recreo, Torre la Piñata, Piso 3, Oficina 3–A, Boulevard Sabana Grande, Caracas, Venezuela; tel 58 212 761 6647;
fax 58 212 761 6148; e-mail:
curacaoturismo@cantv.net

The Marine Environment

THE NATURE OF CORALS AND REEFS

Tropical reefs are built mainly from corals, primitive animals closely related to sea anemones. Corals are basically a stomach with a mouth surrounded by tentacles. Most of the coral types that contribute to reef construction are colonial; that is, numerous individuals – polyps – come together to create what is essentially a single compound organism. The polyps produce calcareous skeletons; when thousands of them are present in a single colony they form large, stony (limestone) structures, which accumulate as reefs.

When these corals die, some of their skeleton remains intact, thus adding to the reef. Cracks and holes then fill with sand and the calcareous remains of other reef plants and animals, and gradually the whole lot becomes consolidated, with new corals growing on the surface of the mass. Thus only the outermost layer of the growing reef is actually alive.

Coral reefs are important structures, providing food, shelter and protection for a myriad of fish and other marine life. Corals grow slowly, adding about 1–10cm (0.4–4in) growth in a year. Once over a few years old, they become sexually mature and begin to reproduce. In the ABC islands, over a few nights in September and October, all the coral polyps spawn by releasing eggs and sperm into the water at the same time. The eggs and sperm fertilize with eggs or sperm of the same species to form a larva known as a planula. These planulae are planktonic; they float around in the ocean until they find somewhere suitable to settle to then begin or continue the growth of reefs.

Corals can be classified as hermatypic (reef-building) or ahermatypic (non reef-building). The shapes they create as they grow vary enormously according to the species and to the place on the reef where they are growing. Colonies range in size from those that are a few centimetres in diameter to those that are giants, several metres across and many hundreds of years old. Some are branched or bushy, others tree-like, others in the form of plates, tables or delicate leafy fronds, and yet others are encrusting, lobed, rounded or massive.

Microscopic single celled blue-green algae (plants) called zooxanthellae are of great importance to the growth and health of stony corals and other marine animals such as anemones. Living in symbiosis with the coral, they are packed in their millions into the living tissues of all reef-building corals. Although reef corals capture planktonic organisms from the water, particularly at night, a significant amount of their food comes directly from the products of photosynthesis manufactured by the zooxanthellae. It is for this reason that the most prolific coral growth is in the shallow, well-lit water that zooxanthellae prefer.

In late 1995 there was extensive bleaching (loss of zooxanthellae) of both corals and anemones in the Caribbean, to depths of at least 40m (130ft). Local divers dated the problem to late September or early October when water temperatures climbed to 33°C (91°F). In 1996 the water temperatures returned to normal and most of the zooxanthellae returned; the major reef-building coral, the mountainous star coral, recovered its colour.

Fringing Reefs

In theory, coral reefs can develop anywhere where the underlying rock has at some time been close enough to the water surface for corals to become established and grow. Sea levels may have risen or fallen considerably since then and other geological changes may have occurred to lower or raise the coral. The reefs around the ABC islands are of the fringing kind. Fringing reefs occur in shallow water near to land. Typically they extend to depths of 9–20m (30–65ft) and then drop off quite steeply, sometimes steeper than 70° – referred to as a wall.

In some areas the drop-off exhibits 'spur-and-groove' formations that run perpendicular to the shore, caused by the constant swell of the waves. The 'spur' is a ridge of stony coral that harbours sponges and gorgonian sea fans, sea plumes, sea rods and sea whips; the 'groove' is a lower-lying chute of sand and coral rubble.

In shallow water above the drop-off you will find elkhorn, staghorn and fire coral, gorgonians and small fish, while over the drop-off, in deeper water, many other species are found.

REEF LIFE

On most reefs your attention is likely to be held initially by the fish life. On a single dive, concentrated observation would reveal over 50 species, but that is only part of the story – many inhabitants are hidden from view within the complex framework of the reef.

The back reef and lagoon fill the area between the shore and the seaward reef. Here the seabed is usually a mixture of sand, coral rubble, limestone and living coral colonies. The water depth varies from a few metres to 50m (165ft) or more, and the size of the lagoon can be anywhere from a few hundred to thousands of square metres. Sites within lagoons are obviously more sheltered than those that are on the seaward side of the reef, and are also more affected by sedimentation. Most of the corals are of the delicate, branching type and you may encounter beds of sea-

---

Opposite: *Healthy reefs and clear water continue to attract divers year after year to the ABC islands.*

CARIBBEAN COASTAL MARINE PRODUCTIVITY PROGRAMME

The Caribbean Coastal Marine Productivity Programme (CARI-COMP) is a regional effort to study the interaction between the land and the sea, monitoring its changes and collecting scientific information to be used in its management. The programme covers coral reefs, mangroves and sea-grass beds, and involves no less than thirteen islands, including Bonaire and Curaçao, plus eight mainland countries.

CARICOMP's centre is based in Jamaica: CARICOMP, c/o Centre for Marine Sciences, University of the West Indies, Mona, Kingston 6, Jamaica; tel 876 9271609; fax 876 9771033.

---

grasses, the only flowering plants to occur in the sea.

Although some typical reef fish are absent from this environment, there is no shortage of interesting species. There are roving predators – snappers, wrasse, trigger-fish and others – on the look-out for prey, and there are the bottom-dwelling fish – flounders, rays etc – that burrow into the sand until completely hidden, emerging only when they need to feed.

Most divers ignore the shoreward zones of the reef and head straight for sites on the reef front, on the basis that here they are most likely to see spectacular features and impressive displays of marine life. Brightly lit, clean water provides ideal growing conditions for corals, and the colonies that they form help create habitats of considerable complexity. There is infinite variety, from shallow gardens of delicate branching corals to walls festooned with sponges and gorgonian sea plumes, sea rods, sea whips and sea fans. Under shaded overhangs, whether they are small crevices or large caves, orange *Tubastrea* cup corals will have some of their colourful polyps spread out feeding.

The top 20m (66ft) or so of the seaward reef is especially full of life. Here small damselfish, chromis and sergeant majors swarm around the coral, darting into open water to feed on plankton. Butterflyfish show their arrays of spots, stripes and intricate patterns as they probe into crevices or pick at coral polyps – many have elongated snouts especially adapted for this delicate task. In contrast, you can see surgeonfish grazing the algae and parrotfish biting and scraping at the coral, leaving characteristic white scars.

Open-water species such as barracuda, jacks, snappers and sharks cover quite large areas when feeding, and wrasse often forage far and wide over the reef. There are also many species that are more localized and these can be highly territorial.

Fish-watching can provide endless pleasure, but there are plenty of other things to see. Any bare spaces in the reef can soon be colonized, and in some places the surface is covered with large organisms that may be tens or even hundreds of years old. These sedentary

reef-dwellers rely primarily on water-borne food. Corals and their close relatives – anemones, sea fans and black corals – capture planktonic organisms using their tiny stinging cells. Sponges and tunicates strain the plankton as seawater passes through special canals in their body-walls. Other organisms have rather different techniques, the Christmas tree worm, for example, filters out food with the aid of its beautiful feathery 'crown' of tentacles.

As well as the fish and sedentary organisms, there is a huge array of other life forms to observe on the reef. Tiny crabs live among the coral branches and larger ones wedge themselves into appropriate nooks and crannies, often emerging to feed at night. Spiny lobsters hide in caverns, coming out to hunt under the cover of darkness. Gastropod molluscs are another type of marine creature seldom seen during the day, but they are often plentiful, especially on the shallower parts of the reef.

Some of the more easily spotted of the mobile invertebrates are the echinoderms, most primitive of which are the feather stars, sporting long delicate black arms. Their well-known relatives, the sea urchins, include the black, spiny variety that lives in shallow reef areas and is a potential hazard to anyone walking onto the reef.

Whether brilliantly attractive or frankly plain, whether swiftly darting or fixed to the spot, all the life forms you find on the reef are part of the reef's finely balanced ecosystem. Remember you are not! You are an intruder, albeit hopefully a friendly one. It is your obligation to cause as little disturbance and destruction among these creatures as possible.

CONSERVATION AWARENESS

Corals grow slowly, so if they are damaged or removed they may require years to recover or be replaced. In the natural course of events, storm-driven waves from time to time create havoc on coral reefs but some human activities are similarly destructive, especially coral quarrying and the indiscriminate collection of corals to sell as marine curios. Fortunately neither of the latter occur on the ABC islands' reefs.

Over-fishing is a further hazard to reef environments, and has already led to declining populations of target species in some areas. Another way that over-fishing can cause grave damage is through altering the balance of local ecosystems; for example, decreasing the populations of herbivorous fish can lead to an explosive increase in the algae on which those species feed, so the corals of the reef may become overgrown and suffer.

Some areas are being damaged by pollution, especially where reefs occur close to large centres of human population. Corals and other reef creatures are sensitive to dirty, sediment-laden water, and are at risk of being smothered when silt settles on the bottom. Sewage, nutrients from agricultural fertilizers and other organic materials washed into the sea encourage the growth of algae, sometimes to the extent that – again – corals become overgrown.

If left to themselves coral reefs are very resilient systems. Often referred to as the tropical rainforests of the oceans, coral reefs provide shelter, nutrients, and breeding grounds for thousands of fish and invertebrate species. Coral reefs and their symbiotic partners have existed in relative harmony for thousands of years – but, as with the rainforests, we now threaten their survival.

Protecting the Reefs

One outcome of the growing awareness of environmental issues has been the growth of 'ecotourism'. The main underlying principle is often summarized as 'take nothing but photographs, leave nothing but footprints', but even footprints – indeed, any form of touching – can be a problem in fragile environments, particularly among corals. A better way to think of ecotourism is in terms of managing tourism and the tourists themselves in such a way as to make the industry ecologically sustainable. The necessary capital investment is minimal, and thereafter much-needed employment becomes available for the local population. In the long term the profits from this sustainability can be much greater than the income from fishing.

Although divers, as well as many dive operators and resorts, have been at the forefront in protecting reefs and marine ecosystems, we all need somewhere to eat and sleep. If a small resort is built without a waste-treatment system, the nearby reefs may not be irreparably damaged; but if those same reefs start to attract increasing numbers of divers and spawn further resorts, strict controls become necessary.

In such discussions of ecotourism we are looking at the larger scale. It is too easy to forget that 'tourists' and 'divers' are not amorphous groups but collections of individuals, with individual responsibilities and capable of making individual decisions. Keeping reefs ecologically sustainable depends as much on each one of us as it does on the dive and resort operators.

Here are just some of the ways in which you, as a diver, can help preserve the reefs that give you so much pleasure:

Try not to touch living marine organisms with either your body or your diving equipment. Be particularly careful to control your fins, since their size and the force of kicking can damage large areas of coral. Don't use deep fin-strokes next to the reef, since the surge of water can disturb delicate organisms.

Learn the skills of good buoyancy control – too much damage is caused by divers descending too rapidly or crashing into corals while trying to adjust their buoyan-

cy. Make sure you are properly weighted and learn to achieve neutral buoyancy. If you haven't dived for a while, practise your skills somewhere where you won't cause any damage.

Avoid kicking up sand. Clouds of sand settling on the reef can smother corals. Snorkellers should be careful not to kick up sand when treading water in shallow reef areas.

If you are out of control and about to collide with the reef, steady yourself with your fingertips on a part of the reef that is already dead or covered in algae. If you need to adjust your diving equipment or mask, try to do so in a sandy area well away from the reef.

Never stand on corals, however robust they may seem. Living polyps are easily damaged by the slightest touch. Never pose for pictures or stand inside giant basket or barrel sponges.

Don't move marine organisms around to photograph or play with them. In particular, don't hitch rides on turtles or manta rays: it causes them considerable stress.

Don't feed fish. It may seem harmless but it can upset their normal feeding patterns and provoke aggressive behaviour – and be unhealthy for them if you give them food that is not part of their normal diet.

Take great care in underwater caverns and caves. Avoid crowding a cave, and don't stay too long: your air bubbles collect in pockets on the roof of the cave, and delicate creatures living there can 'drown in air'.

On any excursion, whether with an operator or privately organized, make sure you take your garbage back for proper disposal on land.

Avoid boats that have bad oil leaks, or discharge untreated sewage near reefs.

Don't participate in spear fishing – it is now banned anyway in the ABC islands. Elsewhere, if you live on a boat and rely on spear fishing for food, make sure you are familiar with all local fish and game regulations and obtain any necessary licensing.

Don't collect or buy shells, corals, starfish or any other marine souvenirs.

REEF CARE CURAÇAO

Reef Care Curaçao was formed by a group of conservation enthusiasts in 1992. Their aim is to improve public awareness of the reefs, actively become involved in reef protection and carry out research projects.

Among their ongoing activities are beach clean-up campaigns, research into coral and sponge spawning, a Reef Alarm Help Line and an educational programme for underprivileged children known as 'Kids for Coral'.

If you encounter any violations of the reefs or any unusual events connected with them, telephone the Reef Alarm Help Line on 3216666. Prospective donors and volunteers can contact Reef Care Curaçao on tel 599 9 8693220;fax 599 9 8693323; email: reefcare@cura.net

Sergeant major, 10–18cm (4–7in), *Abudefduf saxatilis*

COMMON FISH AND INVERTEBRATES

Chromis, damselfish and **sergeant major**
(family Pomacentridae)

Some members of the family (eg. *Stegastes*) farm their own patch of algae, aggressively driving away other herbivores. Others form large aggregations to feed on plankton. Their eggs are often defended aggressively by the males.

Spotted drum, 15–28cm (6–11in), *Equetus punctatus*

Drums (family Sciaenidae)

Spotted drums are timid fish that usually hide under small overhangs or in holes, only coming out to feed at night. They have an unusually long front dorsal fin, black and white bars on the head and their rear dorsal and tail fins are black with white spots. The juveniles have an even longer front dorsal fin.

Whitespotted filefish, 25–45cm (10–18in), *Cantherhines macroceros*

Filefish (family Monacanthidae)

The commonest filefish seen off the ABC islands is the whitespotted filefish, which has an obviously extended belly appendage and scalpels like a surgeonfish at the base of its tail.

Graysby, 15–30cm (6–12in), *Cephalopholis cruentata*

Groupers/sea bass (family Serranidae)

Groupers range from just a few centimetres long to the massive giant grouper, 3.5m (12ft) long. They vary enormously in colour; grey with darker spots is the most common. Movement is slow except when attacking prey, which is carried out with remarkable speed. All groupers are carnivorous, feeding on invertebrates and other fish. The Goliath Grouper (*Epinephelus itajara*) is the largest of the species found in the ABC islands.

French grunt, 15–30cm (6–12in), *Haemulon flavolineatum*

Grunts and **margates** (family Haemulidae)

Grunts are often confused with snappers but, except for margate, are generally smaller and do not have canine teeth. The name comes from the noise produced in their throats when their teeth are grinding. This noise is then amplified by their air bladder.

Lizardfish/sand diver (family Synodontidae)
Lizardfish are named after their lizard-like heads. They lie motionless and camouflaged on the bottom waiting for prey to swim by. They will not move even if you approach closely with a camera.

Lizardfish/sand diver, 20–45cm (8–18in), *Synodus intermedius*

Moray eels (family Muraenidae)
This ancient family of fish have gained their undeserved reputation for ferocity largely because, as they breathe, they open and close the mouth to reveal their numerous sharp teeth. They do not have fins or scales. Moray eels hide the rear portion of their bodies in a selected coral crevice and are fairly inactive during the day. They emerge at night to feed.

Spotted moray eel, 45–90cm (18–36in), *Gymnothorax moringa*

Parrotfish (family Scaridae)
So-called because of their sharp, parrot-like beaks and bright colours, parrotfish are among the most important herbivores on the reef. Many change colour and sex as they grow. The terminal-phase males develop striking coloration in comparison with the drab initial-phase males and females. These fish consume considerable amounts of coral limestone when feeding.

Redband parrotfish, 18–28cm (7–11in), *Sparisoma aurofrenatum*

Pufferfish/balloonfish/burrfish (family Tetraodontidae)
These small to medium-size omnivores feed on algae, worms, molluscs and crustaceans. Pufferfish are found all the way down the reef to depths of around 30m (100ft). They are slow moving but when threatened, they inflate themselves into big, round balls by sucking water into the abdomen, so that it becomes almost an impossible task for predators to swallow them.

Porcupine pufferfish, 30–90cm (12–36in), *Diodon hystrix*

Soapfish (family Grammistidae)
Named after a toxic, soap-like mucus that they secrete, soapfish are the height of inactivity, often resting on the bottom or leaning against ledges. They are so lazy that divers can approach them closely. Soapfish hunt at night.

Greater soapfish, 13–33cm (5–13in), *Rypticus saponaceus*

OTHER FISH AND INVERTEBRATES

Anemones (phylum Cnidaria, order Actiniaria)
Sea anemones come in many different shapes and sizes. Their tentacles have stinging nematocysts that paralyse any small fish or invertebrates that brush against them and then draw the prey to the mouth at the centre of the anemone's disc. Some species of crab, shrimp and fish can live in symbiosis with anemones without being stung by the nematocysts. Anemones can move slowly and will fight other anemones nearby; they can also retract their tentacles for protection.

Angelfish (family Pomacanthidae)
A close relative of the butterflyfish and equally as beautiful, angelfish browse on sponges, algae and corals using their minute, brush-like teeth. Their vibrant colouring varies according to the species, like those of the butterflyfish and they were once thought part of the same family. However, they are distinguishable by a short spike extending from the gill cover. Angelfish are territorial in habit and tend to occupy the same caves or ledges for a period of time. Large angelfish species produce loud a drumming noise when agitated.

Barracuda (family Sphyraenidae)
With their elongated silvery body and sinister-looking jaws, barracuda look rather fearsome. Though they rarely threaten divers (but have a habit of following them about), it is wise to approach large, lone individuals with caution. Barracuda are effective reef predators; they tend to school when young, but hunt singly or in pairs when mature.

Bigeyes (family Priacanthidae)
As their name suggests, these small, nocturnal fish have large eyes. Effective predators, they hover in holes in the reef or under overhangs during the day and venture further afield to feed at night.

Butterflyfish (family Chaetodontidae)
Among the most colourful of reef inhabitants, butterflyfish have compressed, thin bodies, usually with a stripe through the eye and sometimes with a dark blotch near the tail: this serves as camouflage and confuses predators, who lunge for the wrong end of the fish. Butterflyfish can also swim backwards to escape danger. Many species live as mated pairs and have territories.

Calcareous tube worms (phylum Annelida, family Serpulidae)
Divers easily notice Christmas tree worms because of their colour and beauty. They live in calcareous tubes embedded in live corals, the two fan-shaped spiral whorls, called radioles, protrude from the tubes with a sharp spine above the mouth. The worms withdraw instantly when approached and a hard structure called an operculum closes over the tube opening.

Cardinalfish (family Apogonidae)
The nocturnal counterpart of the damselfish in terms of sheer abundance, at night cardinalfish actively feed on small shrimps and crabs. In some species the males incubate the eggs inside their mouths.

Crabs (phylum Crustacea, order Decapoda)
Crabs have evolved reduced abdomens and tails. The first pair of legs have grown claws that are used for fighting or posturing and the manipulation of objects such as when feeding. The other four pairs of legs enable the animal to rapidly move sideways. Most species are small and prefer to remain hidden. Some such as the yellowline arrow crab usually only come out at night.

Feather stars (phylum Echinodermata, class Crinoidea)
Often referred to as 'living fossils' as they have changed little according to fossil records, feather stars have bodies with five arms that divide to give them long arms in multiples of five. Numerous short appendages cover each arm to give a feather-like appearance and catch passing food in the current. These arms adhere tightly to anything that comes into contact with them and are said to be the original idea behind Velcro. As with sea stars the arms can regenerate if broken off. Some crinoids can swim short distances but they usually walk on short jointed legs called cirri.

Flounders (family Bothidae)
Flounders are flatfish that lie on their sides – within weeks of birth, the eye on the underside migrates to the exposed side and the exposed pectoral fin acts like a dorsal fin. Flounders can change their colour to blend in with the bottom and partially bury themselves in the sand or mud. They glide over the seabed with an undulating motion. The peacock flounder has blue spots and the unusually long exposed pectoral fin is often erect while the fish is swimming.

Goatfish (family Mullidae)
Bottom dwellers, goatfish are easily recognized by a pair of barbels under their chin, which they use to rummage in the sand for prey. They are usually found in small groups or large shoals.

Gobies (family Gobiidae)
The goby is a 'bottom dweller' and has the ability to remain stationary and undetected on the seabed for long periods of time. They have large protruding eyes, which are raised above the level of the head, and powerful jaws which enable them to snatch prey and dart back to safety. The goby family is one of the most successful, with literally hundreds of species. In fact new species of these small, secretive fish are being discovered all the time.

Gorgonians (phylum Cnidaria, order Gorgonacea)
Gorgonians is the preferred name for the octocorals that are often mistakenly called 'soft corals' by Caribbean dive masters because they are flexible and often appear bushy. Gorgonians include sea fans, sea plumes, sea rods and sea whips. Sea fans are always set perpendicular to the current so that their polyps, which are so close together as to be almost touching, can efficiently sieve the current for food.

Jacks, palometas, permits and **rainbow runners** (family Carangidae)
Jacks are open water (pelagic) fish, though shoals often pass over reefs while following the current in search of prey. A few species find it productive to remain near reefs, such as horse-eye jacks, palometas and permits. Cruising outer reef slopes, they dash in to catch unwary prey. They are usually in small groups but are sometimes seen in large shoals.

Sea cucumbers (phylum Echinodermata, class Holothuroidea)
Sea cucumbers are sausage-shaped with a mouth at one end and an anus at the other. Like other echinoderms they have a water-vascular system, which operates their tube-feet by hydraulic pressure. The skeletons of sea cucumbers consist of small spicules within their leathery body-wall. Taking in sediment through the mouth as they crawl across the reef, extracting organic debris and voiding the waste sand through their anus, they shift large amounts of sand.

Soldierfish and **squirrelfish** (family Holocentridae)
These are predominantly red fish that hide under overhangs or in crevices during the day and come out to feed at night.

Snappers (family Lutjanidae)
They are called snappers because they snap their jaws when hooked on a line. Snappers are often associated with grunts, but snappers have prominent canine teeth while grunts do not. Snappers are nocturnal predators that hang around singly or in small groups during the day.

Sponges (phylum Porifera)
The basic sponge structure is made up of a collection of cells that enclose canals and chambers that open to the outside and inside through pores. The form is supported by a skeleton of calcareous or siliceous spicules and a matrix of fibres. Water is drawn through the outer pores and as it passes through the canals, food and oxygen are filtered out. The water exits into the sponge's interior cavity and out through its excurrent openings. Sponges are responsible for much of the colour visible on Caribbean reefs.

Surgeonfish (family Acanthuridae)
Grazers of algae, surgeonfish have spines like scalpels at the base of their tails. They can be solitary but often shoal in large groups.

Triggerfish (family Balistidae)
These medium to large fish, with flattened bodies and powerful teeth, feed on crustaceans and echinoderms on the mid-reef. When a triggerfish is threatened it squeezes itself into a crevice and erects its first dorsal spine. Locking it into place with a second, smaller spine, this first dorsal spine stays wedged until the 'trigger' is released.

Trumpetfish (family Aulostomidae)
Expert at changing colour to blend in with a background, trumpetfish are always solitary. They often hide among branching corals or gorgonian sea rods, lining up their bodies with the branches even if they are vertical. They closely shadow fish such as pufferfish to sneak up on prey.

Tunicates/sea squirts (phylum Chordata, class Ascidiacea)
Tunicates, also called sea squirts, come in many colours and are often translucent. Their habit of filtering food is similar to that of sponges but when disturbed they can close their siphons quickly. Solitary tunicates are called simple ascidians, while those that exist as colonies of many individuals are called compound tunicates. Some species are only joined at their bases while others are completely embedded in a common tunic. In some species their excurrent siphons open into a single, shared chamber.

Yellowfin mojarras (family Gerreidae)
Yellowfin mojarras swim slowly or hover over the sand and dig for small invertebrates.

Wrasse/hogfish (family Labridae)
This is a colourful and conspicuous group of fish, easily recognized by shape and the bird-like way of swimming. Most wrasse constantly move about and can change sex from female to male.

Underwater Still Photography

Underwater photography requires some technical competence and dedication. The new digital cameras are more forgiving in that you can discard any failures without having to pay for them, but underwater photography can work out expensive. You cannot change films, memory cards or prime lenses underwater, so if you have a clear idea of what you wish to photograph before you take the plunge, you are likely to get better results. Another possibility is to have a zoom lens on a housed camera. If the water is calm, you can carry two camera outfits, one for wide-angle and another for close-up or macro. In strong currents a non-reflex camera will be smaller and therefore easier to handle.

DEDICATED UNDERWATER CAMERAS

There are several waterproof non-reflex cameras, both film and digital, that do not need waterproof housings, but if you want to use the best lenses at this level you will have to find a Nikonos V film camera, which has a Through-The-Lens (TTL) automatic exposure system and dedicated flash guns (strobes) made by Nikon and other manufacturers. This camera is now discontinued but there are still plenty of them around because they are so popular.

Prime lenses for the Nikonos that are manufactured by Nikon range from 15mm to 80mm in focal length, but these must be changed in air. The 35mm and 80mm lenses can also be used in air, but they are really only useful underwater when fitted to extension tubes of close-up outfits. The 28mm lens should be considered as the standard lens.

Independent companies supply lenses, lens converters, extension tubes and a housing for fish-eye and super wide-angle land camera lenses to fit the Nikonos. Lens converters are convenient and can be changed underwater. Some cameras make good use of these with converters for wide-angle and macro. The Nikonos close-up kit can also be changed underwater. The lack of reflex focusing makes it difficult to compose pictures and it is easy to cut off part of a subject.

HOUSED CAMERAS

Huge increases in the technical advances of land cameras are the main reason for the demise of the Nikonos. Land cameras are used underwater in specialist metal or Plexiglas waterproof housings. There are advantages and disadvantages to each system. Metal housings are strong, reliable, work well at depth and will last a long time if properly maintained. They are heavy to carry, especially when travelling by air, but buoyant in water. Their high cost is justified if you are using an expensive camera needing the extra protection.

Plexiglas housings are cheaper but more fragile, and require careful handling, both above and below the water. Some models compress at depth, making the control rods miss the camera controls. These control rods can be adjusted

to work at depths, but then do not function properly near to the surface. Most underwater photographs are taken near to the surface, so this drawback is not serious. These housings are lightweight to carry on land, but often too buoyant in the water, where you have to attach extra weights to them.

'O' Rings and Other Equipment

Underwater cameras, housings, flash guns and cables have 'O'-ring seals to keep the water out. These and their mating surfaces or grooves must be kept scrupulously clean. 'O'-rings should be lightly greased with special grease to prevent flooding. When not in use, it is best to store any user-removable 'O'-rings off the unit to avoid them becoming flattened. The unit itself should then be sealed in a plastic bag to keep out moisture. User-removable 'O'-rings on cameras and flash synchronization cables are best replaced every 12 months. Non-user-removable 'O'-rings on the Nikonos should be serviced every 12–18 months, while those on housing usually last the life of the housing.

Housings without controls, which are designed for fully auto cameras, require flash films or with digital, higher ISO ratings to obtain reasonable shutter speeds and lens apertures in the low ambient light underwater. When balancing flash with daylight, cameras with faster flash synchronization speeds, $1/125$ or $1/250$ of a second, give sharper results by avoiding the double images associated with fast-moving fish.

Masks hold your eyes away from the viewfinder, so buy the smallest volume mask you can wear. Cameras fitted with optical action finders or eyepiece magnifiers are useful in housings, but this is not so important with autofocus systems.

Light refraction through your mask and through the camera lens causes objects to appear one-third closer and larger than in air. Reflex focusing or visually estimated distances remain correct, but if you measure distances by ruler, these must be reduced by a third when setting the lens focus if it is inscribed in 'in-air' distances. If you are using a waterproof housing with a flat port (window) in front of the lens, refraction increases the focal length of the lens and decreases its sharpness, due to the individual colours of light being refracted at different angles and speeds (chromatic aberration). This is most pronounced with wide-angle lenses, which should be corrected by using a convex dome port. Dome ports require lenses to be able to focus on a virtual image at around 30cm (1ft), so you may have to fit supplementary positive dioptre lenses to some camera lenses.

FLASH

Water acts as a cyan (blue/green) filter, cutting back red, so colour film will have a blue/green cast. For available light photography, different filters are sold to correct this in either temperate or tropical waters, but they reduce the already limited amount of light available. Flash will put back the colour and increase apparent sharpness. Modern flash guns (strobes) have TTL automatic exposure systems. Underwater, large flash guns have good wide-angle performance usable up to 1.5m (5ft). Smaller flash guns have a narrow angle and only work up to 1m (40in), diffusers widen the angle covered, but you lose at least one F-stop in output. Most land flash guns are more advanced than underwater flash guns, and they can be housed for underwater use (refer to flash guns for digital cameras, page 163).

Flash guns used on or near to the camera will light up suspended matter in the water like white stars in a black sky (back scatter). The closer these particles are to the camera, the larger they will appear. The solution is to keep the flash as far as possible above and to one side of the camera. Two narrow-angle flash guns, one on each side of the camera and each pointing slightly outwards but with their light output overlapping in the centre, often produce a better result than a single wide-angle flash gun. However, the result will be a little flat as two flash guns of the same power will not give the modelling light that photographers rely on to distinguish features by showing shadows.

When photographing divers, remember the golden rule that the eyes within the mask must be lit and in focus. Flash guns with a colour temperature of 4500° Kelvin will give more accurate skin tones and colour by replacing some of the red that the water has filtered out. In a multiple flash set-up, the prime flash gun will meter by TTL if this is available, and unless it has TTL-Slave, any other flash gun connected will give its pre-programmed output, so this should be set low to achieve modelling light. TTL-Slave flash guns should have a lower output than the main flash for the same reason.

Multiple-segment matrix flash exists with some land cameras in housings that are connected to housed matrix-metering flash guns. With other TTL systems, although the ambient light metering may be multiple-segment matrix, the flash metering is by a single segment in the centre of the frame. This means that flash on smaller off-centre foreground subjects may not be correctly metered with these systems (see also flash with digital cameras, page 164).

Although objects appear closer to both your eye and the camera lens underwater, the flash must strike the subject directly to illuminate it. Narrow-angle flash guns must therefore be aimed behind the apparent subject, to hit the real subject. Built-in aiming/focusing lights or a torch strapped to the flash will aid both this problem and focusing during night photography. Built-in aiming/focusing lights are best powered by separate batteries, or the main flash battery will not last for a complete dive. Fish scales reflect light in ways that vary with the angle of the fish to the camera. Silver fish reflect more light than coloured fish and black fish almost none at all, so you should bracket exposures. With automatic flash guns do this by altering the film speed ISO setting on the camera.

The easiest way to balance flash with the ambient available light is to use TTL flash with the camera on

aperture priority metering. Take a meter reading of the mid-water background that agrees with your chosen flash synchronization speed, set your flash to TTL and it will correctly light the subject. If you do not have multi-segment matrix flash, then your subject should be in the central part of the frame. If you use manual exposure, using an aperture half a stop higher than the meter recommends will give a darker background and make the subject stand out more. At distances of less than 1m (40in) most automatic flash guns tend to overexpose, so you must allow for this.

PHOTOGRAPHIC SUBJECTS

What you photograph depends on your personal interests. Macro photography with extension tubes and fixed framers is easiest to get right: the lens-to-subject distance and flash-to-subject distance are fixed, and the water sediment is minimized. Expose a test film at a variety of exposures with a fixed set-up and the best result will be the exposure to use for all future pictures for this setting and film, or on digital cameras, the ISO speed set.

Some fish are strongly territorial. Surgeonfish, triggerfish and sharks will make mock attacks on a perceived invader, and these situations can make strong pictures if you are brave enough to hold your ground. Manta rays are curious and will keep coming back if you react quietly and do not chase after them. Angelfish and butterflyfish will swim off when you first enter their territory, but if you remain quietly in the same place they will usually return and allow you to photograph them. Remember that if an eye is in the picture it must be lit and sharp; it is acceptable for the rest of the animal to be slightly blurred.

Diver and wreck photography are the most difficult. Even with apparently clear water and wide-angle lenses there will be back scatter, and flash is essential to light a diver's mask. Note that when the sun is at a low angle, or in choppy seas, much of the light fails to enter the water. To take advantage of the maximum light available it is best to photograph two hours either side of the sun's highest point. Sunlight can give spectacular effects underwater: keep the sun behind you and on your subject.

Night photography underwater is another world. Focusing quickly in dim light is difficult and many subjects will disappear when lit up, so pre-set the controls. Many creatures only appear at night and some fish are half asleep, making them more approachable.

DIGITAL CAMERAS AND THEIR USE UNDERWATER

Digital cameras are gradually taking over from film cameras because without the cost of film they appear to work out cheaper. They appeal to underwater photographers because they can get a lot more shots onto a memory card than they could on a film. They can discard any failures and can keep on photographing a subject until they get it right so long as it does not move. However, electronics give more problems in a saltwater environment, you have to carry a portable computer or several memory cards to download the images and, if used professionally (i.e. heavily), the camera's service life is only about three years so that the saving in film costs is soon negated. Digital cameras also often produce images that lack the punch, contrast or sparkle that a film-based model can deliver; the results can be wish-washy and lack detail in the highlights; and you may have to 'up' the colour depth and contrast with image manipulation software.

Files of the images are stored in a variety of file formats, e.g. uncompressed as TIFFs (Tagged Image File Format) or compressed as JPEGs (Joint Photographic Experts Group), which can reduce the file size by 8 or 10 to 1 if required. Some modern cameras allow storage as RAW – the raw data as it comes directly off the sensor. There is no standard for this – it uses the proprietary software of the manufacturer, but it has the best quality as no adjustments have yet been made to the image.

Digital and optical zoom

Digital zoom is electronic enlargement of the image coupled with cropping to emulate 'zooming in' closer with the lens, whereas in reality all that is being done is enlargement of the pixels (picture elements). An optical zoom 'brings the subject closer' optically before recording the image on the sensor – thus giving better resolution and a higher quality result.

Image capture, noise, temperature, ISO speeds and white balance

Noise is the visible effect of electronic interference and usually appears as coloured lines across an image. Two of the major causes are temperature, where high equals worse and low equals better. Try not to let the camera get hot, and try to use a slower ISO speed. All digital cameras, including video cameras, have an automatic white-balance setting that enables the camera to calculate the correct colour balance for an image. Some have pre-set values for different types of lighting, either by colour temperature or professional models, or such settings as sunny, cloudy, incandescent or fluorescent lighting on amateur models. For underwater use some divers use the 'cloudy' setting, or you may have to experiment with 'manual', using a white plastic card as the subject. Some divers use the RAW image format for the freedom of adjusting the white balance setting after a dive.

Flash with digital cameras

Most digital cameras are not compatible with normal TTL flash guns as they cannot read the flash reflected off film.

This is addressed with either a light sensor on the camera body to judge proper exposure, or with special flash guns for different digital cameras, many of which send out several pre-flashes and read their intensity when they are reflected back from the subject (DTTL). You can still use manual flash, shoot the picture, review the picture, make any necessary adjustments and shoot the picture again, but this takes time and the subject may have moved. You can delete any shots that were not correctly exposed. There are answers to TTL flash problems for underwater photography. One is to house a land flash gun that is dedicated to your digital camera. The problem with this method is that the land flash guns will not cover the field of view of very wide-angle lenses, though they are fine for close shots. Alternatively, some manufacturers of wide-angle underwater flash guns now have models with special electronic circuitry for use with the newest digital cameras, but they are still compatible with the popular film cameras used underwater, including the Nikonos. As a third option, the Fuji S2 Pro digital camera will work with all standard Nikonos-compatible underwater flash guns. Because of this and the fact that it is based on the Nikon F80/N80 camera body and utilizes Nikkor lenses, this camera has become popular for use in a waterproof housing.

Shutter lag

Most cheaper digital cameras suffer from 'shutter lag'. There is a time lag between pressing the shutter release and the shutter actually firing because the camera has to change mode and write to memory or the storage media. This means that if you are aiming for an expression on a face or a moving fish, it can be lost by the time that the shutter fires. This makes action photography difficult. More expensive cameras speed things up by saving to a buffer (extra memory).

Image storage

At the higher definition settings, underwater photographers require a large-capacity memory card to hold a reasonable number of pictures before they have to return to the surface and dowload them to a storage medium. Another problem is storage and accessibility of the images. Those who store negatives or transparencies in transparent viewpacks can view 36 frames of film by eye and know what is there very quickly. Viewing them on a computer is nowhere near as fast, and if you are not sure of where a particular image is stored, finding it can be a slow business even with special software. There is also a problem with hard disk storage space: a 40Gb hard drive is soon full and you have to resort to saving images to CDs, which deteriorate over time.

Digital cameras and their batteries

Unlike film cameras, some digital cameras can consume their battery power very quickly. There are two types of camera: those that accept standard AA-size batteries, and those that use a rechargeable proprietary battery of a different shape. AA-compatible cameras usually ship with disposable alkaline batteries. These make acceptable emergency back-ups, but rechargeable batteries perform better and have longer lives.

Health and Safety for Divers

The information on first aid and safety in this part of the book is intended as a guide only. It is based on currently accepted health and safety guidelines, but it is merely a summary and is no substitute for a comprehensive manual on the subject – or, even better, for first aid training. We strongly advise you to buy a recognized manual on diving safety and medicine before setting off on a diving trip, to read it through during the journey, and to carry it with you to refer to during the trip. It would also be sensible to take a short course in first aid.

We urge anyone in need of advice on emergency treatment to see a doctor as soon as possible.

WHAT TO DO IN AN EMERGENCY

- Divers who have suffered any injury or symptom of an injury, no matter how minor, related to diving, should consult a doctor, preferably a specialist in diving medicine, as soon as possible after the symptom or injury occurs.
- No matter how confident you are in making a diagnosis, remember that you are an amateur diver and an unqualified medical practitioner.
- If you are the victim of a diving injury do not let fear of ridicule prevent you from revealing your symptoms. Apparently minor symptoms can mask or even develop into a life-threatening illness. It is better to be honest with yourself and live to dive another day.
- Always err on the conservative side when treating an illness or an injury. If you find that the condition is only minor you – and the doctor – will both be relieved.

FIRST AID
The basic principles of first aid are to:
- do no harm
- sustain life
- prevent deterioration
- promote recovery.

If you have to treat an ill or injured person:
- First try to secure the safety of yourself and the ill or injured person by getting the two of you out of the threatening environment: the water.
- Think before you act: do not do anything that will further endanger either of you.
- Then follow a simple sequence of patient assessment and management:
  1 Assess whether you are dealing with a life-threatening condition.
  2 If so, try to define which one.
  3 Then try to manage the condition.

Assessing the ABCs:
Learn the basic checks – the ABCs:
A: for AIRWAY (with care of the neck)
B : for BREATHING
C: for CIRCULATION
D: for DECREASED level of consciousness
E: for EXPOSURE (a patient must be exposed enough for a proper examination to be made).

- **Airway (with attention to the neck):** check whether the patient has a neck injury. Are the mouth and nose free from obstruction? Noisy breathing is a sign of airway obstruction.

- **Breathing:** look at the chest to see if it is rising and falling. Listen for air movement at the nose and mouth. Feel for the movement of air against your cheek.

- **Circulation:** feel for a pulse (the carotid artery) next to the windpipe.

- **Decreased level of consciousness:** does the patient respond in any of the following ways?
    A - Awake, aware, spontaneous speech.
    V - Verbal stimuli: does he or she answer to 'Wake up'?
    P - Painful stimuli: does he or she respond to a pinch?
    U - Unresponsive.

- **Exposure:** preserve the dignity of the patient as much as you can, but remove clothes as necessary to carry out your treatment.

Now, send for help
If, after your assessment, you think the condition of the patient is serious, you must send or call for help from the nearest emergency services (ambulance, paramedics). Tell whoever you send for help to come back and let you know whether help is on the way.

Recovery position
If the patient is unconscious but breathing normally there is a risk that he or he she may vomit and choke on the vomit. It is therefore critical that the patient be turned on one side into the recovery position. This is illustrated in all first aid manuals.

If you suspect injury to the spine or neck, immobilize the patient in a straight line before you turn him or her on one side.

If the patient is unconscious, does not seem to be breathing, and you cannot feel a pulse, do not try to turn him or her into the recovery position.

Do **NOT** give fluids to unconscious or semi-conscious divers.

If you cannot feel a pulse

If your patient has no pulse you will have to carry out CPR (cardiopulmonary resuscitation). This consists of techniques to:
• ventilate the patient's lungs (expired air resuscitation)
• pump the patient's heart (external cardiac compression).

CPR (cardiopulmonary resuscitation)

Airway

Open the patient's airway by gently extending the head (head tilt) and lifting the chin with two fingers (chin lift). This lifts the patient's tongue away from the back of the throat and opens the airway. If the patient is unconscious and you think something may be blocking the airway, sweep your finger across the back of the tongue from one side to the other. If you find anything, remove it. Do not try this if the patient is conscious or semi-conscious because he or she may bite your finger or vomit.

Breathing: EAR (expired air resuscitation)

If the patient is not breathing you need to give the 'kiss of life', or expired air resuscitation (EAR) – you breathe into his or her lungs. The percentage of oxygen in the air you expire is enough to keep your patient alive.
1 Pinch the patient's nose to close the nostrils.
2 Place your open mouth fully over the patient's mouth, making as good a seal as possible.
3 Exhale into the mouth hard enough to make the chest rise and fall. Give two breaths, each over one second.
4 If the patient's chest fails to rise, try adjusting the position of the airway.
5 Check the patient's pulse. If you cannot feel one, follow the instructions under 'Circulation' below. If you can, continue breathing for the patient once every five seconds, checking the pulse after every ten breaths.
• If the patient begins breathing, turn him or her into the recovery position (see page 165).

Circulation

If, after giving expired air resuscitation, you cannot feel a pulse, you should try external cardiac compression:
1 Kneel next to the patient's chest.
2 Place your hands in the chest's centre, rather than spend time placing your hands using other methods.
3 Place the heel of your left hand just above your two fingers in the centre of the breast bone.
4 Place the heel of your right hand on your left hand.
5 Straighten your elbows.
6 Place your shoulders perpendicularly above the patient's breast bone.
7 Compress the breast bone 4–5cm (1½–2in) to a rhythm of 'one, two, three . . .'
8 Carry out 30 compressions.
Continue giving cycles of 2 breaths and 30 compressions. Carry on with a ratio of 30:2 compressions to breaths.

The aim of CPR is to keep the patient alive until paramedics or a doctor arrive with the necessary equipment.

Check before you dive that you and your buddy are both trained in CPR. If not, get some training – it could mean the difference between life and death for either of you or for someone else.

DIVING DISEASES AND ILLNESSES

Acute decompression illness

Acute decompression illness is any illness arising from the decompression of a diver – in other words, by the diver moving from an area of high ambient pressure to an area of low pressure. There are two types of acute decompression illness:
• decompression sickness (the bends)
• barotrauma with arterial gas embolism.

It is not important for the diver or first aider to be able to differentiate between the two conditions because both are serious, life-threatening illnesses, and both require the same emergency treatment. The important thing is to be able to recognize acute decompression illness and to initiate emergency treatment. The box on page 167 outlines the signs and symptoms to look out for.

The bends (decompression sickness)

Decompression sickness or the bends occurs when a diver has not been adequately decompressed. Exposure to higher ambient pressure underwater causes nitrogen to dissolve in increasing amounts in the body tissues. If this pressure is released gradually during correct and adequate decompression procedures, the nitrogen escapes naturally into the blood and is exhaled through the lungs. If the release of pressure is too rapid, the nitrogen cannot escape quickly enough and bubbles of nitrogen gas form in the tissues. The symptoms and signs of the disease are related to the tissues in which the bubbles form and it is described by the tissues affected – joint bend, for example.

Symptoms and signs include:
• nausea and vomiting
• dizziness
• malaise
• weakness
• pains in the joints
• paralysis
• numbness
• itching of skin
• incontinence.

Barotrauma with arterial gas embolism

Barotrauma is the damage that occurs when the tissue surrounding a gaseous space is injured following a change in the volume of air in that space. An arterial gas embolism is a gas bubble that moves in a blood vessel; this usually leads to the obstruction of that blood vessel or a vessel further downstream.

Barotrauma can occur in any tissue surrounding a gas-filled space. Common sites and types of barotrauma are:
- ears (middle ear squeeze) ⇢ burst ear drum
- sinuses (sinus squeeze) ⇢ sinus pain/nose bleeds
- lungs (lung squeeze) ⇢ burst lung
- face (mask squeeze) ⇢ swollen, bloodshot eyes
- teeth (tooth squeeze) ⇢ toothache.

Burst lung is the most serious of these since it can result in arterial gas embolism. It occurs following a rapid ascent during which the diver does not exhale adequately. The rising pressure of expanding air in the lungs bursts the delicate alveoli – air sacs in the lungs – and forces air into the blood vessels that carry blood back to the heart and, ultimately, the brain. In the brain these air bubbles block blood vessels and obstruct the supply of blood and oxygen to the brain. This causes brain damage.

ROUGH AND READY NON-SPECIALIST TESTS FOR THE BENDS

If you suspect a diver may be suffering from the bends, carry out these tests. If the results of your checks do not seem normal, the diver may be suffering from the bends and you must take emergency action. Take the appropriate action outlined on page 166 even if you are not sure of your assessment – the bends is a life-threatening illness.

1 Does the diver know:
who he/she is?
where he/she is?
what the time is?
2 Can the diver see and count the number of fingers you hold up? Hold your hand 50cm (20in) in front of the diver's face and ask him/her to follow your hand with his/her eyes as you move it from side to side and up and down. Be sure that both eyes follow in each direction, and look out for any rapid oscillation or jerky movements of the eyeballs.
3 Ask the diver to smile, and check that both sides of the face have the same expression. Run the back of a finger across each side of the diver's forehead, cheeks and chin, and ask whether he/she can feel it.
4 Check that the diver can hear you whisper when his/her eyes are closed.
5 Ask the diver to shrug his/her shoulders. Both should move equally.
6 Ask the diver to swallow. Check that the adam's apple moves up and down.
7 Ask the diver to stick out his/her tongue at the centre of the mouth – deviation to either side indicates a problem.
8 Check the diver has equal muscle strength on both sides of the body. You do this by pulling/pushing each of the diver's arms and legs away from and back toward the body, asking him/her to resist you.
9 Run your finger lightly across the diver's shoulders, down the back, across the chest and abdomen, and along the arms and legs, feeling upper and underside surfaces. Check that the diver can feel your finger moving along each surface.
10 On firm ground (not on a boat) check that the diver can walk in a straight line and, with eyes closed, stand upright with feet together and arms outstretched.

The symptoms and signs of lung barotrauma and arterial gas embolism include:
- shortness of breath
- chest pain
- unconsciousness.

Treatment of acute decompression Illness:
- ABCs and CPR (see pages 165-6) as necessary
- position the patient in the recovery position (see page 165) with no tilt or raising of the legs
- give 100 per cent oxygen by mask or demand valve
- keep the patient warm
- remove to the nearest hospital as soon as possible – the hospital or emergency services will arrange for recompression treatment.

Carbon dioxide and carbon monoxide poisoning

Carbon dioxide poisoning can occur as a result of skip breathing (diver holds breath on SCUBA), heavy exercise on SCUBA or malfunctioning rebreather systems. Carbon monoxide poisoning occurs as a result of exhaust gases being pumped into cylinders or hookah systems due to the compressor air intake being downwind of exhaust fumes.

Symptoms and signs of carbon monoxide poisoning include:
- blue colour of the skin
- shortness of breath
- loss of consciousness.

Treatment of carbon monoxide poisoning:
- get the patient to a safe environment
- ABCs and CPR (see pages 165-6) as necessary
- 100 per cent oxygen through a mask or demand valve
- get the patient to hospital.

Head injury

Any head injury should be treated as serious.

Treatment of a head injury:
- the diver must surface and do no more diving until a doctor has been consulted
- disinfect the wound
- if the diver is unconscious, contact the emergency services
- if breathing and/or pulse have stopped, administer CPR (see page 166)
- if the diver is breathing and has a pulse, check for bleeding and other injuries, and treat for shock (see page 169)
- if the wounds permit, put the injured person into the recovery position and, if possible, give 100 per cent oxygen
- keep the patient warm and comfortable and monitor pulse and respiration constantly.

Hyperthermia (raised body temperature)

A rise in body temperature results from a combination of overheating, normally due to exercise, and inadequate fluid intake. A person with hyperthermia will progress through heat exhaustion to heat stroke, with eventual collapse. Heat stroke is an emergency: if the diver is not cooled and rehydrated he or she will die.

Treatment of hyperthermia:
• move the diver as quickly as possible into a cooler place and remove all clothes
• call the emergency services
• sponge the diver's body with a damp cloth and fan him or her manually or with an electric fan
• if the patient is unconscious, put him or her into the recovery position (see page 165) and monitor the ABCs as necessary
• if the patient is conscious you can give him or her a cold drink.

Hypothermia (low body temperature)

Normal internal body temperature is just under 37°C (98.4°F). If for any reason it falls much below this – usually, in diving, because of inadequate protective clothing – progressively more serious symptoms may follow, and the person will eventually die if the condition is not treated rapidly. A drop of 1C° (2F°) causes shivering and discomfort. A 2C° (3F°) drop induces the body's self-heating mechanisms to react: blood flow to the hands and feet is reduced and shivering becomes extreme. A 3C° (5F°) drop results in memory loss, confusion, disorientation, irregular heartbeat and breathing and eventually death.

Treatment of hypothermia:
• move the diver as quickly as possible into a sheltered and warm place; *or:*
• prevent further heat loss: use an exposure bag; surround the diver with buddies' bodies; cover his or her head and neck with a woolly hat, warm towels or anything else suitable
• if you have managed to get the diver into sheltered warmth, remove wet clothing, dress your patient in warm, dry clothing and wrap him or her in an exposure bag or blanket; however, if you are still in the open, the diver is best left in existing garments
• if the diver is conscious and coherent administer a warm shower or bath and a warm, sweet drink
• if the diver is unconscious, check the ABCs (see page 165), call the emergency services, make the patient as warm as possible, and treat for shock (see page 169).

Near-drowning

Near-drowning is a medical condition in which a diver has inhaled some water – water in the lungs interferes with the normal transport of oxygen from the lungs into the bloodstream. A person in a near-drowning condition may be conscious or unconscious.

Near-drowning victims sometimes develop secondary drowning, a condition in which fluid oozing into the lungs causes the diver to drown in internal secretions, so all near-drowning patients must be monitored in a hospital.

Treatment of near-drowning:
• get the diver out of the water and check the ABCs (see page 165); depending on your findings, begin EAR or CPR (see page 166) as appropriate
• if possible, administer oxygen by mask or demand valve
• call the emergency services and get the diver to a hospital for observation, even if he/she appears to have recovered from the experience.

Nitrogen narcosis

Air contains about 80 per cent nitrogen. Breathing the standard diving mixture under compression can lead to symptoms very much like those of drunkenness (nitrogen narcosis is popularly known as 'rapture of the deep'). Some divers experience nitrogen narcosis at depths of 30–40m (100–130ft). Down to a depth of about 60m (200ft) – which is beyond the legal maximum depth for sport-diving in the UK and the USA – the symptoms are not always serious; but below about 80m (260ft) a diver is likely to lose consciousness. Symptoms can occur very suddenly. Nitrogen narcosis is not a serious condition, but a diver suffering from it may do something dangerous.

Treatment of nitrogen narcosis: the only treatment for this condition is to get the diver to ascend immediately to shallower waters.

TRAVELLING MEDICINE

Many doctors decline to issue drugs, particularly antibiotics, to people who want them 'just in case'; but a diving holiday can be ruined by an ear or sinus infection, especially in a remote area or on a live-aboard boat, where the nearest doctor or pharmacy is a long and difficult journey away.

Many travelling divers therefore carry with them medical kits that could lead the uninitiated to think they were hypochondriacs. Nasal sprays, ear drops, antihistamine creams, anti-diarrhoea medicines, antibiotics, sea-sickness remedies . . . Forearmed, such divers can take immediate action as soon as they realize something is wrong. At the very least, this may minimize their loss of diving time.

Always bear in mind that most decongestants and remedies for sea-sickness can make you drowsy and therefore should never be taken before diving.

Shock

Shock is a medical condition and not just the emotional trauma of a frightening experience. Medical shock results from poor blood and oxygen delivery to the tissues. As a result of oxygen and blood deprivation the tissues cannot carry out their functions. There are many causes; the most common is loss of blood.

Treatment for medical shock:
This is directed at restoring blood and oxygen delivery to the tissues:
• check the ABCs (see page 165)
• give 100 per cent oxygen
• control any external bleeding by pressing hard on the wound and/or pressure points (the location of the pressure points is illustrated in first-aid manuals); raise the injured limb or other part of the body
• use a tourniquet only as a last resort and only on the arms and legs
• if the diver is conscious, lay him/her on the back with the legs raised and the head to one side; if unconscious, turn him or her on the left side in the recovery position (see page 165).

MARINE-RELATED AILMENTS

Sunburn, coral cuts, fire-coral stings, swimmers' ear, sea-sickness and bites from various insects are perhaps the most common divers' complaints – but there are more serious marine-related illnesses you should know about.

Cuts and abrasions

Divers should wear appropriate abrasive protection for the undersea environment. Hands, knees, elbows and feet are the areas most commonly affected. The danger with abrasions is that they become infected, so all wounds must be thoroughly washed and rinsed with freshwater and an antiseptic as soon as possible after the injury. Infection may progress to a stage where antibiotics are necessary. If the site of an apparently minor injury becomes inflamed, and the inflammation spreads, consult a doctor immediately – you may need antibiotics to prevent the infection spreading to the bloodstream.

Swimmers' ear

Swimmers' ear is an infection of the external ear canal caused by constantly wet ears. The condition is often a combined fungal and bacterial infection. To prevent it, always dry your ears thoroughly after diving. If you know you are susceptible to the condition, insert drops to dry out the ear after diving. If an infection occurs, the best treatment is to stop diving or swimming for a few days and apply ear drops such as:
• 5 per cent acetic acid in isopropyl alcohol; *or*
• aluminium acetate/acetic acid solution.

FIRST-AID KIT

Your first-aid kit should be waterproof, compartmentalized and sealable, and, as a minimum, should contain the following items:
• a full first-aid manual – the information in this appendix is for general guidance only
• contact numbers for the emergency services
• coins for telephone
• pencil and notebook
• tweezers
• scissors
• 6 large standard sterile dressings
• 1 large Elastoplast/Band-Aid fabric dressing strip
• 2 triangular bandages
• 3 medium-size safety pins
• 1 pack sterile cotton wool
• 2 50mm (2in) crepe bandages
• eyedrops
• antiseptic fluid/cream
• bottle of vinegar
• sachets of rehydration salts
• sea-sickness tablets
• decongestants
• painkillers
• anti-AIDS pack (syringes/needles/drip needle)

Sea or motion sickness

Motion sickness can be an annoying complication on a diving holiday involving boat dives. If you suffer from motion sickness, discuss the problem with a doctor before your holiday – or at least before boarding the boat. But bear in mind that many medicines formulated to prevent travel sickness contain antihistamines, which make you drowsy and will impair your ability to think quickly while you are diving.

Biting insects

Some regions are notorious for biting insects. Take a good insect repellent and some antihistamine cream to relieve the effects.

Sunburn

Be sure to take plenty of precautions against sunburn, which can cause skin cancer. Many people get sunburned on the first day of a holiday and spend a very uncomfortable time afterwards recovering. Pay particular attention to the head, the nose and the backs of the legs. Always use high-protection factor creams, and wear clothes that keep off the sun.

Tropical diseases

Visit the doctor before your trip and make sure you have the appropriate vaccinations for the regions you intend to visit on your trip.

Fish that bite

- **Barracuda** These very rarely bite divers, although they have been known to bite in turbid or murky, shallow water, where sunlight flashing on a knife blade, a camera lens or jewellery has confused the fish into thinking they are attacking their normal prey.

  Treatment: clean the wounds thoroughly and use antiseptic or antibiotic cream. Bad bites will also need antibiotic and anti-tetanus treatment.

- **Moray eels** Probably more divers are bitten by morays than by all other sea creatures added together – usually through putting their hands into holes to collect shells or lobsters, remove anchors, or hide baitfish. Once it bites, a moray often refuses to let go, so you may have to persuade it to by gripping it behind the head and exerting pressure with your finger and thumb until it opens its jaw. You can make the wound worse by tearing your flesh if you pull the fish off.

  Treatment: thorough cleaning and usually stitching. The bites always go septic, so have antibiotics and anti-tetanus available.

- **Sharks** Sharks rarely attack divers, but should always be treated with great respect. Their attacks are usually connected with speared or hooked fish, fish or meat set up as bait, lobsters rattling when picked up, or certain types of vibration, such as that produced by helicopters. The decomposition products of dead fish (even several days old) seem much more attractive to most sharks than fresh blood. Grey reef sharks can be territorial. They often warn of an attack by arching their backs and pointing their pectoral fins downward. Other sharks often give warning by bumping into you first. If you are frightened, a shark will detect this from the vibrations given off by your body. Calmly back up to the reef or boat and get out of the water.

  Treatment: a person who has been bitten by a shark usually has severe injuries and is suffering from shock (see page 169). If possible, stop any bleeding by applying pressure. The patient will need to be stabilized with blood or plasma transfusions before being moved to hospital. Even minor wounds are likely to become infected, so the diver will need antibiotic and anti-tetanus treatment.

- **Triggerfish** Large triggerfish – usually males guarding eggs in 'nests' – are aggressive and will attack divers who get too close. Their teeth can go through rubber fins and draw blood through a 4mm (1/6in) wet suit.

  Treatment: clean the wound and treat it with antiseptic cream.

Venomous sea creatures

Many venomous sea creatures are bottom dwellers – they hide among coral or rest on or burrow into sand. If you need to move along the sea bottom, shuffle along, so that you push such creatures out of the way and minimize the risk of stepping directly onto sharp venomous spines, many of which can pierce rubber fins. Antivenins require specialist medical supervision, do not work for all species, and need refrigerated storage, so they are rarely available when they are needed. Most of the venoms are proteins of high molecular weight that break down under heat.

General treatment: tie a broad bandage at a point between the limb and the body and tighten it. Remember to release it every 15 minutes. Immerse the limb in hot water (perhaps the cooling water from an outboard motor if no other supply is available) at 50°C (120°F) for two hours, until the pain stops. Several injections around the wound of local anaesthetic (such as procaine hydrochloride), if available, will ease the pain. Young or weak people may need CPR (see page 166). Remember that venoms may still be active in fish that have been dead for 48 hours.

- **Cone shells** Live cone shells should never be handled without gloves: the animal has a mobile, tubelike organ that shoots a poison dart. This causes numbness at first, followed by local muscular paralysis, which may extend to respiratory paralysis and heart failure.

  Treatment: tie a bandage between the wound and the body, tighten it, and release it every 15 minutes. CPR (see page 166) may be necessary.

- **Fire coral** Corals of the genus *Millepora* are not true corals but members of the class Hydrozoa – i.e., they are more closely related to the stinging hydroids. Many people react violently from the slightest brush with them – producing blisters sometimes as large as 15cm (6in) across, which can last for as long as several weeks.

  Treatment: bathe the affected part in methylated spirit or vinegar (acetic acid). Local anaesthetic may be required to ease the pain, though antihistamine cream is usually enough.

- **Fireworms** These worms with white hairs along their sides display bristles when touched. These easily break off in the skin, causing a burning feeling and intense irritation.

  Treatment: bathe the affected part in methylated spirit, vinegar (acetic acid) or hot water.

- **Jellyfish** Most jellyfish sting, but few are dangerous. When seasonal changes are favourable you can encounter the Portuguese man-of-war (*Physalia physalis*). It is highly toxic and continued exposure to the stinging cells may require hospital treatment. Sea wasps (*Carybdea alata*) can be found in shallow warm water at night and are attracted to light. They often swarm and stings can be severe, causing muscle cramps, nausea and breathing difficulties. Whenever the conditions are favourable for thimble jellyfish (*Linuche unguiculata*), there is always the chance of much smaller and almost invisible micro-organisms in the water column. Wear protection such as a wet suit or a Lycra skin suit.

Treatment: in the event of a sting, the recommended treatment is to pour acetic acid (vinegar) over both animal and wounds and then to remove the animal with forceps or gloves. CPR (see page 166) may be required.

- **Scorpionfish** These are not considered dangerous in Caribbean waters, but care should always be taken of the spines on top of their dorsal fin.

Treatment: inadvertent stinging can be treated by bathing the affected part of the body in very hot water.

- **Sea urchins** The spines of some sea urchins are poisonous and all sea urchin spines can puncture the skin, even through gloves, and break off, leaving painful wounds that often go septic.

Treatment: for bad cases bathe the affected part of the body in very hot water. This softens the spines, making it easier for the body to reject them. Soothing creams or a magnesium sulphate compress will help reduce the pain, as will the application of the flesh of papaya fruit. Septic wounds need to be treated with antibiotics.

- **Stinging hydroids** Stinging hydroids often go unnoticed on wrecks, old anchor ropes and chains until you put your hand on them, when their nematocysts are fired into your skin. The wounds are not particularly serious but they are extremely painful, and large blisters can be raised on sensitive skin, which can last for some time.

Treatment: bathe the affected part in methylated spirit or vinegar (acetic acid). Local anaesthetic may be required to ease the pain, though antihistamine cream is usually enough.

- **Stinging plankton** You cannot see stinging plankton, and so cannot take evasive measures. If there are reports of any in the area, keep as much of your body covered as you can.

Treatment: bathe the affected part in methylated spirit or vinegar (acetic acid). Local anaesthetic may be required to ease the pain, though antihistamine cream is usually enough.

- **Stingrays** Stingrays vary considerably in size from a few centimetres to several metres across. The sting consists of one or more spines on top of the tail; although these point backward they can sting in any direction. The rays thrash out and sting when they are trodden on or caught. The wounds may be large and severely lacerated. Large stingrays have barbs that can pierce the heart. It is essential to control bleeding by leaving them in position until the casualty reaches specialist medical help.

Treatment: clean the wound and remove any spines. Bathe or immerse in very hot water and apply a local anaesthetic if one is available; follow up with antibiotics and anti-tetanus.

Cuts
Underwater cuts and scrapes, especially those caused by coral, barnacles and sharp metal, will usually, if they are not cleaned out and treated quickly, go septic; absorption of the resulting poisons into the body can cause more serious conditions. After every dive, clean and disinfect even the smallest wounds. Larger wounds may refuse to heal unless you stay out of seawater for a couple of days. Surgeonfish have sharp fins on each side of the caudal peduncle; they use these to lash out at other fish with a sweep of the tail, and occasionally to defend their territory against a trespassing diver. Their 'scalpels' may be covered in toxic mucus, so wounds must be cleaned and treated with antibiotic cream. As a preventive measure against cuts in general, the golden rule on the reef is: do not touch. Be sure you learn good buoyancy control so that you can avoid touching anything unnecessarily – never forget for an instant that every area of the coral you touch will inevitably be killed.

Bibliography

George, J. and George, J. David: *Marine Life – An Illustrated Encyclopedia of Invertebrates in the Sea* (1979), Harrap, London, UK

Humann, Paul: *Reef Fish Identification (Florida, Caribbean, Bahamas)* (1992), New World Publications Inc, Florida, USA

Humann, Paul: *Reef Creature Identification (Florida, Caribbean, Bahamas)*, (1992), New World Publications Inc, Florida, USA

Humann, Paul: *Reef Coral Identification (Florida, Caribbean, Bahamas)* (1993), New World Publications Inc, Florida, USA

Lewbel, George S.: *Diving and Snorkeling Guide to Curaçao* (1988), Pisces Books, PBC International, New York – (now Lonely Planet)

Lieske, Ewald and Myers, Robert: *Collins Pocket Guide to Coral Reef Fishes of the Indo Pacific and Caribbean* (1994), Harper Collins, London

Mulder-Cudmore, Cynthia: *DIP Take The Plunge – The Official Curaçao Island Dive Guide* (1996), Curaçao Tourism Development Bureau

Schnabel, Jerry and Swygert, Susan L.: *Diving and Snorkeling Guide to Bonaire* (1991), Pisces Books, Gulf Publishing Company, Houston, Texas – (now Lonely Planet)

Wells, Sue et al: *Coral Reefs of the World* (3 volumes, 1988), United Nations Environmental Program/International Union for Conservation of Nature and Natural Resources, Gland, Switzerland and Cambridge, UK

Wells, Sue and Hanna, Nick: *The Greenpeace Book of Coral Reefs* (1992), Blandford Cameron Books, Dumfriesshire, Scotland

Wood, Elizabeth M (1983): *Corals of the World*, T.F.H. Publications, Neptune, N.J.

PAPIAMENTO

Golio, E. R.: *Papiamemtu Textbook* (6th edition), DeWit Stores NV, Oranjestad, Aruba

Mansur, Jossy M: *Papiamento/English Dictionary*, Edicionnan Classico Dario, Oranjestad, Aruba

Ratzlaff, Betty: *Papiamento/English Dictionary*, TWR Dictionary Foundation, Bonaire

GENERAL

Dawood, Dr. Richard (1992): *Travellers' Health - How To Stay Healthy Abroad* (3rd edition), Oxford University Press, Oxford, UK

Index